THE MACMILLAN BOOK OF CANADIAN PLACE NAMES

WILLIAM B. HAMILTON

The Macmillan Book of
Canadian Place Names

MACMILLAN OF CANADA
TORONTO

PROVINCIAL FLOWERS BY WILLI SCHIFFERS

Alberta: *Wild Rose*; British Columbia: *Pacific Dogwood*;
Manitoba: *Prairie Crocus*; New Brunswick: *Purple Violet*;
Newfoundland: *Pitcher Plant*; Nova Scotia: *Mayflower*; Ontario:
Trillium; Prince Edward Island: *Lady's Slipper*; Québec: *Madonna
Lily*; Saskatchewan: *Prairie Lily*; Yukon Territory: *Fireweed*;
Northwest Territories: *Mountain Avens*

Canadian Cataloguing in Publication Data

Hamilton, William B., 1929-
   The Macmillan book of Canadian place names

Bibliography: p.
ISBN 0-7705-1524-X

1. Names, Geographical – Canada. I. Title.
II. Title: Canadian place names.

FC36.H35   917.1'003   C77-001618-9
F1004.H35

Printed in Canada for
The Macmillan Company of Canada Ltd.
70 Bond Street, Toronto
M5B 1X3

Contents

Preface

It is nearly fifty years since George Armstrong compiled *The Origin and Meaning of Place Names in Canada*. From 1930 onward no other general treatment of Canadian toponymy has appeared, although several provincial and local studies have been published. When the present volume was projected it was thought that a revision of the Armstrong volume would be sufficient; however, it became obvious that more was required. Great progress has occurred in place-name research in recent years. Armstrong's method of selection was haphazard, and the earlier publication predated the entry of Newfoundland into Confederation. The *Macmillan Book of Canadian Place Names* is the result.

No one is more aware than the writer of the problems inherent in *any* manageable selection from among the more than three hundred thousand recorded place names in this country. Three broad categories were used as a measure to determine entry. (1) *Size*: The major centres of population and the most important physical features – rivers, mountains, lakes, etc. – have, it is hoped, been included. (2) *History*: Those places which have had some significant bearing on the development of Canada also qualified for entry. Port Royal, Nova Scotia; Dollard-des-Ormeaux, Quebec; Batoche, Saskatchewan; and Craigellachie, British Columbia, exemplify this classification. (3) *Human Interest*: This final category is more difficult to define. Simply stated it includes a broad selection of those places most likely to provoke

the question: "What is the meaning of *that* name?" The reader
might like to check the following entries as examples: Flin Flon,
Manitoba; Punkeydoodles Corner, Ontario; Chibougamau, Quebec; or Joe Batt's Arm, Newfoundland. The end result is a compila-
tion of some twenty-five hundred entries that provide a representative sample of the rich tapestry of Canadian place names.

Obviously, in a general work of this kind I have had to lean
heavily on the research of others, and due acknowledgement is
given in the Bibliography. More formal recognition is scattered
throughout the text to those whose theories and interpretations
were particularly illuminating. When several competing explanations exist for the origin of a given place name, I have included
the one that, on the basis of investigation, appears to be the most
plausible or historically sound. When doubt remained, a summa-
ry of the major interpretations has been given. Future research
will inevitably nullify some of the conclusions reached, and I
would be pleased to receive comments from anyone with information to share. These may be forwarded to me in care of the
publisher.

Detailed thanks are due to so many people that one must risk
the offence of seeming ingratitude in not attempting to list
names. An important side benefit in compiling this book has
been the opportunity to undertake research in all parts of Canada. I am grateful to the many archivists, librarians, local histori-
ans, government officials, and others, who gave freely of their
time in answering my queries. I should like to thank the 1974-5
staff of the Toponymy Division, Department of Energy, Mines
and Resources, for the welcome granted an outside researcher.
All members of the Division contributed in no small measure to
the completion of the book. In particular, Mr. Alan Rayburn, Executive Secretary, Canadian Permanent Committee on Geographical Names, displayed infinite patience and courtesy in dealing
with endless questions. While he was generous enough to read
portions of the manuscript, any sins of omission or commission
are those of the writer. The staff of the Manuscript and Map
Rooms of the Public Archives of Canada and of the National Li-
brary were, as always, helpful in solving seemingly insoluble rid-

the features; pioneers, war casualties, and historical events connected with the area; names from native languages currently or formerly identified with the general area.

PRINCIPLE 10 AMERINDIAN AND INUIT NAMES
Names of Amerindian (Indian) and Inuit (Eskimo) origin will be recorded according to a recognized Romanized orthography or according to the considered opinion of recognized linguistic authorities.

PRINCIPLE 11 FORM AND CHARACTER OF NAMES
Forms that should be avoided are:
(a) unnatural or incongruous combinations of words, including combinations of words of different languages and fusions of Christian and surname elements;
(b) cumbersome and unpronounceable names;
(c) corrupted or modified names;
(d) obscene or blasphemous names;
(e) discriminatory or derogatory names from the point of view of race, sex, colour, creed, political affiliation, or other social factors;
(f) names that could be construed as advertising particular commercial or industrial enterprises.

PRINCIPLE 12 QUALIFYING TERMINOLOGY
Qualifying words may be used in an area to distinguish between two or more features with identical names. Such words may be derived from other local features or may be terms such as "upper", "new", "west branch", and "big". Wherever possible new names should be distinctive.

PRINCIPLE 13 GENERIC TERMINOLOGY
When a geographical name includes both a specific and a generic element, the generic term must be appropriate to the nature of the feature. Its position shall be dictated by euphony and usage. The generic term shall be recorded in the language having priority of local usage or origin, although publishers may choose the

relative term in the language of their maps and publications.

PRINCIPLE 14   NAMES OUTSIDE CANADA
Geographical names in foreign countries should be rendered in forms adopted by each country, except where there are recognized English or French equivalents established by appropriate international authorities.

Procedures

PROPOSALS
Except in exceptional circumstances the Committee itself does not initiate naming. Most new names approved by the Committee are derived from the general public and from organizations. Such names should be for specific geographical features.

Individuals or organizations contemplating the publication of geographical names should submit proposals well in advance of publication dates. The consideration of new names may require considerable time, particularly when local investigation is required. The publication of unauthorized names will not necessarily result in official recognition.

New proposals should be for specific geographical features.

Descriptive names and names relating to the history of an area are preferred. The following information, accompanied by adequate documentation, will facilitate prompt decisions:
a)   location by latitude and longitude, specifying map consulted;
b)   identification on map indicating precise extent;
c)   photographs or sketches;
d)   reasons for proposals;
e)   origin;
f)   evidence that features are unnamed.

CHANGES
Reliable, preferably documented, information concerning corrections in the use, spelling, or application of toponyms on maps and charts and in other publications is welcomed by the Committee.

dles. Special thanks must also be extended to Mr. Ken McVey, Executive Editor, Trade Division, Macmillan of Canada, for his suggestions and constructive comments. Above all, I am indebted to my wife, who for years tolerated a preoccupation with place-name research and has given me the encouragement to continue my writing. To her this book is dedicated.

THE MACMILLAN BOOK OF CANADIAN PLACE NAMES

The Tapestry of Place Names

Place names form a permanent register or index of the course and events of a country's history; they are fossils exposed in the cross-section of that history, marking its successive periods; and so lasting are they that records in stone or brass are not to be compared with them for endurance.[1]

William Francis Ganong (1864–1941)

The map of Canada reveals a rich tapestry of place names. The pattern is one of infinite variety, colourful contrasts, and an interwoven texture which has withstood the test of centuries. The early strands rely heavily on European and Amerindian sources, on successive threads of settlement and exploration, and on wide variations in topography. Entwined throughout one finds a summation of the country's historical, linguistic, and folk heritage. Port aux Basques and the Miramichi, Sept Îles or Sorel, HaHa Bay and the Gatineau, Niagara-on-the-Lake or Mississauga, Swift Current and Drumheller, Uranium City or Axel Heiberg Island, Kelowna and Kamloops – all indicate something of Canada's total composition and richly variegated design.

There was a time when the study of place names was looked upon as an antiquarian hobby; however, more recently it has evolved as a specialized field of inquiry. Place names are investigated because of the valuable insight they provide into history, for the evidence they give of linguistic change, and for the clues they provide concerning the cultural and social development of the country. They are useful in tracing settlement patterns and perceptions of past landscapes and in charting early political attitudes and issues. Then, too, they are important for the interest they evoke, since all people are concerned with names and naming.

It has been reliably estimated that over three hundred thousand official names are to be found on lists maintained by the Canadian Permanent Committee on Geographical Names. Annually, about twenty-five thousand new ones are recorded in an effort to recognize approximately two million geographical features as yet unnamed. These figures indicate the magnitude of the task of merely keeping track of current place names in Canada. In addition, the names and variations of names which have disappeared from maps and official lists are also important in interpreting present-day names.

During the early years of Canadian history the assigning of place names was largely accidental. Fishermen and mariners, explorers and mapmakers, adventurers and voyageurs, pioneers and politicians, all took part in haphazard naming. Not surprisingly, wide variations in spelling, in interpretation, and in actual location, were commonplace. It was not until the latter part of the nineteenth century that agitation for a formalized procedure became widespread. By this time both Britain and the United States had established a series of rules for the orthography of place names. The American Board on Geographical Names, established on September 4, 1890, was charged with the responsibility of adjudicating "all unsettled questions" concerning nomenclature. The need for a similar body in Canada was evident. Regularly, groups such as the Dominion Land Surveyors Association urged the federal government "to formulate some scheme or set of rules for the guidance of geographers and surveyors in naming geographical features and for use in compiling government maps". Before any action, the Minister of the Interior, Edgar Dewdney (a surveyor and civil engineer in private life), invited several government departments to form a voluntary association for revising place names in the North West Territories. Although the idea received support, it became clear that government legislation was necessary. Unfortunately, the 1890s were politically unsettled years, and nothing happened until after the advent of the Laurier government in 1896.

On December 18, 1897, an order-in-council was passed which established the Canadian Board on Geographic Names:

> His Excellency, by and with the advice of the Queen's Privy Council for Canada, is pleased to create a "Geographic Board" to consist of one member for each of the Departments of the Geological Survey, Railways and Canals, Post Office and Marine and Fisheries, such member being appointed by the Minister of the Department; of the Surveyor General of Dominion Lands, of such other members as may, from time to time, be appointed by Order in Council, and of an officer of the Department of the Interior, designated by the Minister of the Interior, who shall act as Secretary of the Board; and to authorize the Board to elect its Chairman and to make such rules and regulations for the transaction of its business as may be requisite.
>
> His Excellency is further pleased to order and direct that all questions concerning geographic names in the Dominion which arise in the Departments of the Public Service shall be referred to the Board, and that all Departments shall accept and use in their publications the names and orthography adopted by the Board.[2]

Named to the first Board were: Major F. Gordeau, Deputy Minister of Marine and Fisheries; Edouard G. Deville, Surveyor General; E. V. Johnson from the Department of Railways and Canals; James White of the Geological Survey of Canada; and William Smith, representing the Postmaster General; while A. H. Whitcher of the Department of the Interior served as secretary of the committee. Later Dr. S. E. Dawson, Queen's Printer, and Lieut.-Col. W. P. Anderson, Chief Engineer of the Department of Marine and Fisheries, were added to round out the membership. In developing early priorities, establishing rules of nomenclature, and attempting to standardize map designations, the need for co-operation with provincial authorities became obvious. Accordingly, in 1899 a further order-in-council granted the provinces and the North West Territories the right to name representatives to the Board.

There was little change in the overall structure of the Board until 1948, when the designation Canadian Board on Geographical Names was adopted to prevent confusion with other federal agencies. A further change occurred in 1961 when the present title, Canadian Permanent Committee on Geographical Names, was adopted (hereafter CPCGN). Membership is still drawn from related federal authorities, along with representatives from the provinces. Close liaison is maintained with the four provinces which have established boards of their own: Newfoundland (whose Nomenclature Board dates back to 1904), Quebec, Ontario, and Alberta. Responsibilities and functions of the Committee are broadly defined as dealing with "... all questions of geographical nomenclature affecting Canada", and the undertaking of "... research and investigation into the origin and usage of geographical names". In addition, the Committee has adopted for its guidance several basic principles of nomenclature (see p. 15).

While it might appear that the major preoccupation of the CPCGN is co-ordinating decisions concerning names, publishing gazetteers, or mediating interprovincial and national problems, considerable toponymic research has been undertaken. During the first years of the century, annual reports listing approved names with locational descriptions and a brief note on origins were issued.* In the more than seventy-five years that the Committee has been in operation, three names stand out in the field of toponymic investigation: James White (1863–1928); Robert Douglas (1881–1930); and, in the present period, Alan Rayburn. White, a member of the original Board and later its chairman, had a long association with the geographical profession in Canada. First appointed geographer with the Geological Survey, he became, in 1899, Chief Geographer with the Department of the Interior. With this background, an interest in researching Canadian place names was almost axiomatic. During 1904–6, as Chief Ge-

*The more important volumes are included in the select bibliography at the end of this volume.

ographer, he dispatched letters to all postmasters in the country inquiring as to the derivation of local place names. Much of the material collected in this survey is still to be found in the files of the Toponymy Division, Department of Energy, Mines and Resources. Robert Douglas, whose untimely death at the age of forty-nine cut short an outstanding career in place-name research, served for many years as secretary of the Geographic Board of Canada. The best tribute to his work is simply that much is still authoritative. The Depression of the 1930s, followed by the Second World War, meant that little priority was given to place nomenclature. It was not until after the reorganization of 1948 that serious work was again undertaken. Important monographs on a wide range of topics were produced by J. Keith Fraser, by Gordon Delaney, and more recently by Alan Rayburn, all of whom in turn have served as executive secretary of the CPCGN. Today, toponymic research, like related fields, has become more organized and thorough than the sometimes indiscriminate efforts of earlier years. Emphasis on field research, modern linguistic interpretations, and in-depth historical investigation, have all had their impact on recent works by Rayburn such as *Geographical Names of Prince Edward Island,* Ottawa, 1973, and a companion volume, *Geographical Names of New Brunswick,* published in 1975. So painstaking has been the research that these two studies will remain the definitive authorities for some time to come. Indeed, a casual glance at either of the last-mentioned will give the reader some idea of the man-hours required and the nature of the problems and difficulties encountered. It was just this situation that led Robert Douglas to wryly observe: "The trouble with place names is that people think they can write a book on the subject without burning the midnight oil. It may be possible to become a barber in a week but not to write a book on place names."[3]

Aside from the sheer magnitude of keeping track of a large number of names, and of other names that have disappeared, there are still major hurdles to overcome. Officially, this is a bilingual country, which in itself creates questions of procedure and consistency. As well, all provinces have a say in approving new place names within their boundaries. Thus, nomenclature has the intricacy of a delicate federal-provincial issue. The geographic extent of the country, coupled with the fact that large areas are unsettled, presents an obstacle both to the assignment of names and to research.

That this is not a new situation is borne out in a comment made by Sir William Van Horne while the building of the Canadian Pacific Railway was in progress:

> In giving names to stations we had to reject all names which were preoccupied in Canada, all which contained a combination of so-called "spaced" letters in the Morse telegraphic alphabet and which were likely to be blurred in transmission, and all names having a close resemblance either in print or handwriting or in Morse alphabet because such names result in frequent errors in booking passengers and in handling freight. . . . We had further to reject, as a rule, names not easily pronounced. . . . I am not particularly proud of our station names as a whole for there is not much originality in them. When we were building at the rate of 100 or more miles per month the stations frequently ran ahead of the names.[4]

Some of the most interesting and euphonious Canadian place names are attributable to Amerindian and Inuit sources. Unfortunately, many of these are difficult to relate to the English or the French language and consequently have often been disregarded in favour of more traditional names. Although this situation has sparked controversy on more than one occasion, it captured the headlines in 1975 when the Quebec government recommended a series of new names for lakes in the northern region of the province. All designations honoured seventeenth-century inhabitants of Quebec, with the exception of two which commemorated Huron Indians associated with Samuel de Champlain. Since neither group – French or Huron – had had an association with the area, and since the features in question already possessed Inuit names, protests were launched. If this trend were to be continued, the Northern Inuit Association went on record as suggesting that certain locations in southern Canada might appropriately be renamed. Thus, Sanikuvik, roughly translated as "large garbage dump", was facetiously suggested for Montreal.

Various procedures have been tried for evolving new place names and for replacing earlier names. From the standpoint of the CPCGN, all such changes must fall within the guidelines listed on pages 15-18. A source frequently tapped for previously un-named features in some sections of the country has been casualty lists of Canadian servicemen who paid the supreme sacrifice in the Second World War. More than nine thousand new names have been added to the map of Canada as a result of the decision to honour the memory of fallen servicemen. Not all casualties could be commemorated in this way, as every effort had to be made to avoid name duplication, especially within a single prov-ince. Occasionally, residents of a given area mount campaigns for name changes, sometimes politicians assign names with little thought of the consequences, and not infrequently pressure groups lobby for changes. From time to time a note of partisan-ship may enter the debates, although at all times such overtures are scrupulously side-stepped by the Permanent Committee. Thus, the complaint of a Northern Ontario resident was merely noted and filed. The writer lamented that ". . . many lakes and streams in this district were named after good tories who contrib-uted nothing but tory chaos. [Our family] has worked for the Liberal party since confederation and it is only because of my employment with the provincial government until retirement that I was unable to expose myself too much. But I still voted the proper way and this includes my family."[5] The nature of the whole problem and the complexities involved can best be indica-ted by citing a few case studies.

During 1934, the four-hundredth anniversary of the arrival of the explorer Jacques Cartier was marked. In line with the interest inspired by the occasion, a three-cent commemorative stamp with a view of Cartier on board ship was issued on July 1, 1934. Cairns were unveiled and appropriate ceremonies arranged. Early in the year the Ligue des Intérêts Nationaux (League of National Interest) petitioned the Board on Geographic Names that North-umberland Strait (which separates Prince Edward Island from the mainland) be renamed Cartier Strait in honour of its discoverer.

At first the suggestion was dismissed on the ground that North-umberland Strait was an old and established name. In rebuttal the League pointed out that ". . .if the name Northumberland is ancient and respectable. . .is not that of Cartier still more respectable?" It soon became evident that the matter was one which would not disappear. In an effort toward resolution, the Board asked for comments from its members in the Maritimes and decided to delve into the claim that Cartier discovered the strait. All replies received from the region were negative. The Premier of Prince Edward Island, W. J. P. MacMillan, was of the opinion that confusion would result from the suggested change and that this would "counteract any sentimental merit which would attach to the name Cartier". The Nova Scotian representative, Harry Piers, elaborated upon a more general problem. To make such a change ". . .however worthy the intention and notable the occasion would open the way for all sorts of changes in the names of geographic features and this would gradually result in the replacement of well established names long used on maps, charts, legal documents and in literature by names which have become perhaps unfortunately, merely ones of historic interest."[6]

Meanwhile, extensive archival research was undertaken and it was uncovered that Cartier had never sailed though the strait, that he merely crossed the north end of it and, mistaking the expanse of water for a bay, had named it for St. Lunarius since he sailed into the "bay" on July 1, 1534, the day of St. Lunarius. With all the evidence in, the Board ruled, on June 12, 1934, that the name Northumberland Strait would stand. Absence of any measure of local support, combined with the problems inherent in such a major name change, sealed the fate of the campaign by the Ligue des Intérêts Nationaux.

A name change which created a more violent outburst and which was rejected by both local and national groups occurred in 1946. Prime Minister Mackenzie King decided that Castle Mountain, located in Banff National Park, would be renamed Mount Eisenhower in honour of the Allied commander in Europe during the Second World War. Castle Mountain, a towering 9,076-foot peak resembling a parapeted fortress, had been on the maps since at least 1858, when it was spotted by Sir James Hector, a member of the famous Palliser expedition. King's decision, conveyed in a memo dated January 9, 1946, was reluctantly accepted. However, this was not the first time that a place name had been assigned by prime-ministerial edict. In 1929, King's Christmas present to Miss Ishbel MacDonald, daughter of British Prime Minister Ramsay MacDonald, was mentioned in his diary: ". . . a telegram [today to] Ishbel telling her the government has named a mountain between Banff and Lake Louise, Mount Ishbel, after her. . . . a peak 10,300 feet high. This will give great pleasure to her father."[7]

This 1929 decision, concerning a previously unnamed peak, passed virtually unnoticed. Mount Eisenhower, on the other hand, became a matter of national controversy as letters, telegrams, and petitions poured in from all parts of the country. The Alpine Club of Canada protested: "While we recognize the kind thought that prompted such action. . .surely there is some better way of doing honour to [Eisenhower] than by renaming a landmark which is so fittingly named. . . . We earnestly hope that other great peaks which have become well known and beloved will remain inviolate."[8] Ski clubs, mountain-climbing organizations, and ordinary citizens joined the fray "to protect a name assigned by nature thousands of years ago". Equally impressive was the unanimity of editorial comment on the issue, while the few voices raised in favour of the move merely hoped that it might encourage more American tourists to visit the area. The Vancouver *Province* struck a prophetic note: ". . .the gesture will be futile. No one who has ever seen Castle Mountain will call it anything but Castle Mountain. The mountain named itself in the first instance. . .its battlemented towers, its buttresses, its crenellated crags shout Castle! Castle! Castle! all day long. They can never be made to say 'Eisenhower'."[9]

Subsequent events have supported the view of the editorial. Thirty years of repetition of the new name on maps, charts, and official documents has not erased the memory of Castle Mountain. Each year protests are mounted with the CPCGN, and recently a movement was launched to leave Eisenhower as a designation for one of the peaks, retaining the old name for the mountain.

That it is still an emotion-tinged issue is borne out by a 1971 correspondent: "Now that Mackenzie King is no longer with us, could your committee not take the popular step of restoring the old name? Generations of Western Canadians will call you blessed if you do."[10] There is little doubt that acquiescence to this name change was probably the most unpopular decision in the history of the Committee.

Mackenzie King was not the only prominent politician to interfere with the policies and procedures of the CPCGN. In most other instances the changes sought have not achieved notoriety or any measure of publicity, usually because suggested designations were for minor, unnamed features, and sometimes because prior consultation was undertaken. The outstanding exception was a decision of Newfoundland Premier J. R. Smallwood to honour the memory of Sir Winston Churchill by renaming the Hamilton River in Labrador. As Smallwood tells it: "I had been to the funeral of Churchill in London, Edmund de Rothschild taking me in his car to the lying in state at Westminster. He was deeply affected, and so was I. I told him that I thought that the least Newfoundland could do to honour Churchill's name was to call our great falls and river after him."[11] Not only was there no consultation with the CPCGN on the matter, but the change disregarded procedures outlined in the legislation which established the Newfoundland Nomenclature Board. Specifically, three points were at issue: Canada already possessed a Churchill River, and confusion could result, the previous name was one of longstanding usage, and appropriate bodies had not been called on for advice or recommendations. After Smallwood's public announcement it was too late, and although the change was subsequently approved by the Newfoundland legislature, an air of controversy continued to surround the issue. The *Cape Breton Post* was particularly outspoken: "When Newfoundland entered Confederation it took on certain obligations in relation to the entire Canadian picture as well as the tangible advantages that Mr. Smallwood is quick to point out to the voters of his province. One of the obligations should be a proper respect for established names on the map of Canada and its corollary to be original in the choice of new place names."[12] In both the Mount Eisenhower and Churchill River cases, few people questioned the motive of honouring these men; the unanimity of protest came in the manner and the locale in which these changes of name were carried out. The hands of the CPCGN were tied, for, after the fanfare of public announcements, it was difficult if not impossible to retract the change. All it could do was to go on record "that well established names which have proved satisfactory should not be changed and that if it is desirable to commemorate distinguished persons, that a hitherto unnamed feature be selected."

Not all disputes concerning place names have political over-tones – sometimes the addition or deletion of a single letter can provoke debate. Is Whonnock or Whonock the correct spelling for a town in the Fraser Valley of British Columbia? Of Amerindian origin, both forms were used until 1939, when an attempt was made by postal authorities to standardize matters by adopting Whonock. Immediately there was a public outcry, and a petition bearing 217 signatures (in favour of Whonnock) was forwarded to Ottawa. The question was raised in the House of Commons by the Member for Fraser Valley, H. J. Barber. To those who suggested that this was an insignificant matter, Mr. Barber replied: "We have not reached the stage in this country where some central authority is going to dictate such matters to a community." And again: "What would happen if someone tried to take one 't' out of Ottawa?"[13] As with many similar cases, it became necessary to undertake exhaustive research to determine the most authoritative spelling. The documentary evidence revealed that, from 1879 onward, Whonock was most frequently used, and the shortened form was adopted; however, local residents have continued to use Whonnock.[14]

Wawa, Ontario, another Amerindian name, also inspired a lengthy debate. In 1948 executives of Algoma Steel Corporation decided that the name should be changed to Jamestown in honour of Sir James Dunn, who held a controlling interest in the company. Numerous public-opinion polls were taken, and on all occasions the suggested change was not accepted. Eventually, the United Steel Workers Local collected a petition bearing over a thousand names supporting the change to Jamestown. This was sufficient evidence for the postal authorities, and the name of the post office was changed accordingly. The townspeople refused to accept the decision and finally, on December 15, 1953, a formal plebiscite was held in an effort to settle the matter. Jamestown lost by a substantial margin, the name reverted to the euphonious Wawa, and this form was officially adopted by the CPCGN on April 17, 1960.

Sometimes commercial interests have become involved in suggesting changes in place names. LaRivière, Manitoba, was named for Alphonse LaRivière (1842–1925), a prominent journalist and politician. In 1964 it was proposed that the name be changed to Seekaywye, a word purporting to be of Cree origin but in reality a mere rendering of the call letters of a Winnipeg radio station. Although there was some local support for the change, it was soon evident that opposition was mounting. A protest was launched by the Association d'Éducation des Canadiens Français du Manitoba, which pointed out the singular contribution of La-Rivière to the development of the province. The suggested change did not have the support of the Manitoba provincial authorities and it was emphasized that the proposal contravened CPCGN guidelines (see 11f). The matter was finally settled by the CPCGN on October 5, 1964, when official sanction for the name change was refused. LaRivière remains on the map.

Canada has witnessed in recent years a steady movement toward the ideal of a bilingual and bicultural country. Not unexpectedly, in light of our history, this development has inspired considerable criticism and even hostility. Some Canadians would willingly block almost every move in the direction of language equality, while others, very aware of years of indifference and inactivity, have shown themselves to be unusually sensitive on the matter. Inevitably, place-name changes and suggested changes have figured in these linguistic skirmishes. Over the years some place names of undoubted French origin have been replaced either by new English names or English translations of the original. Lac-St-Pierre, a widening of the St. Lawrence River near Trois-Rivières, was named by Samuel de Champlain on June 29, 1603,

St. Peter's Day; however, for years it was listed on all federal maps as Lake St. Peter. The justification was simply that a general policy of wholesale translation of English nomenclature, no matter how valid the historical and linguistic arguments, would be detrimental to the safety of shipping. In the case of Lac-St-Pierre this was hardly a legitimate point, and the French form was given approval on June 18, 1965. The present policy of the CPCGN regarding names in Quebec is to accept the decision of the Geographic Board of Quebec unless it can be demonstrated that their wishes are at odds with the guidelines adopted by all provinces.

A classic example of English–French difficulties in place nomenclature erupted over the official designation for Harrington Lake in the Gatineau region of Quebec. The case would, in all probability, have passed unnoticed were it not for the acquisition by the federal government in 1958 of a sizeable acreage on the shore of the lake. The estate, to be used as a summer residence for the prime minister, focused national attention on the site. When the matter came before the House of Commons, Quebec members pointed out that Lac Mousseau was the accepted local name for the lake. A compromise, suggested by J. W. Pickersgill and accepted by Paul Comtois, the minister responsible, designated the location as Harrington Lake (Lac Mousseau) in the English text and Lac Mousseau (Lake Harrington) in the French version.[15] On the surface it might appear that historical research would reveal which of the two competing names was the more accurate. However, the more research, the more entangled the rival claims became. It was established that a settler by the name of Heatherington (later spelled Harrington) had occupied land on the lakeshore as early as 1827, and the name Lake Harrington appeared on maps and plans from 1850 onward. Valid confirmation of the designation Lac Mousseau was also made. Louis Mousseau settled on the lakeshore in 1867, and his descendants retained title to their land until 1905. Thus there was no clear-cut historical precedent on which to base a final decision.

In 1962 the question surfaced again when the Quebec authorities informed the CPCGN that Lac Mousseau (Lac Harrington) was the provincially approved name. This was ratified by the CPCGN and is now the official name for the lake. After the establishment of the prime minister's summer residence, the Historical Society of the Gatineau took an active part in researching the rival name claims. When the final designation became known they put forward the suggestion that, since both the Harrington and Mousseau families had unquestioned associations with the area, "the creek which draws from Lac Philippe into Lac Mousseau into Lac Meech be named Harrington Creek". This was unacceptable to La Commission de Géographie de Québec and the name Ruisseau Mousseau was officially adopted for this drainage feature. Perhaps the least that can be said is that Lac Mousseau (Lac Harrington) is now a thoroughly bilingual place name; however, oral tradition dies hard, and Prime Minister Pierre Trudeau still referred, as late as 1977, to his summer residence as being located at Harrington Lake. Sensitivity on the language issue is particularly noticeable in the Ottawa–Hull region. For example: Hull is not a popular place name with many residents of Quebec and from time to time suggestions have been put forward to replace it with Ville Montcalm, Ville Montferrand, or the more neutral Amerindian Asticou.[16] In 1976 the suggestion was put forward that the Ottawa–Hull area should be officially designated the National Capital Region. This was later decided against by government sources, much to the relief of the *Ottawa Journal.* In commenting on the controversy, the newspaper chided the government: "Ottawa will always be Ottawa. . . . It isn't the seat of government that needs changing. It's the head. At least we presume it is the government's head that keeps coming up with so many schemes causing concern in the country."[17]

From the foregoing examples the deduction can be made that place names become fixed following one of two major patterns. Those oldest and more enduring "than records in stone or brass" can best be described as having originated through evolutionary means. The name of the country – Canada – falls in this category (see entry for same).[18]

The second method of naming is affirmation by government decree – either in the replacement of old names or in the assigning of new ones. While this approach is normally commendable, it can be carried to exaggerated lengths. Some of the most banal and bland of Canadian place names may be traced to this source. In the final analysis it is people, and the people most directly concerned, who can best adjudicate the acceptability of place names. Changes will only become established and accepted if backed by the popular will.

PRINCIPLES AND PROCEDURES ADOPTED BY CPCGN*

PRINCIPLE 1   NAMES GOVERNED BY STATUTORY AUTHORITY
The names of municipalities, territorial divisions, reserves, parks and other legal entities as created by, or a result of, legislation by the appropriate government shall be accepted by the Committee.

PRINCIPLE 2   NAMES GIVEN BY OTHER AGENCIES
Postal authorities, railway companies, major utilities, and resource development companies should seek the advice and the endorsement of the Committee concerning the use of geographical names connected with their operations.

PRINCIPLE 3   NAMES IN PUBLIC USE
First consideration should be given to names with established public use. Unless there are good reasons to the contrary, this principle should prevail.

PRINCIPLE 4   PRESERVATION OF NAMES
Established names that have proved acceptable and satisfactory should not be changed or altered.

PRINCIPLE 5   UNIFORMITY FOR SINGLE ENTITIES
Names applying to various service facilities (e.g. post offices, stations) should conform with the names of the communities which they serve. When proposing names for physical and cultural fea-

*Canadian Permanent Committee on Geographical Names, *Principles and Procedures* (Ottawa, Department of Energy, Mines and Resources, 1976).

tures, the complete entity to which each name applies should be determined to avoid the approval in the future of different names for sections of the same entity. It is not necessary, however, to extend the names of streams to the uppermost headwaters if large lakes intervene.

PRINCIPLE 6   DUPLICATION OF NAMES

Where established duplicated names and names similar in sound or spelling tend to cause confusion, the Committee will seek local assistance to achieve distinctions among them. Duplication of new names to the extent that it may result in confusion should be avoided.

PRINCIPLE 7   LANGUAGE AND ORTHOGRAPHY

Words of common origin for associated features should be uniform in spelling. The adoption of both English and French forms for the specific part of a name should be avoided, although they may be accepted where sanctioned by established usage. The spelling and accenting of names should agree with the rules of the language in which they are written. Hyphenation and the genitive apostrophe should be approved only when they are well established and in current usage.

PRINCIPLE 8   PERSONAL NAMES

Personal names should not be used unless it is in the public interest to honour a person by applying such a name to a geographical feature. Names should be derived from persons who have significantly contributed to the area of the features selected. The application of a personal name during the lifetime of the person concerned should only be made in exceptional circumstances. Ownership of land should never in itself be grounds for the application of the owner's or donor's name to a geographical feature.

PRINCIPLE 9   PREFERRED SOURCES FOR NAMES

In approving names for previously unnamed features the following sources are recommended: descriptive names appropriate to

NOTES

1. W. F. Ganong, "A Monograph on the Place Nomenclature of the Province of New Brunswick", *Transactions of the Royal Society of Canada*, 2d ser. (1896), p. 176.
2. *The Canada Gazette*, June 25, 1898 (3324)
3. CPCGN 204-1, Vol. I, R. Douglas to J. Wallace, November 7, 1924.
4. PAC MG30 D9, Vol. V, W. Van Horne to G. Johnson, November 23, 1897.
5. CPCGN 42/A/SE.
6. CPCGN 11/L.
7. PAC MG26 J13, Vol. XXXV, December 21, 1929.
8. CPCGN 82/0, Alpine Club of Canada to Mackenzie King, January 10, 1946.
9. *Vancouver Province*, January 22, 1946.
10. CPCGN 82/0, G. F. G. Stanley to Gordon Delaney, June 15, 1971.
11. Joseph Smallwood, *I Chose Canada* (Toronto: Macmillan of Canada, 1973), p. 461.
12. *Cape Breton Post*, February 10, 1965.
13. *House of Commons Debates*, May 24, 1939. See also CPCGN 92/G/1.
14. An unsuccessful attempt was launched in 1930 to change the spelling of Moncton, New Brunswick, to Monckton, the correct version of the name of Robert Monckton (1726–82), for whom the city was named. Monckton was senior brigadier-general under General James Wolfe and was wounded at the Battle of the Plains of Abraham in 1759. CPCGN 21/I/2.
15. *House of Commons Debates*, June 18, 1959.
16. *Ottawa Journal*, May 22, 1975.
17. *Ibid.*, February 7, 1976.
18. For a detailed explanation of the various theories surrounding the name Canada, see: Mark M. Orkin, *Speaking Canadian English* (Toronto: General Publishing Co., 1970), p. 159-74. Note also *A Dictionary of Canadianisms* (Toronto: W. J. Gage Limited, 1967).

Canada

Although time has indelibly imprinted "Canada" on the map of the northern half of the continent of North America, numerous other names were suggested for the proposed confederation in 1867. Among these were: Albertsland, Albionora, Borealia, Britannia, Cabotia, Colonia, Efisga (a combination of the first letters of England, France, Ireland, Scotland, Germany, and Aboriginal lands), Hochelaga, Norland, Superior, Transatlantia, Tuponia (an acrostic for the United Provinces of North America), and Victorialand. The debate was placed in perspective by Thomas D'Arcy McGee, who declared (February 9, 1865), "I read in one newspaper not less than a dozen attempts to derive a new name. One individual chooses Tuponia and another Hochelaga as a suitable name for the new nationality. Now I ask any honourable member of this House how he would feel if he woke up some fine morning and found himself instead of a Canadian, a Tuponian or a Hochelagander." Fortunately for posterity, McGee's wit and reasoning, along with common sense, prevailed, and on July 1, 1867, "the provinces of Canada, Nova Scotia, and New Brunswick" became "one Dominion under the name of Canada".

While the *Dictionary of Canadianisms* lists ten possible explanations for the word (ranging from Spanish *Acan Nada* to a form of *Canara* or *Canata*, a place name in southern India), the generally accepted origin may be traced to the writings of Jacques Cartier in 1536. While sailing up the St. Lawrence River, Cartier noticed that the Indians referred to their settlements as *kanata,* which, from its repetition, the French took to be the name of the entire country. Such it was destined to become in 1867.

Alberta

 The district of Alberta was created in 1882, and enlarged to become a province of Canada on September 1, 1905. The name was suggested by the Marquess of Lorne, Governor General of Canada from 1878 to 1883, in honour of his wife, H.R.H. Princess Louise Caroline Alberta, daughter of Queen Victoria.

ACADIA VALLEY   Named in 1910 by settlers from Nova Scotia. *See* Nova Scotia *entry*

AIRDRIE   Site selected about 1893 by the Canadian Pacific Railway; named for a town in Lanarkshire, Scotland.

ANDREW   Name honours the first postmaster in the district, Andrew Whitford. Post office opened in 1902.

ASSINIBOINE, MOUNT   Named for the Assiniboine tribe of Stony Indians who frequented the area. In translation: "those who cook by placing hot stones in water". *See* Manitoba *entry*

ATHABASCA   Of Cree origin. Early spellings: Araubaska (Peter Pond) and Athapescow (Arrowsmith). Various interpretations of the meaning: "where there are reeds" (Douglas); "meeting place of many waters" (Voorhis). Town was first called Athabasca Landing about 1889; name changed to Athabaska in 1904 and changed back to Athabasca in 1948. The provisional district of Athabasca was established in 1882, embracing the northern parts of modern Alberta and Saskatchewan.

BANFF   Name suggested by John H. MacTavish, Land Commissioner of the Canadian Pacific Railway, for Banff, an ancient resort town in Scotland near the birthplace of Sir George Stephen, Baron Mount Stephen, president of the railway from 1881 to 1888.

BARRHEAD   Named in 1913 by the directors of a local co-operative for Barrhead, Renfrewshire, Scotland, a town where the co-operative idea flourished.

BASHAW   Named for Eugene Bashaw, an early settler. Post office dates from 1910.

BASSANO   Probably traceable to Marquis de Bassano, a prominent shareholder in the Canadian Pacific Railway.

BEAVERLODGE   Name taken from the nearby river of the same name. Possibly a descriptive.

BELLEVUE   Name suggested by the mountain setting. First applied to a mining camp and later transferred to the town in 1907.

BENTLEY   Named for an early settler, George Bentley. Post office opened in 1901.

BLACK DIAMOND   Descriptive, for the coal beds found in the vicinity. Suggested by Addison McPherson, an early pioneer (Mardon). First post office opened in 1907.

BLACKFALDS   Early name, Waghorn (for Walter Waghorn, postmaster), changed in 1903 to Blackfalds, after Blackfaulds, a Scottish hamlet.

BLAIRMORE   For Andrew G. Blair (1844–1907), Premier of New Brunswick from 1883 to 1884 and federal Minister of Railways from 1896 to 1903. Townsite named in 1898.

BONNYVILLE   Early name, St. Louis de Moose Lake, changed in 1910 to commemorate the Rev. François Bonnin, the first Catholic priest in the district.

BOWDEN   Assigned in 1892 for Bowden, near Manchester, England. The early name was Lonepine, referring to a landmark adjacent to the Edmonton Trail.

BOW RIVER   On Thompson's map of 1792. Possibly an English translation of the Cree word for "bow", since wood for bow-making was plentiful in the vicinity. Also Bow Island.

BRAZEAU, MOUNT   Named for Joseph E. Brazeau, a Hudson's Bay Company officer, who served at Rocky Mountain House from 1858 to 1859 and at Jasper House from 1861 to 1862.

BROOKS   Name assigned in 1903 in honour of N. E. Brooks, divisional engineer of the Canadian Pacific Railway.

CALGARY   The North West Mounted Police established Fort Brisebois (named for its commanding officer) at the junction of the Bow and Elbow rivers in 1875. The name was later changed to Calgary, from the name of a location on the Isle of Mull, Scotland. Exact interpretation of the original Gaelic is lost; however, a meaning once ascribed, "clear running water", is incorrect. May possibly refer to a stone enclosure since there is an outcropping on Mull which, from a distance, resembles a stone dyke.

CALMAR   For the Swedish seaport town of Kalmar, the birthplace of an early resident in the district. Post office established in 1900.

CAMROSE   Probably for Camrose in Pembrokeshire, Wales; but may also be a coined name for the wild roses that grow along the bank or "cam" of Stoney Creek, which flows through the town.

CANMORE   Probably after Malcolm Canmore (?–1093), King Malcolm III of Scotland.

CARDSTON   Honours Charles Ora Card (1839–1906), son-in-law of Brigham Young. Card was first president of the Mormon Church in Canada and was responsible for a migration from Utah to this area in 1887.

CASTLE MOUNTAIN   *See* Eisenhower, Mount

CASTOR   The adjacent Castor Creek implies the presence of beaver in the area (French = *castor*; Latin = *Castor canadensis*).

CHOWN, MOUNT   After the Rev. Samuel Dwight Chown (1853–1933), General Superintendent of the Methodist Church, and a strong supporter of Church Union in 1925.

CLAIRE LAKE   Originally Clearwater Lake in Sir Alexander Mackenzie's *Journal* of 1792. Thompson's map (1814) describes this condition of the lake.

CLARESHOLM   Assigned in the early 1890s for the home in Medicine Hat of Superintendent Niblock of the C.P.R. and his wife, Clare.

COALDALE   Named for the residence of Elliott T. Galt (son of Sir Alexander Tilloch Galt), general manager of the Alberta Railway and Irrigation Company.

COCHRANE   After Senator M. H. Cochrane (1823–1903), president of the British America Ranch Company.

COLD LAKE   Undoubtedly a descriptive designation. The name appears first as Coldwater Lake on Turnor's map (1790).

COLEMAN   Name assigned in 1904 by the president of the International Coal and Coke Company, A. C. Flumerfelt, for his daughter.

COLEMAN, MOUNT   Named in honour of Dr. Arthur Philemon Coleman (1852–1939), geologist, who explored the territory between the North Saskatchewan and Athabasca rivers.

COLUMBIA, MOUNT   Name traceable to Columbia River. *See* British Columbia entry

CORONATION   Designated by the Canadian Pacific Railway to mark the coronation of King George V and Queen Mary, June 22, 1911.

CORONATION, MOUNT   Commemorates the coronation of King Edward VII and Queen Alexandra, August 9, 1902.

CROWSNEST   Pass, river, lake, and village. Name probably refers to the nesting place of crows. It is less likely attributable to the Crow Indians, a group of whom were surprised and captured "in their nest" by members of the Blackfoot tribe. The pass was first noted by Blakiston in 1858.

DEVON   Name stems from the Devonian geological formation. Devon Mountain takes its name from the same source.

DIADEM, PEAK   A descriptive term for the "diadem of snow" which crowns the peak. Name assigned by J. Norman Collie, who scaled the mountain in 1898.

DIDSBURY   For Didsbury, now a part of the city of Manchester, England.

DRAYTON VALLEY   Originally called Power House; present name was assigned in 1920 and was taken from a village in Berkshire, England.

DRUMHELLER   Honours Samuel Drumheller, a pioneer in the mining of coal in the province.

EAST COULEE   A term applied to the dry bed of a stream or ravine.

EDITH CAVELL, MOUNT   The mountain, first known as Montagne de la Grande Traverse, was noted in 1859 by Dr. Hector of the Palliser expedition. The new name was approved and adopted March 7, 1916, to commemorate Edith Cavell (1865–1915), an English nurse, executed during the First World War.

EDMONTON   Name taken from Fort Edmonton, built in 1795 farther down the North Saskatchewan River than the present city. The fort was destroyed in 1807, but was relocated within the site of the present city limits by the Hudson's Bay Company some time before 1819. The fort is reputed to have been named by William Tomison for Edmonton, now part of metropolitan

London, England, in honour of the birthplace of John Peter Pruden, a clerk of the Hudson's Bay Company (Holmgren).

EDSON   The original name, Heatherwood, was changed in 1911 to honour Edson Joseph Chamberlain (1852–1924), president of the Grand Trunk Railway from 1912 to 1917.

EISENHOWER, MOUNT   For General Dwight Eisenhower, Supreme Allied Commander during the Second World War. Details in the opening chapter.

ELK POINT   Named by an early settler for a community in South Dakota (Holmgren).

EVANSBURG   For Harry Marshall Erskine Evans (1876–1973) of Edmonton (Holmgren). Post office dates from 1914.

EXSHAW   For one of the directors of a local cement company, a relative of Sir Sandford Fleming.

FAIRVIEW   Named Waterhole about 1910 because of an abundance of water for stock. Name changed in 1914 to Fairview for the farm of an early settler.

FALHER   Honours the Rev. C. Falher, an early missionary in the community.

FORBES, MOUNT   Assigned by James Hector after James David Forbes (1809–68), a Scottish scientist, who was professor of natural philosophy at Edinburgh University and later principal of St. Andrews.

FORESTBURG   First named Duxbury; incorporated in 1919 and renamed Forestburg, possibly for Forestburg, South Dakota.

FORT CHIPEWYAN   Of Cree origin, designating an Athapaskan-speaking band. The word may be translated as "pointed skins", probably referring to the manner in which the Chipewyans prepared beaver pelts. Originally a North West Company (later a Hudson's Bay Company) trading post. On Arrowsmith's map of 1832.

FORT MACLEOD   Site selected in 1874 by Col. James Farquharson Macleod (1836–94), later Commissioner of the North West Mounted Police. Known for some years as Macleod; original name restored in 1952.

FORT MCMURRAY   The North West Company established a fort on this site in 1790 known as Fort of the Forks (earliest mention in Thompson's *Journal* of 1799). Taken over by the Hudson's Bay Company in 1821, it was rebuilt in 1870 and named in honour of William McMurray (1822–77), then factor at Île-à-la-Crosse.

FORT SASKATCHEWAN   Site of a North West Mounted Police post established in 1875. *See* Saskatchewan *entry*

FORT VERMILION   North West Company trading post established in 1798; became part of Hudson's Bay Company in 1821; appears on Arrowsmith's map of 1857. Name refers to the red ochre or ferruginous deposits in the vicinity.

FRANK   Honours H. L. Frank, who opened the first coal mine in the region. A rock slide here on April 29, 1903, claimed seventy lives.

GLEICHEN   Named for Count Albert Edward Wilfred Gleichen (1833–91), financial backer of the C.P.R., who travelled to the railhead at Calgary in 1883.

GRAND CENTRE   When the community was established in 1937 "it was hoped it would become the centre of a prosperous area" (Rayburn).

GRANDE CACHE   Derived from the French *cacher*, "to hide". The word *cache* was used locally to describe a secret hiding place (probably for supplies).

GRANDE PRAIRIE   The name is French for "big prairie", indicating an open stretch of country.

GRIMSHAW   Honours Dr. M. E. Grimshaw (?–1929), a pioneer physician in the Peace River District.

GROUARD   Formerly Lesser Slave Lake post office. Name changed in 1909 to commemorate Mgr. Emile Jean-Baptiste Marie Grouard (1840–1931), pioneer missionary and Vicar Apostolic of Athabaska Diocese from 1910 to 1930.

HANNA   For David Blythe Hanna (1858–1938), railway builder and president of the Canadian National Railways from 1918 to 1922. The original name of the community was Cooperville.

HECTOR, MOUNT   Named by Dr. G. M. Dawson in 1884 in honour of Sir James Hector (1834–1907), a member of the Palliser expedition.

HIGH LEVEL   Descriptive of the topography of the region between the Peace and Hay rivers.

HIGH PRAIRIE   Describes the nature of the surrounding countryside. Post office opened in 1910. Early name, Prairie River.

HIGH RIVER   For nearby Highwood River, which takes its name from "tall trees", an English translation of the Blackfoot *Ispitsi*. So called because the trees on the river bank may be seen from a distance.

HILLCREST   Named for a local industry, Hillcrest Collieries Ltd., established by Charles P. Hill. Scene of a coal-mining disaster which killed 198 men on June 19, 1914.

HINTON   The name first appeared as Hinton Trail to mark the route from Jasper to the Yukon. The trail, and later the town, was named for W. D. Hinton, general manager of the Grand Trunk Railway.

HOLDEN   Honours James B. Holden (1876–1956), one-time member of the Alberta legislature. Known as Vermilion Valley until 1907.

HUNGABEE, MOUNT   A Stony Indian word roughly translated as "chieftain"; refers to the dominating aspect of the peak in relation to nearby mountains.

INNISFAIL   Community was known as Poplar Grove, before 1893, when it was renamed for Innisfail in Argyllshire, Scotland. The town was incorporated in 1903.

JASPER   The name is taken from Jasper House, a nearby North West Company trading post named for Jasper Hawes, the clerk in charge. Mentioned by Milton and Cheadle in *North West Passage By Land,* 1832. Also Jasper National Park and Jasper Lake.

JOFFRE, MOUNT   Honours Marshal Joseph Joffre (1852–1931), Commander-in-Chief of the French Army during the First World War.

KANANASKIS PASS   The pass was named by Palliser (1863) after a legendary Indian. The river takes its name from the pass.

KILLAM   Named for Albert Clements Killam (1849–1908), Chief Justice of Manitoba from 1899 to 1903, judge of the Supreme Court of Canada from 1903 to 1905, and first Chief Commissioner of the Board of Railway Commissioners for Canada from 1905 to 1908.

KING EDWARD, MOUNT   For King Edward VII (1841–1910), who succeeded to the throne upon the death of Queen Victoria in 1901.

KITCHENER, MOUNT   After Field-Marshal Horatio Herbert Kitchener (1850–1916), who served as British Secretary of State for War from 1914 to 1916.

LAC LA BICHE   The lake noted on Turnor's map (1790) bears the French name for "red deer lake" or "lake of the red doe". Mackenzie (1793) has Red Deer Lake. The townsite was established in 1915 on the location of an earlier Hudson's Bay Company fort.

LACOMBE   Commemorates the work of Father Albert Lacombe (1827–1916), a member of the Oblate Order and one of the first Roman Catholic missionaries in the Northwest. Lacombe played a prominent role in the uprising of 1885 by assuring the neutrality of the Blackfoot.

LAKE LOUISE   The lake was first called Emerald (Dawson map, 1884); name changed to honour H.R.H. Princess Louise Caroline Alberta, fourth daughter of Queen Victoria and wife of the Governor General, the Marquess of Lorne. *See provincial entry for* Alberta

LAMONT   After John Henderson Lamont (1865–1936), politician and jurist, who was appointed a member of the Supreme Court of Canada in 1927.

LEDUC   For Abbé Hippolyte Leduc (1842–1918), a pioneer missionary in the Northwest Territories, and later in Alberta.

LETHBRIDGE   Name assigned in 1885 for William Lethbridge (1824–1901), first president of the Northwest Coal and Navigation Company Ltd. The town was first called Coal Banks.

LLOYDMINSTER   The district was originally the site of an all-British colony, which was founded by the Rev. I. M. Barr

(1849–1937) and named Barrview. The colony was later taken over by the Rev. George Exton Lloyd (1861–1940), after whom the town is named.

LUNETTE PEAK   A descriptive (French *lunette* diminutive of *lune* "moon") for a peak south of Mount Assiniboine.

LYALL, MOUNT   Named after Dr. David Lyall, a surgeon and a naturalist, who was a member of the Boundary Commission from 1858 to 1862.

MC LENNAN   After Dr. J. K. McLennan, an official of the Edmonton, Dunvegan, and British Columbia Railway (now Northern Alberta Railway).

MAGRATH   Named for Charles A. Magrath (1860–1949), Dominion Topographical Surveyor and M.P. for Medicine Hat from 1908 to 1911. He served on the International Joint Commission from 1911 to 1914, and was its chairman from 1914 to 1936.

MANNING   The community was named in 1947 for Ernest C. Manning, Premier of Alberta from 1943 to 1968 and Senator from 1970.

MANNVILLE   For Sir Donald Mann (1853–1934), railroad contractor and vice-president of the Canadian Northern Railway.

MAYERTHORPE   The name of the post office, established in 1915, honours R. I. Mayer, the first postmaster. "Thorpe" is from the Old English for hamlet or village.

MEDICINE HAT   A translation of the Blackfoot *saamis*, "the headdress of a medicine man". The name was mentioned in a report of the North West Mounted Police in 1882. Various apocryphal stories have arisen as to its origin; however, the translation theory is probably correct. See *Alberta Historical Review*, Summer, 1965.

MERCOAL   A compound of portions of the name of a prominent local firm, McLeod River Hard Coal Company, Ltd.

MICHICHI   Takes its name from the Cree word for "hand". A reference to the nearby Hand Hills.

MIRROR   Named in 1911 for the *Daily Mirror*, an English newspaper. The Grand Trunk Pacific Railway advertised in this newspaper, hence the name (Holmgren).

MORINVILLE   Founded in 1891 by Abbé Jean-Baptiste Morin (1852–1911) and named in his honour.

MUNDARE   William Mundare, an early settler and station agent, gave his name to the post office and the railway station when the town was established in 1906.

NANTON   For Sir Augustus Nanton (1860–1925), financier and director of the Canadian Pacific Railway. Name adopted in 1902 in preference to Mosquito Creek.

OKOTOKS   Originally called Dewdney for Edgar Dewdney (1835–1916), federal Minister of the Interior; name changed March 1, 1897, to Okotoks, a Blackfoot word meaning "big rock valley". The term refers to a large glacial erratic south of the town.

OLDS   Named in 1893 for George Olds, traffic manager of the Canadian Pacific Railway. The community was formerly known as Lone Pine.

ONOWAY   Generally considered to be a misspelling of Onaway, a character in *Hiawatha* by Henry Wadsworth Longfellow. Post office established in 1904.

OYEN   Early name, Bishopburg, was changed in 1912 to honour Andrew Oyen, an early settler.

PEACE RIVER   Takes its name from Peace Point. On this location the Cree and Beaver Indians settled a jurisdictional dispute (from an entry in Mackenzie's *Journal* for October 13, 1792). Turnor's map (1790) records "Beaver Indian River by the Canadians called Peace River".

PENHOLD   Name assigned by the Canadian Pacific Railway, before 1893, after a hamlet in Scotland.

PICTURE BUTTE   A translation of a Blackfoot place name meaning "beautiful hill". A butte is a hill, usually with a flat top. Near the top of Picture Butte many stones were found, with Indian signs, pictures, and patterns on them (Rayburn).

PINCHER CREEK   A number of stories, with varying details, have evolved as to the origin of the name; however, there is agreement that it originated with the discovery in 1874 of a pair of pincers lost by an earlier prospecting party. It was officially listed as a place name in the *Geological Survey Report*, 1880.

PONOKA   Name taken from the Blackfoot word for elk. Briefly referred to as Siding 14 in early railroading days.

PROVOST   The Scottish title which applies to the head of a municipal corporation or burgh. Post office established in 1908.

RALSTON   Named by the Department of National Defence in 1949 to mark the career of J. L. Ralston (1881–1948), who served as Minister of National Defence from 1940 until his resignation in 1944.

RAYMOND   After Raymond Knight, who was part of the Mormon migration from Utah. Use of the word "stampede" (for an exhibition of skills associated with ranching) is reputed to have been suggested by Knight for the first Raymond Stampede in 1902.

REDCLIFF A descriptive name which refers to the red cliffs and outcroppings of shale on the nearby South Saskatchewan River.

RED DEER Town and river. Early Scottish settlers confused elk (found in numbers locally) for the red deer of their homeland. The original Cree name may be translated as Elk River.

REDWATER Town and river. This is a descriptive name, originally Vermilion River on Thompson's map (1814) and later changed to avoid confusion with Vermilion and Fort Vermilion. *See* Fort Vermilion

ROCKY MOUNTAIN HOUSE Name derived from the popular designation for the mountains. *See* British Columbia *entry*. David Thompson established his headquarters here in 1799. Both the Hudson's Bay Company and the North West Company were active in the region. The community appears as Acton House or Rocky Mountain House on the Arrowsmith map of 1857.

RUNDLE, MOUNT Named by Sir James Hector in 1859 after the Rev. Robert Terrill Rundle (1811–96), a prominent Methodist missionary in western Canada.

RYCROFT The post office was originally known as Spirit River. The name was changed to Roycroft in 1920 to honour R. H. Roycroft, a prominent local citizen, and was altered to Rycroft in 1933.

RYLEY Named in 1908 for G. V. Ryley, who served the Grand Trunk Pacific Railway as Land Commissioner.

ST. ALBERT After the patron saint of Father Albert Lacombe (1827–1916) and dating from January 14, 1861, when Bishop A. A. Taché selected the location as the site for a mission.

ST. PAUL Originally known as St. Paul de Métis when it was a mission station established by Father Lacombe (see above). The name was changed in 1936 upon the town's incorporation.

SEDGWICK   Honours Robert Sedgwick (1848–1906), Deputy Minister of Justice and later, from 1893 to 1906, a judge of the Supreme Court of Canada.

SIR DOUGLAS, MOUNT   Named for Field-Marshal Sir Douglas Haig (1861–1928), Commander-in-Chief of the British Army in France during the First World War.

SMOKY LAKE   Originated with a translation of an Amerindian phrase meaning "smoking lake", for a vapour caused by smouldering coal beds in the area.

SNOW DOME   A descriptive name which emphasizes the dominant feature of the mountain.

SPIRIT RIVER   Name formed from a translation of the Cree *chip-si-pi*, meaning "ghost" or "spirit".

STETTLER   Originally Blumenau, for a German colony in Brazil. The name was changed in 1906 to honour Carl Stettler (1861–1919), a native of Switzerland, who emigrated to the United States in 1887 and to Alberta in 1903.

STONY PLAIN   May be a descriptive for boulders found in the region, or may possibly have developed because the area was once frequented by Stony Indians.

STRATHMORE   Named for Claude Bowes-Lyon, Earl of Strathmore (1824–1904). His granddaughter Elizabeth married the Duke of York, later King George vi.

STUTFIELD MOUNTAIN   Honours Hugh Stutfield, a member of the English Alpine Club and joint author with J. Norman Collie of *Climbs and Explorations in the Canadian Rockies.*

SUNDRE   After Sondre in Norway, the birthplace of an early settler.

SYLVAN LAKE   Palliser's map of 1859 gives the name Swan Lake for the location. Probably a descriptive. The town of Sylvan Lake dates from 1907.

TABER   Generally considered to have been taken from Mount Tabor (Judges 4:14) or the word tabernacle. Other sources have suggested that the name may be traced to a Senator Tabor of Colorado.

TEMPLE, MOUNT   Named by Dr. G. M. Dawson for Sir Richard Temple, who led the British Association Expedition to the Rocky Mountains in 1884.

THREE HILLS   The name refers to the fact that three hills running northwest to southeast are a dominant physical characteristic of the region. Post office dates from 1904.

THREE SISTERS   A descriptive coined by Dr. G. M. Dawson in 1886 for three similar peaks in the same ridge.

TOFIELD   After an early settler, Dr. James H. Tofield. Post office established in 1898.

TROCHU   Community founded by Col. Armand Trochu (1857–1930), son of General Louis Jules Trochu (1815–96), who led the forces defending Paris in 1870. Incorporated as a village in 1911 and as a town in 1962.

TURNER VALLEY   Named for two brothers, Robert and James Turner, who established homesteads in this area in 1886.

TWINS, THE   A descriptive for "a doubleheaded mountain". Name assigned by Stutfield and Collie in 1898.

TWO HILLS   From the presence of two hills located near the town. Post office established in 1914.

VALLEYVIEW   Undoubtedly descriptive of the local topography of the Little Smoky River Valley.

VAUXHALL   After a district in London, England, that is located on the south bank of the Thames River.

VEGREVILLE   In honour of Abbé Valentin Végréville (?–1903), a late-nineteenth-century missionary in the West.

VERMILION   Town, lake, and river. *See also* Fort Vermilion. Named for red ochre deposits in the region. The first name of the town was Breage, after a town in Cornwall, England. The name was changed in 1906.

VIKING   The area was settled by immigrants from Norway. The name was selected in 1904 by popular vote.

VULCAN   The name was selected by officials of the Canadian Pacific Railway in 1910; for the Roman god of fire.

WAINWRIGHT   Originally Denwood, the name was changed June 1, 1908, to honour William Wainwright (1840–1914), senior vice-president of the Grand Trunk Pacific Railway.

WATERTON LAKES   Named by Thomas Blakiston, a member of the Palliser expedition, for Charles Waterton (1782–1865), prominent British naturalist. The river and national park take their names from the lakes.

WESTLOCK   Post office known as Edison until 1913. The present name is a compound of the names of the original owners of the townsite, Westgate and Lockhart.

WETASKIWIN   The name is derived from the Cree *witaskiwinik,* which may be translated as "place of peace" or "hills of peace".

WHISKEY GAP   A community on the Alberta–Montana border. The name is indicative of smuggling activities once carried on in the area.

WHITECOURT   Named in 1909 for Walter L. White, the first postmaster, the "court" being derived from Green Court, twenty-six miles northeast, where White had picked up mail from 1905 to 1909 (Rayburn).

WOOLLEY, MOUNT   Named by J. Norman Collie in 1898 for Herman Woolley, a prominent mountain climber.

British Columbia

 Much of the mainland region was originally known as New Caledonia; however, this name (duplicated in the South Pacific) was discarded in favour of British Columbia. The designation appears to have originated with Queen Victoria and was officially proclaimed in 1858. Columbia (after the Columbia River which was named by the American Captain Robert Gray for his ship *Columbia*) had previously been loosely applied to the southern portion of the colony.

ABBOTSFORD   Possibly for Abbotsford, the residence of Sir Walter Scott near Melrose, Roxburghshire, Scotland, but more probably after Henry Abbott (brother of Sir John Abbott, Prime Minister from 1891 to 1892), general superintendent of the Pacific Division, Canadian Pacific Railway. *See* Abbotsford, Quebec

AGASSIZ   Honours Captain Lewis Agassiz, prospector in the Cariboo gold fields, who in 1867 took up farming in the Fraser Valley.

ALBERNI   Alberni Canal named in 1791 for Don Pedro de Alberni, who attempted to establish a Spanish base at Nootka. Name applied to the settlement in 1861 by Captain George Richards.

ALBREDA   Name dates from the Milton-Cheadle expedition of 1862–3. For a relative of Viscount Milton, Lady Albreda Lyveden.

ALERT BAY   Originates with H.M.S. *Alert*, reputed to be the first steam vessel to visit the area.

ALICE ARM   Commemorates Alice Mary Tomlinson, wife of the Rev. Robert Tomlinson, who represented the Church Missionary Society in the area from 1867 to 1879. Alice Rock in Alice Arm had its name assigned by the Geographic Board of Canada in 1898.

AMOR DE COSMOS CREEK   Marks the career of Amor De Cosmos (1825–97), born William Alexander Smith (in Windsor, Nova Scotia), Premier of British Columbia from 1872 to 1874, federal M.P. for Victoria from 1871 to 1882.

ARISTAZABAL ISLAND   Name assigned by Lieutenant-Commander Jacinto Caamaño of the Spanish navy in 1792. The meaning of the name is unknown.

ARMSTRONG   Named in 1892 for W. C. Heaton Armstrong

(1853–1917), British financier, who negotiated funding for the Shuswap and Okanagan Railway and who visited the community about 1892.

ASHCROFT   Name assigned in 1862 by Clement Francis Cornwall (1836–1910) to his ranch, Ashcroft Manor, named for the home of his family in Ashcroft, Gloucestershire, England. Cornwall served as a Senator from 1867 to 1881, and as a Lieutenant-Governor of British Columbia from 1881 to 1887.

ATLIN   Lake and town. An adaptation of the Amerindian *ahtlah*, meaning "stormy water", "lake of storms", or "big water". Once a colourful gold-rush town.

BABINE LAKE   Incorporates the French word for large or protruding lip. Applied by early voyageurs to the females of the Carrier (Amerindians), who were noted for the custom of wearing labrets or lip ornaments.

BARKERVILLE   Named for William Barker (?–1894), a Cornish sailor who jumped ship in 1858 to take part in the Cariboo gold rush. Barker made a strike in 1862 valued at $600,000, only to die in poverty. Restoration of the town as a living museum began in 1959.

BEGBIE, MOUNT   Honours Sir Matthew Baillie Begbie (1819–94), noted frontier judge and Chief Justice of British Columbia from 1870 to 1894.

BELLA COOLA   River and settlement. Named after a local Salish-speaking tribe.

BRYCE, MOUNT   After British statesman Viscount James Bryce (1838–1922), one-time president of the Alpine Club of London, England.

BURNABY   Island, lake, mountain, and municipality. Marks the contribution of Robert Burnaby (1828–78), who was active in the early political and economic life of the province.

BURNS LAKE   Named in 1866 for Michael Byrnes, a surveyor for the Collins Overland Telegraph scheme. The project was later abandoned because of the success of transoceanic cable lines. *See* Telegraph Creek

CASSIAR MOUNTAINS   Derived from the Nahanni *kaska* or *kasha*, sometimes translated as "creek" or "small river". Jenness asserts that the word is Tahltan for either (1) "long moss hanging from tree", or (2) "rags wrapped around the feet". The only certainty is its Amerindian origin.

CASTLEGAR   The name is often credited to Castlegar, County Galway, Ireland; however it may be a corruption of "Castle Garden" (CPCGN files).

CHAPMAN CAMP   After F. Chapman, one-time superintendent of construction for the Consolidated Mining and Smelting Company at Kimberley (Akrigg).

CHETWYND   Originally known as Little Prairie; renamed in honour of Ralph Chetwynd (1890–1957), who served first as provincial Minister of Railways and later as Minister of Agriculture.

CHILLIWACK   The name of an Amerindian tribe. The exact meaning is in dispute but is generally interpreted as *Chill-a-waak*, "going back up", a reference to the return home "after a visit to the mouth of the Fraser River" (Akrigg).

CLEMENCEAU, MOUNT   After the French statesman Georges Clemenceau (1841–1929). Name suggested by A. O. Wheeler on November 16, 1921.

CLINTON   Name assigned in 1863 to mark the career of Henry Pelham Clinton, Duke of Newcastle (1811–64), who visited Canada while serving as Colonial Secretary. Formerly called Cut-off Valley and 47 Mile House.

COLUMBIA   River which flows across the international boundary. Originally Rio de San Roque, rediscovered in 1792 by Captain Robert Gray and named after his ship, the *Columbia*.

COMMITTEE PUNCH BOWL   Lake on Alberta–British Columbia boundary. Named by Sir George Simpson on October 17, 1824, in honour of the London Board of the Hudson's Bay Company. "... At 6 a.m. got to the Committee's Punch Bowl where the people had a glass of rum each and ourselves a little wine which was drunk to the health of their honours with three cheers" (*Alberta Historical Review*, Autumn 1974).

COMOX   An abbreviation of an Amerindian word for "abundance", indicative of the supply of berries and game found in the district.

COQUITLAM   Derived from the Salish tribal name, *Kawayquitlam*, which may be translated as "small red salmon". For the sockeye salmon common to the area.

COURTENAY   The town is named for the nearby river, which in turn was named for Captain George Courtenay, R.N., who served on the Pacific station from 1846 to 1849.

COWICHAN   From the presence in the area of the Cowichans, a division of the Coast Salish people. Usually translated as "between two rivers" or "the warm land".

CRAIGELLACHIE   The location where the "last spike" of the Canadian Pacific Railway was driven in 1885. For a community in Morayshire, Scotland.

CRANBROOK   An early settler, Col. James Baker, named his landholding Cranbrook Farm for his birthplace, Cranbrook, in Kent, England.

CUMBERLAND   Originally known as Union for the Union Coal Company, the town changed its name in 1898 for Cumberland, England.

DAWSON CREEK   Named for George Mercer Dawson (1849–1901), prominent geologist, who became Director of the Geological Survey of Canada in 1895. The Dawson range and Mount Dawson were also named in his honour. *See also* Dawson, Y.T.

DELTA   Descriptive of the alluvial tract of land at the mouth of the Fraser River.

DUNCAN   After William Chalmers Duncan, a native of Sarnia, Ontario, and an early settler in the area. City incorporated in 1912.

ENDERBY   First called Lambly's Landing for an early settler, Robert Lambly. Name changed in 1887 to Enderby, for a village in Lincolnshire, England.

ESQUIMALT   Of Amerindian origin, the name is derived from *Is-whoy-malth*, indicating "a place gradually shoaling". Originally Puerto de Cordova in honour of the Viceroy of Mexico.

FAIRWEATHER, MOUNT   A mountain on the British Columbia–Alaska boundary, so named by Captain James Cook, who enjoyed "fair weather" there in 1778.

FERNIE   For William Fernie (1837?–1921), an early settler and prospector in the Kootenay district. The community was first known as Coal Creek.

FIELD   Named in 1884 for Cyrus W. Field (1819–92), projector of the first Atlantic cable, who is reported to have visited the area.

FORT LANGLEY   Honours Thomas Langley, Director of the Hudson's Bay Company. Here, the colony of British Columbia was proclaimed on November 19, 1858.

FORT ST. JAMES   Originally a North West Company post built by John Stuart and Simon Fraser in 1806. Served briefly as the capital of the fur-trading district of New Caledonia and is one of the oldest settlements in the province.

FORT ST. JOHN   Five different forts (dating from 1805 to 1806) were constructed at various times near the modern location. The site of the present town was established in 1925. Both Fort St. James and Fort St. John were named by the North West Company for reasons unknown today.

FRASER RIVER   The largest river in British Columbia was named about 1813 by David Thompson (1770–1857) in honour of Simon Fraser (1760?–1839), the superintendent of the then district of New Caledonia. The river was discovered in 1793 by Alexander Mackenzie; however, Fraser explored the river from its source to its mouth. *See* Thompson River

FRUITVALE   A coined word to denote the prevalence of fruit farming in the region. Established in 1899.

GARIBALDI, MOUNT   Named about 1860 by Captain George Richards of H.M.S. *Plumper*, a survey ship, for Italian patriot Giuseppe Garibaldi (1807–82).

GEORGIA, STRAIT OF   Honours King George III and was conferred by Captain Vancouver on June 4, 1792. The original designation, The Gulf of Georgia, was changed in 1865 to The Strait of Georgia.

GIBSONS LANDING   From the presence of George William Gibson (1829–1913), one of the early settlers in the area. Post office is called Gibsons.

GILFORD ISLAND Named for Richard James Meade, Viscount Gilford (1832–1907), Commander of H.M.S. *Tribune*, which saw duty on the Pacific station in 1864.

GOLDEN Originally The Cache, the name Golden City was chosen as a counterpart to Silver City (which is near the present Mount Eisenhower). This was later shortened to Golden by postal authorities.

GOODSIR, MOUNT Applied by James Hector of the Palliser expedition in 1858. Probably for John Goodsir (1814–67), professor of anatomy at Edinburgh University. Name approved on March 1, 1904.

GRAHAM ISLAND Largest and northernmost island of the Queen Charlotte group. Discovered by John Perez in 1774 and named in 1853 for Sir James Robert Graham (1792–1861), then First Lord of the Admiralty.

GRAND FORKS First known as Grande Prairie, this town changed its name upon incorporation in 1897 to the descriptive Grand Forks from the confluence of the Granby and Kettle rivers. It may also have been named for a mining camp in Colorado (CPCGN files).

GREENWOOD The first settler, Robert Wood, devised the name in 1895, indicating that the townsite was covered with green timber.

HARRISON HOT SPRINGS Spa at the south end of Harrison Lake. Named for Benjamin Harrison, one-time deputy-governor of the Hudson's Bay Company. Although long known by Amerindians, the first official record of the springs was published in the *Victoria Gazette*, December 30, 1858.

HAWKESBURY ISLAND Name assigned by Captain George Vancouver for Sir Charles Jenkinson, Baron Hawkesbury

(1727–1808), who served as President of the Board of Trade.

HAY RIVER   A descriptive name derived from the abundance of hay and grass along the banks of the river.

HAZELTON   From the presence of large numbers of hazelnut trees in the vicinity.

HECATE STRAIT   Named after H.M.S. *Hecate* of the British Columbia coast survey of 1860–2.

HELMET, THE   A peak northeast of Mount Robson, so named by J. H. Scattergood in 1900 because of its resemblance to a helmet.

HOMATHKO RIVER   After Salish tribe living on Bute Inlet. The word may be translated as "ice water" (Akrigg).

HOPE   The original Hudson's Bay Company fort, built in 1848–9, was named Hope in the hope or expectation that an all-British fur-brigade trail north of the 49th parallel might be developed. May also have been named for John Hope, a chief factor of the Hudson's Bay Company.

HOUSTON   Bestowed (as a result of a newspaper poll) in honour of John Houston, early reporter and journalist in Prince Rupert.

HOWE SOUND   Named in 1792 by Captain Vancouver for Admiral the Rt. Hon. Richard Scope, Earl Howe (1726–99).

HUBER, MOUNT   After Émile Huber, prominent member of the Swiss Alpine Club. Named in 1894.

HUDSON HOPE   Fort Hudson's Hope, a North West Company post, was built in 1805 by Simon Fraser. It is shown on Arrowsmith's map of 1850. Although the exact origin of the

name is unknown, it is possibly for an early prospector who antici-
pated a gold strike in the region.

HUNTER ISLAND   Probably named by Captain George Vancouver after his friend and physician Dr. John Hunter.

ILLECILLEWAET   River and village. The name is Amerindian,
meaning "swift water", and was first applied to the river.

INVERMERE   Although first known as Copper City and later as
Canterbury, the town changed its name in 1912 to Invermere,
"mouth of [Windermere] lake".

JUAN DE FUCA STRAIT   The claim of Juan de Fuca (Apostolos
Valeranos) of having discovered the strait is disputed; however, it
was entered and named, or renamed, in his honour by Captain
Charles William Barkley in 1787.

KAMLOOPS   Although various explanations have been advanced as to the origin of the word, the evidence points to the
Amerindian *kahm-o-loops* or *cume-loups*, usually translated as "the
meeting of the waters" or "meeting place" (for the confluence of
the North and South Thompson rivers).

KASLO   The village, lake, and mountain take their names from
Kaslo River, which was named for John Kasleau, an early prospector.

KELOWNA   Traceable to an Amerindian tribe whose name
means "grizzly bear". The post office was established in 1893 and
the city was incorporated in 1905.

KEREMEOS   Probably a corruption of an Amerindian phrase,
"wind channel in the mountain", descriptive of the wind sweep-
ing through the nearby Similkameen Valley.

KICKING HORSE PASS   Dr. (later Sir) James Hector, a member of the Palliser expedition, which explored the Rocky Mountains seeking a practicable pass for the railway, was the discoverer of Kicking Horse Pass. It was so named because one of Hector's horses gave him a severe kick near this location.

KIMBERLEY   For Kimberley, a diamond-mining centre in South Africa. The name was said to have been assigned about 1896 by Col. Ridpath, an American mining magnate, in the expectation that holdings in this region might prove as valuable as those in South Africa.

KING GEORGE, MOUNT   Honours King George V (seven near-by mountains were named for members of his immediate family).

KING ISLAND   Name bestowed by Captain George Vancouver in 1783 after Captain James King. The two had been midshipmen together on H.M.S. *Discovery* under the command of Captain Cook.

KINNAIRD   Name assigned by Canadian Pacific Railway in 1904 to honour Lord Kinnaird, a shareholder in the company.

KITIMAT   For the Kitimat people. The name is usually translated as "the people of the snow". The town came into prominence in 1951 with the establishment of a smelter by the Aluminum Company of Canada. The post office was approved on June 6, 1952.

KITLOPE LAKE   Takes its name from a branch of the Haisla (Kwakiutl) Amerindians. The name has been translated as "the people of the mountain pass".

KLINAKLINI LAKE   An Amerindian (Chilcotin) word meaning "to turn back on itself".

KOOTENAY RIVER   From the Kootenays, whose name means "water people". Also Kootenay Lake.

LAC LA HACHE   "A French person during the days of gold fever was cutting a hole in the ice, and lost his axe (*hache*) resulting in the name." (CPCGN files)

LADYSMITH   Named by James Dunsmuir in 1900 after the relief of Ladysmith in Natal. *See* Natal

LILLOOET   Town, lake, and river. An Amerindian word which may be translated as "wild onion". Appears on Anderson's map of 1849.

LOUISE ISLAND   Named in 1878 by G. M. Dawson of the Geological Survey of Canada (later Director) in honour of Princess Louise, wife of the then Governor-General, the Marquess of Lorne.

LUMBY   First known as White Valley, the town changed its name in 1894 to Lumby for Moses Lumby (1842–93), one-time vice-president of the Shuswap and Okanagan Railway.

LYTTON   Name assigned on November 11, 1858, by Governor James Douglas for Sir Edward Bulwer-Lytton (1803–73), who served as Secretary of State for the Colonies.

MC BRIDE   In honour of Sir Richard McBride (1870–1917), who served as Premier of British Columbia from 1903 to 1915.

MACKENZIE   Created in 1966 and named for Alexander Mackenzie (1764?–1820), the first white man to cross Canada to the Pacific Ocean.

MARYSVILLE   Name taken from the nearby St. Mary's River. The latter was named by the Oblate fathers of St. Eugene's Mission in honour of the Blessed Virgin.

MASSET   Derived from the Haida name, *Maast*, for an island situated in the inlet. It is also said that an officer named Massetta was buried on the island, thus giving rise to the name.

MATSQUI ISLAND　An Amerindian word translated either as "easy travelling" or more probably as "a stretch of higher ground", referring to a nearby campsite.

MERRITT　Earlier names: The Forks or Forksdale. Changed in 1906 for William Hamilton Merritt II (1855–1918), head of a syndicate that held a charter for construction of the Nicola, Kamloops and Similkameen Railway.

MISSION　Founded in 1860–1 as St. Mary's Mission, later known as Mission Junction. Renamed Mission City in 1922. In 1973 Mission City and the District of Mission were amalgamated to become the District Municipality of Mission. The post office was subsequently changed from Mission City to Mission.

MORESBY ISLAND　For Rear-Admiral Sir Fairfax Moresby (1786–1877), who served as Commander-in-Chief of the Pacific station from 1850 to 1853.

MORICE RIVER　For Father Adrien Gabriel Morice, O.M.I. (1859–1938), a prominent missionary in central British Columbia.

NAKUSP　Amerindian for "closed in" or "sheltered" bay. Townsite dates from 1892.

NANAIMO　First named Colville Town, after Andrew Colville, Governor of the Hudson's Bay Company from 1852 to 1856. Gradually the Amerindian name, derived from *sne-ny-mo*, "big strong people or tribe", replaced Colville Town. The name refers to a confederacy of local Amerindian tribes and is in general use on maps after 1860.

NASS RIVER　A Tlingit word for "food depot". Former spellings are Naas and Nasse.

NATAL   Traceable to the wave of patriotism or jingoism which surrounded the South African War, 1899–1902. For the colony of Natal in South Africa, replacing the earlier name, New Michel. *See* Ladysmith

NELSON   Named in 1888 after Hugh Nelson (1830–96), then Lieutenant-Governor of British Columbia.

NEW DENVER   In 1891 named Eldorado by a surveyor. Re-named in 1892 for Denver, Colorado, by Napoleon Fitzstubbs, Gold Commissioner for British Columbia.

NEW WESTMINSTER   The name was suggested in 1858 by Queen Victoria. The town served as capital of British Columbia from 1860 to 1886.

NOOTKA   Island and sound discovered and named by Captain Cook, April 1778. The name is possibly a variation of *nootk-sitl*, which means "to go round" or "to make a circuit".

NORTH VANCOUVER   Named in 1902. Earlier known as Moodyville for Sewell Prescott Moody, a local mill owner.

OAK BAY   A descriptive name, reflecting the prevalence of oak trees in the vicinity.

OKANAGAN   Derived from *Okanogan* or *Okinagen*, the name of a Salish tribe of Amerindians. The exact derivation is uncertain; however, Akrigg suggests that the most likely meaning is "seeing the top or head", in reference to a point on the river from which one can see the summit of Mount Chopaka.

OLIVER   For John Oliver (1856–1927), who served for nine years, from 1918 to 1927, as Premier of British Columbia.

100 MILE HOUSE   Dates from 1862 and was one of the post houses built as public stopping places along the Cariboo Trail and named according to their mileage from Lillooet.

OSOYOOS   Originally *soo-yoos*, an Amerindian descriptive signifying a narrow stretch of land separating two lakes. The addition of the "o" at the beginning of the word was successfully advocated by a local magistrate, Peter O'Reilly.

PARKSVILLE   Named for Frank Parks, first postmaster and early resident of the district.

PEACE RIVER   *See entry under* Alberta

PEACHLAND   Named in 1897 by J. M. Robinson, a promoter of fruit farming and irrigation.

PEMBERTON   Commemorates the career of Joseph Despard Pemberton (1821–93), first Surveyor General of British Columbia and later a member of the Legislative Council of Vancouver Island.

PENTICTON   From the Amerindian *Pentk-tn*, meaning "the always place", in the sense of a permanent abode (Akrigg).

PITT ISLAND   Name assigned by Captain George Vancouver in 1793 for William Pitt the Younger (1759–1806). Though not designated by Vancouver, Pitt River and Pitt Meadows probably honour the same British statesman.

PORCHER ISLAND   Named for Commander E. A. Porcher, R.N., who was in charge of this section of the Pacific station from 1865 to 1868.

PORT MOODY   Named in 1860 by Captain George Richards of H.M.S. *Plumper*, a coastal survey ship, for Colonel Richard Clement Moody (1813–87), one-time Commissioner of Lands and Works for British Columbia. In 1859 Moody selected the site for New Westminster.

POUCE COUP   In translation from the French this means "thumb cut off". Named for a Beaver Indian guide so nicknamed by early voyageurs because he had accidentally lost a thumb.

POWELL RIVER   After Dr. Israel Wood Powell (1836–1915), Superintendent of Indian Affairs for British Columbia from 1872 to 1879.

PRINCE GEORGE   Begun in 1807 as a North West Company post, Fort George was named in honour of King George III. The name was changed to Prince George upon the town's incorporation as a city in 1915.

PRINCE RUPERT   Name chosen in 1906 in an open competition. For Prince Rupert (1619–82), the first Governor of the Hudson's Bay Company. Post office established on November 23, 1906.

PRINCESS ROYAL ISLAND   Assigned by Captain Charles Duncan in 1788 in honour of his ship, the *Princess Royal*.

PRINCETON   Named by Governor James Douglas in 1863 to mark the visit in 1860 to British North America of the Prince of Wales, later King Edward VII.

QUADRA ISLAND   Mountain, island, and hill. Named in 1903 after Juan Francisco de la Bodega y Quadra (1744?–94), a Spanish naval officer who explored the coast of British Columbia in 1755 and 1779.

QUALICUM BEACH   Originated with an Amerindian word indicating the presence of quantities of dog salmon.

QUEEN CHARLOTTE ISLANDS   Dates from 1787 when Captain George Dixon was on a trading cruise along the coast. For his two-hundred-ton vessel, the *Queen Charlotte*.

QUEEN CHARLOTTE SOUND and **STRAIT**   For Queen Charlotte, wife of King George III.

QUESNEL   Town, lake, and river. For Jules Maurice Quesnel (1786–1842), prominent fur trader in the service of the North West Company. He later became a member of the Legislative Council of the United Province of the Canadas. First name of the town was Quesnelle Mouth.

REVELSTOKE   Originally known as Farwell for Arthur Stanhope Farwell, the first settler. When Farwell asked too much money for a station site, the C.P.R. chose a new location and named it in honour of Lord Revelstoke, one of the financial backers of the Canadian Pacific Railway. Post office dates from 1886.

RICHMOND   Most probably for either Richmond in Surrey, or Richmond, Yorkshire, England. Incorporated 1879.

ROBSON, MOUNT   Classified by Akrigg as "a major problem in the study of British Columbia place names". Possibly named for Colin Robertson (1793–1842), an early official of the Hudson's Bay Company. This name was already in popular use in 1863 when the mountain was described by Milton and Cheadle.

ROCKY MOUNTAINS   Earliest reference dates from a 1716 entry in the diary of James Knight, Governor of York Factory. He records that a band of Amerindians told him of a range of mountains so high "they cannot see the tops [sic] without it be clear weather". Referred to as Montagnes de Roche in the *Journal of Legardeur de St. Pierre* (1752).

ROGERS PASS   Named after Major Albert B. Rogers (1829–1889), who discovered the pass in 1881 while exploring for a route through the Selkirks for the Canadian Pacific Railway.

ROOT, MOUNT   For Elihu Root (1845–1937), American statesman remembered in Canadian history as a member of the Alaska Boundary Tribunal of 1903.

ROSSLAND   From the name of an early settler, Ross Thompson. Name changed from Thompson to Rossland in 1894 by postal authorities.

SAANICH   An Amerindian term which may be translated as "fertile" or "good" and refers to the soil.

SALMO   Early maps refer to the Salmo River as the Salmon River. Salmo is the zoological generic term for salmon.

SALMON ARM   Dates from about 1890. Named for the abundance of salmon in the area.

SALTSPRING ISLAND   An early attempt to affix the name "Admiral" (1859) failed, and the older descriptive name was sanctioned by the Geographic Board in 1905. From the presence of saline springs at the north end of the island.

SECHELT   A variation of the Amerindian *se-shalt*, meaning "a place of shelter from the sea" (Akrigg).

SHAGIT RIVER   From Salish tribal name. The meaning is unknown.

SHAWNIGAN LAKE   Exact origin uncertain, possibly a coined word incorporating portions of the names of two early settlers, Shaw and Finnegan.

SHUSWAP LAKE   After a local Salish tribe, *Suxwa'pmux*. The exact meaning of the name is unknown.

SIDNEY   Island named by Captain Richards of H.M.S. *Plumper* in 1859 for Frederick William Sidney, an associate in the Royal Navy. Later applied to other nearby features.

SILVERTON   The village dates from the development of silver mining in the 1890s, hence the name is probably a locally coined word. May be for Silverton, Colorado.

SIMILKAMEEN RIVER An Amerindian word of uncertain origin (Stewart). May be a variation of *Samilkameigh*, possibly meaning "salmon river" (Akrigg), or "swimming river for a two mile stretch of water where the Indians used to camp and swim" (CPCGN files).

SKEENA RIVER Appears on early maps as Ayton's River; however, this did not gain acceptance. Name possibly traceable to the Amerindian *iksh*, "out of", and *shyen*, "the clouds", indicating the source of the river.

SMITHERS Named in 1913 for Sir Alfred Waldron Smithers (1850–1924), a director of the Grand Trunk Pacific Railway.

SPALLUMCHEEN A variation of the Amerindian word for "flat mouth" or "flat meadow" (Akrigg). Rendered as the Okanagan word for "beautiful valley" (CPCGN files).

SPARWOOD Early railway builders found the timber locally "to be suitable for spars" (CPCGN files).

SQUAMISH Named after a local Amerindian tribe whose name may be translated as "mother of the wind". Known as Newport in 1912; however, this name was never accepted locally, and as the result of a contest the name Squamish was restored.

STIKINE RIVER A Tlingit word meaning "great river".

STUART LAKE After John Stuart, an employee of the North West Company, who established a trading post in the area in 1806.

SUMMERLAND Named in 1902 to draw attention to the pleasant climate of the region.

SURREY   Undoubtedly for the county of Surrey in England (because of its geographic proximity to nearby New Westminster).

TADANAC   "T" for Trail, combined with Canada spelled in reverse.

TAKLA LAKE   May be a corruption of *thaitla*, meaning "bottom of the lake" (18th *Annual Report*, G.B.C.).

TAYLOR   For an employee of the Hudson's Bay Company, David Taylor.

TELEGRAPH CREEK   Site where the Collins Overland Telegraph to Asia "was expected to cross the Stikine River".

TELKWA RIVER   Of Amerindian origin, the name may possibly be translated as "rushing water".

TERRACE   First called Littleton, but name was rejected by postal authorities because of possible confusion with Lyttleton, N.B. The new name is descriptive of the manner in which land rises from the river.

TEXADA ISLAND   Designated by the Spanish for Felix de Tejada, Rear-Admiral in the Spanish navy. Rendered by Captain Vancouver as Favada (a misspelling). Present form dates from early nineteenth century.

THOMPSON RIVER   Named by Simon Fraser in 1808 in honour of David Thompson (1770–1857), explorer and geographer. *See* Fraser River

TRAIL   For the Dewdney Trail, which ran overland from Hope to Fort Steele and was completed in 1865. The town was first called Trail Creek or Trail Creek Landing, and the name was shortened to Trail in 1897.

UCLUELET   A variation of a local Amerindian word, *Yu-cluthl-ahts*, meaning "people with the safe landing place" (Walbran).

VANCOUVER   Named for Captain George Vancouver upon the suggestion of Sir William Van Horne: "Vancouver it shall be, if I have the ultimate decision ... and Vancouver it became." (Akrigg)

VANCOUVER ISLAND   On early charts the island is shown as Quadra and Vancouver's Island, later as Vancouver's Island, and finally as Vancouver Island. Named by Captain George Vancouver (1757–98), who explored the Pacific Coast of North America in 1792–4.

VANDERHOOF   For Herbert Vanderhoof, a Chicago publicity agent who mounted a public-relations campaign to encourage emigration to western Canada.

VERNON   Originally Priest's Valley in honour of Father Paul Durieu, the name was later changed in honour of Forbes Vernon, one-time Chief Commissioner of Lands and Works for British Columbia.

VICTORIA   First known as Fort Victoria, the city, like the numerous other locations of the same name, commemorates Queen Victoria (1819–1900). The name was chosen by the Council of the Northern Department (Hudson's Bay Company) at Fort Garry, June 10, 1843.

WADDINGTON, MOUNT   Sometimes referred to as Mystery Mountain because of a difficult ascent, its official name honours Alfred Waddington (1800?–72), author and railway promoter.

WALBRAN ISLAND   For John T. Walbran (?–1913) of the Canadian Fisheries Protection Service. He was the author of *British Columbia Coast Names*, which was published in 1909 and is still a valuable reference on the subject.

WHITEHORN, MOUNT   A descriptive name indicative of the mantle of snow on the mountain.

WHITE ROCK   A descriptive name inspired by a large rock landmark on the beach of Semiahmoo Bay (at the southwestern extremity of the Fraser Valley).

WILLIAMS LAKE   For Chief William of the Sugar Cane Reserve, who warned early settlers of a proposed attack on the settlement. Post office dates from 1861.

YALE   In honour of James Murray Yale (1796?–1871), an employee of the Hudson's Bay Company. Originally Fort Yale.

YELLOWHEAD PASS   Pass and lake. After François Decoigne, a Métis trader who stored furs in the region and was nicknamed Tête Jaune (Yellow Head) because of his blond hair. Nearby Tête Jaune Cache also named for Decoigne.

YOHO   Pass, peak, river, and national park. Name is said to be of Cree origin and is freely translated as "How wonderful".

Manitoba

 Created as a province in 1870, the name was probably first applied to Lake Manitoba. (1) Douglas suggests that the name is of Assiniboine origin: *Mini* and *tobow* meaning "Lake of the Prairie", or in French "Lac des Prairies", the name used by La Vérendrye. (2) The more probable source is the Cree *maniot-wapow*, "the strait of the spirit or *manitobau*". This refers to the roaring sound produced by pebbles on a beach on Manitoba Island in Lake Manitoba. The noise "gave rise to the superstition among the Indians that a *manito* or spirit beats a drum" (Douglas). *See* Manitou

ALTONA   For a former town in Schleswig-Holstein, Germany, which is now part of Hamburg.

ARBORG   The Icelandic word for "town by the river" or "river town".

ASSINIBOIA   The official name of Lord Selkirk's Red River settlement. From 1882 to 1905 this name designated the territory west of Manitoba which now forms part of the provinces of Saskatchewan and Alberta.

ASSINIBOINE RIVER   Discovered by La Vérendrye in 1736. This and Assiniboia take their names from the Amerindian tribe whose name translates "those who cook by placing hot stones in water" (for details see Douglas).

ATHAPAPUSKOW LAKE   This is an adaptation of the Cree word for "rock on both sides".

BEAUSÉJOUR   A French descriptive for "good camping place". *See* Fort Beauséjour, New Brunswick

BERENS RIVER   For Jacob Berens, an Indian chief living there in 1905. Originally called *Omeemee sipi*, "pigeon river".

BINSCARTH   This name is said to be for a farm in the Orkney Islands belonging to a Robert Scarth.

BIRCH RIVER   From the presence of birch trees.

BIRTLE   A contraction of Birdtail, the name of the creek running through the town. It was designated as Birds Tail Rivulet on the Thompson map of 1813–14. The settlement was founded in 1879 and first called St. Clair City.

BISSETT   Honours Dr. E. D. R. Bissett (1890–), who served as federal M.P. for Springfield from 1926 to 1930.

BOISSEVAIN   The place was first known as Cherry Creek. It was renamed in 1886 for Adolph Boissevain, senior partner in a firm "through whom in the early days of the C.P.R. its shares were introduced to the European market" (Douglas).

BOWSMAN   Named by J. B. Tyrrell for Bowsman Moore, an Indian trapper and guide.

BRANDON   Derived from Brandon House, a Hudson's Bay Company post near the present city, which was noted on the Thompson map of 1814 and the Arrowsmith map of 1857. For the Duke of Brandon, a prominent shareholder of the Hudson's Bay Company.

BROOKLANDS   A descriptive name denoting the topography of the area.

BYLOT LAKE   Commemorates the career of Robert Bylot, the Arctic explorer, who sailed with Henry Hudson and William Baffin.

CAMPERVILLE   For Abbé P. Camper, O.M.I., who frequently visited the area.

CARBERRY   Assigned by J. J. Hill in 1882 for Carberry Tower, Musselburgh, Scotland, the home of Lord Elphinstone, a director of the C.P.R.

CARMAN   Named in 1879 for the Rev. Albert Carman (1833–1917), one-time general superintendent of the Methodist Church of Canada. *See* Carmanville, Newfoundland

CHARLESWOOD (Winnipeg)   For a deeply wooded area of St. Charles parish.

CHURCHILL   Town, river, and lake. The name originated with a Hudson's Bay Company post which dated from the 1680s. For

John Churchill, Duke of Marlborough, who was Governor of the Hudson's Bay Company from 1685 to 1691.

CRANBERRY PORTAGE   Possibly a translation of an Amerindian descriptive phrase; the name appears as Cranbury Carrying Place in 1796 (Arrowsmith).

CRYSTAL CITY   Assigned by Thomas Greenway, reputedly for the "clearness of the water in a nearby stream". *See* Dominion City *and* Rapid City

DAUPHIN   Lake, river, and town. Named Fort Dauphin (for the title of the eldest son of the king of France), it was founded in 1741 on the northwest shores of the lake. The name was later applied to the river and the lake. The present town is located some distance from the original Fort Dauphin.

DELORAINE   Named after a village in Roxburghshire, Scotland.

DOMINION CITY   Originally the name was Roseau and Roseau Crossing, but confusion with Roseau, Minn., and Rosseau, Ont., led to its being changed in 1878. "City" was added in keeping with Crystal City and Rapid City.

DUCK BAY   Name assigned because of the numerous wild ducks to be found in the area.

DUFRESNE   Honours the Rev. M. Dufresne, who served as parish priest at Lorette.

EASTERVILLE   The name originated with Donald Easter, one-time chief of the Chemahawin band of Amerindians.

ELKHORN   Designated by survey engineers who placed a pair of elk horns on a hill along the line of the C.P.R. Survey (Douglas).

EMERSON   Townsite established in 1874 and named in 1879, probably for American poet and essayist Ralph Waldo Emerson (1803–82).

ERICKSON   Adopted August 1, 1908, in honour of Albert Erickson, the first postmaster.

FALCON LAKE   Appears on Palliser map 1865 and was named for Pierre Falcon, a Métis balladeer.

FLIN FLON   Name taken from the character Josiah Flintabbatey Flonatin in the novel *The Sunless City* by J. E. Preston-Muddock. A copy of the novel was reputedly found on the site by a prospector in 1913.

FORT GARRY   Originally a post of the Hudson's Bay Company and named after one of its officers, Nicholas Garry. The post office was opened in 1870 and in 1876 the name was changed to Winnipeg.

FORT PRINCE OF WALES   Constructed in 1734 on a point at the entrance to Churchill Harbour. Destroyed by d'Iberville in 1782, it has now been partially restored as a tourist attraction. Named for Prince George William Frederick, later King George III.

GILBERT PLAINS   For an early Métis settler, Gilbert Ross.

GIMLI   Dates from October 1875 and was the first permanent Icelandic settlement in Canada. Named after the home of the gods in Norse mythology.

GLADSTONE   Incorporated as a town in 1882 and named for William Ewart Gladstone, Prime Minister of Great Britain.

GLENBORO   The name is traceable to the first Scottish settlers and is probably for a place name in Scotland.

GODS LAKE   Gods River, Gods Rapids, and Gods Lake Narrows. Probably a translation of the Cree *Manitou* (Douglas).

GRAND RAPIDS   A translation of the Amerindian *misepawistik*, or "rushing rapids".

GRANDVIEW   Assigned because the location "commands a splendid view of that portion of the Gilbert Plains to the south and west of it" (CPCGN files).

GRETNA   A port of entry on the Manitoba–North Dakota border, named by the C.P.R. in 1883 for Gretna Green, Dumfriesshire, on the English–Scottish border.

GRUNTHAL   A descriptive name, this is the German phrase for "verdant vale".

HAMIOTA   First known as Hamilton, for Thomas Hamilton, one of the first settlers. Changed to avoid confusion with Hamilton, Ontario. New name contracted from *Hami*lton with the Sioux word *ota*, "much".

HARTNEY   For James H. Hartney, an early postmaster in the district.

ICELANDIC RIVER   Named in 1875 by an Icelandic expedition as a prelude to later settlement. Originally known as White River, it appears on Arrowsmith's map of 1821, and as White Mud on Palliser's map of 1865. *See* Riverton

KILDONAN   After Kildonan parish, Sutherlandshire, Scotland, the home of many early settlers; it was named by Lord Selkirk in 1817.

KILLARNEY   Lake and town. After Killarney, Ireland.

LAC DU BONNET   First applied to a nearby portage, the name is derived from the Amerindian custom "of laying stones in a circle and crowning them with wreaths of herbage and branches" (Douglas).

LEAF RAPIDS   The town takes its name from the descriptive designation of the rapids. The post office was opened September 20, 1972.

LETELLIER   Commemorates the career of Luc Letellier de St. Just (1820–81), one-time Lieutenant-Governor of Quebec.

LORETTE   For Lorette (now Ancienne-Lorette), Quebec. The parish was noted on a map of 1881.

LUNDAR   Originally Lundi, a name bestowed by an Icelandic settler "after the farm in Iceland from which his bride came". Lundar evolved through a typographical error for the first name (Douglas).

MC CREARY   Commemorates the career of William Forsythe McCreary (1855–1904), who served as Member of Parliament for Selkirk from 1900 to 1904.

MACGREGOR   Assigned by the Marquess of Lorne (1845–1914), Governor General of Canada from 1878 to 1883, in honour of his chaplain, Dr. James Macgregor, of St. Cuthberts Church, Edinburgh. Both of them visited the community in 1882.

MANITOBA, LAKE   *See provincial entry*

MANITOU   Of Amerindian origin meaning "supernatural spirit"; the town was first known as Manitoba City and the name was changed to Manitou in 1881 (Rudnyckyj). *See* Manitoulin, Ontario

MAST RIVER   The local name for the feature is *Mistikokan*, "Mast River". It is a Cree word for a flagstaff or lobstick (a tree trimmed of all but the topmost branches and used as a marker).

MELITA   The classical name for the island of Malta in the Mediterranean. The post office was established in 1884.

MINITONAS   Derived from the Saulteaux word meaning "house of the little god"; it was first applied to a nearby hill.

MINNEDOSA   River and town. The river was called at different times: Rivière St. Pierre, Saskawjewin, Little Saskatchewan, and Rapid. The name of the town was changed from Tanner's Crossing to Minnedosa in 1880. Of Sioux origin (*minne*, "water", and *duza*, "swift water"), it was adopted by the Geographic Board for the river in 1911. *See* Rapid City

MORDEN   Honours Alvey Morden, who was an early settler from Bruce County, Ontario.

MORRIS   Town and river. Known as Scratching River in 1801; the name was changed to mark the career of Alexander Morris (1826–89), who served as Lieutenant-Governor from 1872 to 1877.

MUNK RIVER   For Jens Munk (1579–1628), a Danish nobleman who wintered at the mouth of the Churchill River in 1620.

NARCISSE   Settled first by a group of Russian Jews and named for Narcisse Leven, the president of the Jewish Colonization Association.

NEEPAWA   Derived from an Amerindian word which may be translated as "plenty" or "abundance". The town was so designated in 1873 by the promoters of settlement because of the agricultural potential of the area.

NEJANILINI RIVER   An Amerindian descriptive indicating the presence of wild ducks on the river.

NELSON LAKE   Named by David Thompson after Admiral Horatio Nelson (1758–1805).

NELSON RIVER   Discovered in 1612 and named by Sir Thomas Button in memory of his sailing master, who died while the expedition wintered on the west coast of Hudson Bay.

NINETTE   Said to be named for a popular French actress (the name is a contraction of the name Antoinette). The post office was established in 1884.

NIVERVILLE   Honours Joseph Boucher, Chevalier de Niverville (1715–1804).

NORWAY HOUSE   The site of a Hudson's Bay Company post which was built by Norwegian workmen in 1814.

NOTRE DAME   For Notre-Dame-de-Lourdes, France.

NUELTIN LAKE   Originally *Nu-thel-tin-tu-ch*; the present spelling was adopted January 9, 1945. The name may be translated from the Chipewyan as "sleeping island lake".

PEMBINA   This name is from the Cree word *nipiwina*, meaning "waterberry" or "high bush cranberry" (Johnson Papers, PAC). Others have translated the word as "summer berry".

PILOT MOUND   After the butte or mound which guided pioneers coming over the Emerson Trail in the 1880s. The townsite was established with the coming of the railway in 1884.

PINAWA   Channel and lake. The name is an Amerindian word for "slow" or "calm" and describes the water.

PINE FALLS   A descriptive term which marks the location of a paper mill and hydro community.

PLUM COULEE   The name was mentioned by Thompson in 1797 and possibly attests to the fact that there used to be wild plums growing beside the stream where it flowed through a local coulee, or valley (CPCGN files).

PORTAGE LA PRAIRIE   French for "prairie crossing". Here the fur traders crossed from the Assiniboine River to Lake Manitoba. The location was noted by La Vérendrye in 1739.

POWERVIEW   A coined place name descriptive of the location overlooking a power dam.

PROVENCHER   Marks the career of Joseph Norbert Provencher (1787–1853), who served as Roman Catholic Bishop of St. Boniface from 1847 to 1853.

RAPID CITY   Descriptive name. Prior to 1877 the location was called Ralston's Colony, for John Ralston. The place was renamed for the Minnedosa River (formerly Rapid or Little Saskatchewan River) with its many rapids which flows through the town. *See* Minnedosa

RED RIVER   The name is a translation of the French Rivière Rouge that was used in 1740 or earlier. The French version is itself a translation of the earlier Cree *Miscousipi*, literally "red water river". This feature appears as Red River on Arrowsmith's map of 1796.

RESTON   Named for Reston, Berwickshire, Scotland, from which many of the settlers migrated.

RIVERS   Marks the career of Sir Charles Rivers Wilson, once chairman of the Board of Directors, Grand Trunk Pacific Railway.

RIVERTON   A descriptive which replaced the earlier name, Icelandic River.

ROBLIN   After Sir Rodmond Roblin (1853–1937), who served as Premier of Manitoba from 1900 to 1915. It was first known as Goose Lake.

ROLAND   For Roland McDonald, a farmer and lumber merchant, who settled there in 1880 when the post office was opened.

ROSENFELD   A Mennonite settlement which dates from 1875. The name is German for "rose field".

ROSSBURN   Name bestowed in 1879 to mark the career of R. R. Ross, a settler who arrived in that year from Molesworth, Ontario.

RUSSELL   For General Lord Alexander George Russell, Commander of the British forces in Canada from 1883 to 1888. The early name was Shell River.

ST. ADOLPHE   Originated with Adolphe Turner, an early settler in the district.

STE. ANNE   It is located on the Fort William-to-St. Boniface land-and-water route, which was used extensively prior to the coming of the railway. The name is from that of the parish.

ST. BONIFACE   Name designated by Bishop Joseph Norbert Provencher, who placed a chapel on the Red River "under the patronage of St. Boniface to draw God's blessing on the Swiss–German Catholic settlers of his parish".

ST. CLAUDE   For the town of St. Claude in France.

ST. FRANÇOIS XAVIER   From the name of the Roman Catholic parish; it was formerly called White Horse Plain.

ST. JAMES   After the local parish of the Church of England.

ST. JEAN BAPTISTE   The name commemorates the patron saint of French Canadians.

ST. LAURENT   Name bestowed by Abbé P. Camper, O.M.I., after the St. Lawrence River.

ST. LAZARE   For the patron saint of the parish. This parish was named by Abbé J. Decorby, O.M.I., in 1880.

ST. NORBERT   Established in 1857 and named in honour of Monsignor Joseph Norbert Provencher, first Bishop of St. Boniface.

STE. ROSE DU LAC   An association of the parish name and its location near Lake Dauphin.

ST. VITAL   Honours the career of Rev. Vital Julian Grandin.

SELKIRK   Named for Thomas Douglas, Earl of Selkirk (1771–1820).

SHILO   Derived from the name of an ancient Palestinian town (now in Jordan).

SHOAL LAKE   A translation of the descriptive name, Lac Plat. The lake appears on the Palliser map of 1865.

SNOW LAKE   Possibly named for a local family (Rudnyckyj).

SOURIS   Town and river. Two explanations for the name have been advanced: (1) Most probably, it is a French translation of an earlier Amerindian name for mice; or (2) it is derived from the fact that the river follows a meandering course similar to a mouse's track. Before 1882 the town was called Plum Creek. *See* Souris, Prince Edward Island

SOUTHERN INDIAN LAKE   On the Fidler map of 1814; for the southern Indians, or Crees.

SPRAGUE   For D. E. Sprague, a prominent Winnipeg lumber merchant.

STEINBACH   In 1873 the area was designated by the federal government for Mennonite settlers from south Russia, from which the name was derived.

STONEWALL   Named by O. P. Jackson, a mill operator, for the American general "Stonewall" Jackson (1824–63).

STONY MOUNTAIN   A translation of an earlier Amerindian name (Douglas).

SWAN RIVER   The name is probably a translation of the original Amerindian name of the river. The area was visited by David Thompson in 1797.

TADOULE, LAKE   The name appears as *Tos-da-ool-le* in the T. B. Johnston report of 1890, and as *Tas-da-ool-le* on the Arrowsmith map of 1832. Of Chipewyan origin, it may be translated as "floating charcoal" for the floating cinders and burnt wood resulting from an early forest fire. The modern spelling has been in common usage since 1914.

TEULON   For the wife of C. C. Castle, a resident in Victoria, B.C., in the late 1920s.

THE PAS   Originated with the Cree *opa*, "a narrow place", or *opaskweow*, "narrows between high banks". The location was known to the French as *Pasquia* and *Le Pas*; the expression is descriptive of the Saskatchewan River at this point.

THOMPSON   For John F. Thompson, chairman of the Board of the International Nickel Company; the name was adopted October 16, 1957. Incorporated as a town on January 1, 1967.

TRANSCONA   A coined word which incorporates portions of *Trans*continental and Strath*cona*; the latter is probably derived from the name of Lord Strathcona.

TREHERNE   For George Treherne, an early settler.

TURTLE MOUNTAIN   On Palliser map of 1865. The location was known by the Métis as *Tête de Tortue*, "seeing a resemblance to the buckler of a turtle, its head being represented by the conical mound standing out from one end" (CPCGN files).

TUXEDO   Derived from the Tuxedo Park Co. Ltd., landowners in the district.

VIRDEN   Named Manchester by the C.P.R. in 1882. However, this name was already registered for another place, so Virden, the name of the seat of the Duke of Manchester, was chosen (CPCGN files).

WABOWDEN   For W. A. Bowden, once Chief Engineer for the federal Department of Railways and Canals.

WALES POINT   Named for William Wales (1734?–98), British mathematician and astronomer. He was sent to Churchill by the Royal Society to observe the transit of Venus, June 3, 1769. The name was adopted May 4, 1948.

WAWANESA   Considered to be the Cree word for whippoorwill (Douglas) or for wild goose nest (Rayburn).

WAWAO CREEK   Incorporating the Cree word for snow goose, the name was approved October 31, 1972.

WINKLER   For Valentine Winkler, member of the Manitoba legislature and developer of the town.

WINNIPEG   Capital city of Manitoba, lake, and river. This name is from the Cree *Win-nipi* and may be freely translated as "dirty water" or "murky water". The lake was designated as Sea Lake by Thompson in 1816. Metropolitan Winnipeg, an amalgamation of neighbouring municipalities, was created November 1, 1960, and reorganized as the city of Winnipeg, January 1, 1972.

WINNIPEGOSIS, LAKE   A diminutive of Winnipeg which means "little muddy water".

YORK FACTORY   For the Duke of York, later King James II, second Governor of the Hudson's Bay Company. The port was built in 1684 and is now a national historic site.

New Brunswick

 Originally the territory included in modern New Brunswick was part of Nova Scotia. The American Revolution from 1775 to 1783 resulted in a large influx of Loyalist settlers, and agitation arose for the creation of a new province. On September 10, 1784, the partition took place and the "name was chosen as a compliment to King George III (1760–1820) who was descended from the House of Brunswick". Earlier proposals for naming the new province were: New Ireland (suggested by William Knox, Under-Secretary of State, but rejected "because Ireland was out of royal favour"), and Pittsylvania, for William Pitt.

ALBERT   Now part of village of Riverside–Albert (*see entry for former*). Name taken from that of the county established in 1845 to honour Prince Albert, consort of Queen Victoria. The mineral albertite was discovered a few miles away in 1849, giving rise to Albert Mines.

ALLARDVILLE   Named for Monsignor Jean-Joseph-Auguste Allard (1884–1971), founder of the local mission in the 1930s.

ALMA   The setting is reputed to resemble the Alma River in the Crimea. The parish was established in 1855.

ANDOVER   Probably for Andover, Hampshire, England. *See* Perth–Andover.

AROOSTOOK RIVER   Derived from the Maliseet name *Wool-ahs-took*, translated by Ganong as "good river for everything". Appears as Arassatuk (DeRozier, 1699).

ATHOLVILLE   The railway station was once known as Athol House for a residence built by Robert Ferguson (1768–1851), a native of Blair Atholl, Perthshire, Scotland.

BACK BAY   A local descriptive being on the opposite side of a peninsula from Letete. Post office established in 1872.

BAIE-SAINTE-ANNE   An early Acadian settlement. Possibly named for Sainte-Anne, patroness of the Micmacs.

BAIE VERTE   Of French origin: "... from the salt water grasses which in summer make the bay look like an immense meadow" (Ganong). Variations: Franquelin, 1686 – Baye Verte; Moll, 1715 – Green Bay; Haliburton, 1829 – Bay Verte.

BAKER BROOK   For John Baker, who figured prominently in a Maine–New Brunswick boundary dispute in the 1820s.

BALMORAL   After Balmoral Castle in the parish of Craithie and Braemar, Scotland.

BARACHOIS   *See* Nova Scotia *entry*

BARKERS POINT   Settled in 1825 by Anthony Barker, son of a Loyalist grantee. Amalgamated with the city of Fredericton, 1973.

BARTIBOG RIVER   Honours Bartholomew La Bogue, a Micmac chief, "who was called Balt Bogue by the Indians and Bartabogue by the French and English" (Rayburn).

BATH   Possibly for Bath, Maine, or for the city of Bath, England. Post office dates from 1875.

BATHURST   Assigned in 1826 by Lieutenant-Governor Howard Douglas (1776–1861) for the Colonial Secretary, Henry, third Earl of Bathurst (1762–1834).

BAY DU VIN   Possibly the result of a mistake in transcribing the earlier French name Baie des Vents, a descriptive.

BEAUSÉJOUR   *See* Fort Beauséjour

BERESFORD   From the parish which was named for William Carr Beresford, Viscount Beresford (1768–1854), a prominent English general.

BLACKS HARBOUR   Exact origin unknown, possibly an early family name. Post office dates from 1889.

BLACKVILLE   Marks the career of William Black (1770–1866), who served as administrator of New Brunswick from 1829 to 1831 and was a long-time member of the Legislative Council from 1819 to 1866.

BLISSFIELD   The parish was named for a Loyalist, John Murray

Bliss (1771–1834), judge of the Supreme Court of New Brunswick.

BOCABEC RIVER   Credited by Ganong to the Passamaquoddy *po-ka-besk*, of unknown meaning.

BOIESTOWN   After Thomas Boies, early settler and millowner. Post office established in 1842.

BRANTVILLE   The district is a migratory sanctuary for Brant geese.

BRISTOL   After the city of Bristol, England. Name replaced Kent Station in 1880s.

BUCTOUCHE   Attributed by most authorities to the Micmac *Chebuktoosk*, translated as "big bay". Settlement founded by re-turned Acadians in 1784, although the name is of much earlier origin.

BURNT CHURCH   River, point, and settlement. In 1758 the French settlements in the area were razed by the British. Burnt Church Point marks the site of the mission which was destroyed.

CAMPBELLTON   Undoubtedly in honour of Sir Archibald Campbell (1769–1843), who served as Lieutenant-Governor of New Brunswick from 1831 to 1837. Ganong suggests name may have been "inspired" by Campbeltown, Argyllshire, Scotland. The district was first settled by Scots in 1773.

CAMPOBELLO ISLAND   Named in 1770 by Captain William Owen, to whom a large part of the island had been granted; "... said to have been partly as a pun on the name of the Governor Lord William Campbell [Governor of Nova Scotia from 1766 to 1773, which then included present-day New Brunswick] and partly as descriptive of the island."

CANTERBURY   For Thomas Manners-Sutton (1814–77), later third Viscount Canterbury, who served as Lieutenant-Governor of New Brunswick from 1854 to 1861. Parish erected 1855.

CAPE BALD   *See* Cap-Pelé

CAPE TORMENTINE   Most probably traceable to the French *Cap du Tourment*, "Cape of Storms". Modern spelling dates from Frederick Holland survey of 1791.

CAP-PELÉ   Descriptive. Post office changed from Cape Bald to Cap-Pelé by petition of local residents in 1949. Name approved March 2, 1950.

CARAQUET   Origin unknown. Appears in Denys (1672) as *Caraquet*. Name is of Micmac origin from the word *Ka-la-gue*, translated as "junction of two rivers" (Ganong). Upper Caraquet name changed December 11, 1952, to Haut-Caraquet.

CHALEUR BAY; BAIE DES CHALEURS   Name bestowed by Jacques Cartier, July 10, 1534, "because of the great heat experienced".

CHAMCOOK   From the Passamaquoddy *Skumcook* or *Chamkook*; "Many meanings have been given, but none are certain" (Ganong). May refer to a harbour with a narrow entrance.

CHARLO   The village takes its name from the river. For an early resident, Charles, or "Charlo", Doucet.

CHATHAM   Named by Francis Peabody, about 1800, for William Pitt, Earl of Chatham (1759–1806), Prime Minister of England.

CHIGNECTO BAY   Derived from the Amerindian *sigunikt*, said to mean "foot cloth", possibly alluding to a Micmac legend.

CHIPMAN   After Ward Chipman, Jr. (1787–1851), who served as Chief Justice of New Brunswick from 1834 to 1851.

CHIPUTNETICOOK LAKE   From the Passamaquoddy *Chiputnetikook*, "great fork river", a possible reference to the St. Croix River.

CLOVERDALE   Settlement dates from 1866. Name possibly descriptive.

COCAGNE   Name assigned by Nicolas Denys (1598–1688), who wrote: "I have named this river [Cocagne] because I found there everything with which to make good cheer during eight days of bad weather. . . ." *Cockaigne* is the French equivalent to Utopia – "a land of fabled abundance".

COLES ISLAND (Queens County)   For David Cole, an early Loyalist settler. Post office established 1858.

COLLEGE BRIDGE   From Collège Saint-Joseph-de-Memramcook, founded in 1864 by Abbé Camille Lefebvre and Abbé François Xavier Lafrance. The institution was transferred to Moncton in 1963 to become the nucleus of the Université de Moncton. *See* Pont-Lafrance

COVERDALE   Name first applied to the river, later to the parish, and may be in honour of Miles Coverdale (1488–1569), translator of the Bible and Bishop of Exeter. Town incorporated in 1973, combining Riverview Heights, Bridgedale, and Gunningsville.

DALHOUSIE   Name chosen by Sir Howard Douglas (1776–1861) for the Earl of Dalhousie (1770–1838), who served as Lieutenant-Governor of Nova Scotia from 1816 to 1820 and Governor General from 1819 to 1828. *See* Earltown, Nova Scotia

DEBEC   After George Debec, one of the first settlers in the district.

DEER ISLAND Probably descriptive. Ganong suggests the name may be an English translation of the Passamaquoddy *Edokwemeneek*.

DIEPPE Suggested by the Battle of Dieppe, France, August 19, 1942. Officially adopted May 6, 1946, replacing Leger Corner.

DOAKTOWN After Robert Doak, an early Scottish settler.

DOCHETS ISLAND *See* St. Croix River

DORCHESTER Parish established in 1787. Name marks the career of Sir Guy Carleton, Baron Dorchester (1724–1808), who served as Governor General from 1786 to 1796.

DOUGLASTOWN Originally Gretna Green. Name changed after the great fire of 1825 to honour Sir Howard Douglas (1776–1861), then the Lieutenant-Governor of New Brunswick.

DUNGARVON RIVER For Dungarvan River, Ireland. A local tradition (quoted by Ganong) attributes the naming to Michael Murphy (a native of Dungarvan, Ireland), whose favourite shout during a dance was "I'll make Dungarvan shake." Reputed haunt of a famous ghost, "The Dungarvon Whooper".

Whooper Spring, adjacent to the Dungarvon River, is the supposed site of a murder and "the strange whooping after sundown".

EDMUNDSTON Commemorates the career of Sir Edmund Walker Head (1805–68), who served as Lieutenant-Governor from 1848 to 1854.

EEL RIVER (Chaleur Bay) A descriptive derived from the French designation *Anguille*. Anse à l'Anguille changed to Eel River Cove by petition on October 14, 1950.

ENRAGE, CAPE From the French for "Cape of Rage". May be

for an area of prevailing storms (Ganong) or "for a ledge of rock that gives a rough sea in high winds" (Ganong quoted by Rayburn).

ESCUMINAC   Originated with a local Micmac name, *Eskumunaak*, translated as "lookout place". Rendered as *Escuminac* in the Frederick Holland survey of 1791.

FAIRVILLE   Name bestowed by the Rev. Robert Wilson, a Methodist clergyman, for Robert Fair (1824–1901), a local merchant. "As Lancaster was too indefinite a designation . . . without consulting anyone I called the village Fairville in honour of Mr. Fair." (CNBHS) Now part of Saint John.

FLORENCEVILLE   Named at the time of the Crimean War (1855) to mark the career of Florence Nightingale (1820–1910), the founder of modern nursing.

FORT BEAUSÉJOUR   Dates from the establishment of the fort in 1750. The area was occupied during the French colonial period by Laurent Chatillon, Sieur de Beauséjour, and known as Pointe à Beauséjour, later adopted as the name of the fort.

FREDERICTON   Assigned by order-in-council, February 22, 1785 – "a town at St. Anne's Point, on the River Saint John, to be called Fredericktown after His Royal Highness Prince Frederick, Bishop of Osnaburg". The "k" and "w" were dropped shortly thereafter.

FROSTY HOLLOW   Descriptive for a low-lying area reputed to receive the first frost in the region.

FUNDY, BAY OF   Undoubtedly visited by French, Basque, and Portuguese fishermen from the sixteenth century onward. Formerly thought to be of Portuguese origin, from *fondo* or "deep"; however, more likely an English corruption of the French *fendu*, or "split" – applied first to modern Cape Split at the entrance to

Minas Basin. Known for a time as La Baye Françoise (De Monts, 1604).

GAGETOWN   Name of the Canadian Forces Base is traceable to Gage Township, established in 1765 and named after General Thomas Gage (1721–87).

GANONG, MOUNT   Honours William Francis Ganong (1864–1941), botanist, historian, and foremost authority on New Brunswick nomenclature.

GEARY   Formerly known as New Niagara; name later changed to New Gary and finally to Gary or Geary. Suggested by an early Loyalist settler who lived for a time at Niagara, Ontario.

GIN HILL   "Two workers had their load of logs upset on this hill and a case of Geneva gin ... was partly destroyed; when the horses returned without the men, a search party found them drinking gin at the foot of the hill." (CPCGN files)

GLASSVILLE   Founded in 1861 by the Rev. Charles Gordon Glass, a native of Birse, Scotland.

GONDOLA POINT   Refers to "a small scow or boat used as a ferry on New Brunswick rivers" (Ganong).

GRAND BAY (Saint John River)   A descriptive which dates from the French period. Post office established about 1885.

GRANDE DIGUE   Former spelling, Grandigue, changed March 31, 1944, to Grande Digue. Possibly for a dike (*digue*) which could still be seen in the early twentieth century.

GRAND FALLS (Victoria County)   Also an early descriptive; appears as Grand Sault on early French maps.

GRAND LAKE (Queens County)   Descriptive. The modern

name originated with the Morris survey (1750–61) and may have been assigned by the surveyors.

GRAND MANAN ISLAND   Derived from a combination of Amerindian and French sources – the Malecite-Passamaquoddy *Munanook*, meaning "island", to which the French added the prefix "grand" to distinguish it from Petit Manan in present-day Maine.

GUNNINGSVILLE   Named for the first settler, Hazen Gunning. *See* Coverdale

HAMPSTEAD   Parish established in 1786. Name is a misspelling of Hempstead, Long Island, New York – home of the Loyalist settlers in the area.

HAMPTON   Also a predominantly Loyalist settlement and most probably named for Hampton in New York State. Some evidence to indicate that the name is pre-Loyalist; however, origin is still the same.

HARTLAND   Named in 1874 to honour James R. Hartley, a surveyor who served as M.L.A. for Carleton County. No evidence to support its being named for Rev. Samuel Hartt.

HARVEY   Established in 1837 "... on the road between Fredericton and St. Andrews and very properly named after its founder Sir John Harvey (1777–1852)", Lieutenant-Governor of New Brunswick from 1837 to 1841 (MacNutt).

HAUT-CARAQUET   *See* Caraquet

HAVELOCK   For Sir Henry Havelock (1795–1857), reliever of Lucknow in 1857.

HAWKSHAW   For Howard "Hawk" Shaw, who established a tannery in the area. Post office dates from 1897.

HILLSBOROUGH   Township, 1765; parish, 1786; post office, 1840. After Viscount Hillsborough (1718–93), the Lord Commissioner of Trade and Plantations from 1763 to 1765.

JACQUET RIVER   Probably a variation of the French *Jacques*, for James Doyle, one of the first settlers in the district.

JEMSEG   From the Malecite *Ah-jim-sek*, variously translated as "picking up place", or "depot", since the Malecites used to cache supplies at this location. Ganong credits derivation to the Malecite *Kadjimusek*, or "jumping across place" – "in reference to the narrow part of Grand Lake at the head of Jemseg River".

JOLICURE   A French family name. Early spellings: Jollycoeur and Jolicoeur. Settlement dates from 1770s.

JOURIMAIN, CAPE   Name applied first to the island; later to the cape. Possibly for an early French settler. No verification for the "local tradition that the first settler on the outer island was a German, hence the name gradually corrupted to its present form" (Ganong).

JUNIPER   For *Juniperus L.*, a tree or shrub common to the area. Post office from 1918.

KEDGWICK   A variation of the original Micmac *Madawamkedjwik*, the name was "shortened by the river men to Tom Kedgwick or Kedgwick" (Ganong). Of uncertain meaning. Appears as *Grande Fourche*, "Big Fork", on some maps; however, the older variant prevailed.

KENNEBECASIS   Bay, river, and island. Derived from *Kenepekachichk*, translated by Rayburn as "little long bay place". Not a diminutive of Kennebec in the state of Maine. (Eckstorm)

KESWICK RIVER   Not for Keswick, England, but may be traced to the Malecite *Nookamkeechwak*, or "river of gravel". Modern spelling dates from 1811.

KINGSCLEAR   Marks a clearing made by cutting the king's wood for the benefit of the Royal Navy.

KINGS LANDING   Name selected in 1969 for the historical village established by the New Brunswick government to depict a riverside community of the central Saint John River Valley during the period 1780 to 1870.

KOUCHIBOUGUAC (Kent County)   Bay, river, national park. A corruption, partially through the French, of the Micmac *Pijeboogwek*, meaning "long tideway river" – a descriptive for the length of the river's tidal estuary. Name adopted for the national park in 1971.

LAMÈQUE, BAIE-DE-
LAMÈQUE, ÎLE   Of Amerindian rather than French origin. From the Micmac *Elmugwadasik*, a descriptive reference to the fact that "the head of the tidal river is turned to one side". Name of the island approved by CPCGN in 1974, the result of a local petition. Replaced the earlier Shippegan. *See* Shippegan

LANCASTER   Former city (Saint John West). Name taken from the parish, which was named for Lancaster, Massachusetts.

LÉGERVILLE   After Samuel and Charles Léger, early landholders in the district.

LEPREAU   River and point. Of uncertain origin – probably a corruption of an earlier French designation, *lapereau*, "little rabbit", or *le proe*. Occurs as Pte. aux Napraux (Franquelin, 1686).

LETANG HARBOUR   Derived from the French *l'étang*, "the pond". Havre à Étang (Bellin, 1744).

LEWISVILLE   Possibly for James Lewis, early settler and land-holder. Amalgamated with Moncton, 1973.

LINCOLN   Of Loyalist origin – hence probably suggested by Lincoln, Massachusetts. Ganong asserts that the name was chosen because "of [the town's] proximity to York, as in England".

LOGGIEVILLE   Area was first settled (1790s) by the Logie or Loggie family from Scotland. Modern spelling from 1895. Prior to this, community was known as Black Brook for John Black, who settled there about 1780 (CPCGN files).

LORNEVILLE   Honours the Marquess of Lorne (1845–1914), Governor General from 1878 to 1883.

LOWER NORTH BRANCH LITTLE SOUTHWEST MIRAMICHI RIVER   Descriptive. Cited as the "longest place name in Canada".

MC ADAM   Commemorates the career of John McAdam (1807–93), long-time M.L.A. for Charlotte and later (1872–4) M.P. for the same constituency. Name of McAdam Junction post office changed to McAdam on December 16, 1941.

MACHIAS SEAL ISLAND   Traceable to *Machias*, the name of a river in Maine. Name of Malecite origin, and may be derived from *Mecheyisk*, a reference to the "bad little falls" on the river (Eckstorm). Appears on early maps as Seal Island (Moll, 1715) and Western Seal Island (Frederick Holland, 1791) – the area was once noted for sealing.

MACTAQUAC   Lake, park, stream. From the Malecite *Maktequek*, or "big branch", a possible reference to the Saint John River above tide. The reservoir or lake established by the New Brunswick Electric Power Commission in 1967 stretches sixty-five miles upstream from Mactaquac Dam to above Woodstock.

MADAWASKA RIVER   From the Malecite *Medaweskak*, exact meaning unknown. Has been variously translated as "where one river enters another", "porcupine place", or "mouth of river where there is grass and hay". Modern spelling from about 1791.

MAGAGUADAVIC RIVER   Of Micmac origin, this name is a corruption of *Mageecaatawik*, meaning "big eel place", a reference to a feature of the river "highly important from the Indian point of view" (Ganong). *See also* St. Croix River

MAGNETIC HILL   Descriptive for an optical illusion (the formation of the surrounding countryside makes the slope appear to run in the opposite direction from what it actually does). Named in the 1930s by Muriel Lutes Sikorski and promoted as a tourist attraction.

MAISONNETTE   The French for "little house". Formerly Ste. Jeanne d'Arc, the name was changed on October 1, 1936.

MARYSVILLE   Named by Alexander "Boss" Gibson, local entrepreneur and industrialist, for his wife. Amalgamated with Fredericton in 1973.

MAUGERVILLE   Marks the career of Joshua Mauger (?–1790), a native of Jersey, who established himself in Halifax as a merchant and smuggler. One of the original grantees in the area.

MEMRAMCOOK   River, village, and lake. Name traceable to the Micmac *Amlamkook*, "variegated" or "all spotted", a reference to the many-coloured rocks on the shore near the mouth of the river, Memrancou (Franquelin, 1686).

MILLTOWN   *See* St. Stephen

MINISTERS ISLAND   For the Rev. Samuel Andrews (?–1817), Loyalist and Church of England clergyman, who resided on the island from 1791 to 1817. Summer residence of Sir William Van Horne (1843–1915), first president of the C.P.R., located here.

MINTO   After the Earl of Minto (1845–1914), Governor General from 1898 to 1904.

MIRAMICHI BAY and **RIVER**   Origin unknown; possibly from the Montagnais *Maissimeau Assi*, "the land of the Micmacs". Ganong suggests that it may well be "a greatly altered European form", since the word Micmac is of possible French origin. Miramichy applied to the river by Nicolas Denys in 1672.

MISCOU ISLAND   From the Micmac *Susqu*, meaning "low land" or "boggy marsh". "It forms an admirable descriptive name, for the most striking fact about the physical geography of Miscou is the prevalence of open bogs. . . ." (Ganong)

MISSAGUASH RIVER   Forms part of the boundary between New Brunswick and Nova Scotia. A local Micmac term, usually translated as "muskrat". Musaguash (Morris, 1750); Mesiguash (Des Barres, 1781); Missaguash from 1901 onward.

MONCTON   Formerly "The Bend"; named for Robert Monckton (1726–83), commander of the English expedition against Fort Beauséjour in 1755, later wounded at the Battle of the Plains of Abraham, 1759. Originally spelled with a "k" until 1786, when the letter was omitted by clerical oversight. An unsuccessful campaign was mounted in 1930–1 to replace the "k" (CPCGN files).

NACKAWIC   From the Malecite *Nelgwaweegek*, "straight stream", possibly in reference to how the mouth faces the Saint John River. Village incorporated in 1970.

NASHWAAK RIVER
NASHWAAKSIS   Derived from the Malecite *Nahwijewauk*, which may mean "slow current". Nashwaaksis, "little Nashwaak", amalgamated with Fredericton 1973.

NELSON–MIRAMICHI   Formerly South Nelson, changed to Nelson–Miramichi on April 26, 1968. After Admiral Lord Nelson (1758–1805). *See also* Miramichi

NEPISIQUIT RIVER   Bay, brook, and falls. Appears in *Jesuit Relations* (1643) as *Nepegiguit*, a corruption through the French of the Micmac *Win-peg-ij-oo-ik*, "the river that dashes roughly along" – a reference to the torrential character of the river.

NEWCASTLE   Probably for the Duke of Newcastle (1693–1768), who served as Prime Minister of England from 1754 to 1762.

NEW DENMARK   Founded in 1872 by immigrants from Denmark. Post office name changed from Salmonhurst in 1962.

NICHOLAS DENYS   Commemorates the career of Nicolas Denys (1598–1688), one of the leading figures in seventeenth-century Acadia. In 1654 he was appointed governor of "the coasts and islands of the Gulf of St. Laurence from Canso to Gaspe". Died, probably at Nepisiguit, in 1688. Post office from 1940 to 1970.

NORTHUMBERLAND STRAIT   *See* Prince Edward Island *entry*

NORTON   Parish established in 1795 and possibly is named for Norton, Massachusetts.

ODELL RIVER   Marks the contribution of the Odell family to the history of New Brunswick. Some notable family members were Jonathan Odell (1736–1818) and William Franklin Odell (1776–1844).

OROMOCTO   Headquarters for C.F.B. Gagetown, island, lake, and river. Suggested by a Micmac/Malecite descriptive, *Welamooktook*, "five river". Appears on early maps as Ramouctou and La Rivière du Kamouctou (Freneuse seigneurial grant, 1684).

PASSAMAQUODDY BAY   Traceable to the Amerindian *Peskutam-akadi* or *Peskutumaquadik*, "place where pollock leap entirely out of the water. . .so that the bay seems full of fish – one who has seen such a sight knows that there can be but one explanation for the name." (Eckstorm) The earliest reference is Pessemouquote (*Jesuit Relations*, 1675–7).

PELÉ, CAP   *See* Cap-Pelé

PENNFIELD RIDGE   Parish founded by Quakers in 1786 and named for William Penn (1644–1718), founder of Pennsylvania.

PERTH–ANDOVER   Perth for city in Scotland; Andover for town in Hampshire, England. Joint name approved on July 6, 1970; proclaimed in the *Royal Gazette*, November 1, 1972.

PETITCODIAC RIVER   Of Micmac origin; a corruption of *Pet-koot-koy-ek*, meaning "the river that bends around back", descriptive of its winding course. Petcoucoyee (Franquelin 1686); Pacoudiac (de Couagne, 1749); present spelling from mid nineteenth century.

PETIT ROCHER   From the French, "little rock"; probably descriptive.

PLASTER ROCK   After the reddish gypsum rock prevalent in the region.

POCOLOGAN RIVER   Derived from the Passamaquoddy *Pekelagun*, "enclosed harbour".

POINT DE BUTE   From the French *Pointe à Buot*, probably for a point in Missaguash River. May also be from *Pont à Buot*, "Buot's Bridge". For an early Acadian settler, Pierre Buhot or Buot.

POKEMOUCHE RIVER   Suggested by the Micmac

Pokumoochpetooaak, translated by Rand as "salt water extending inland". R. Pokmouet (Jumeau, 1685).

PONT-LAFRANCE   After the Rev. François Xavier Lafrance (1814–67), one of the founders of Collège Saint-Joseph, who served as parish priest at Tracadie. *See* College Bridge

PORT ELGIN   Named about 1850 in honour of Lord Elgin (1811–63), Governor General from 1846 to 1854. Replaced the earlier name Gaspereaux, from Gaspereau River.

PULL AND BE DAMNED NARROWS   Name arose from the difficulty experienced in rowing against the ebb tide in the Letang River.

PUSH AND BE DAMNED RAPIDS   For a situation similar to that above – the problems encountered in rowing against the on-rushing water.

QUISPAMSIS   Derived from the Malecite for "little lake".

RENFORTH   Given to a Canadian National station in 1903 for an English rower who died following a race there in 1871.

RENOUS   Probably named for a Micmac chief, Sock Renou.

RESTIGOUCHE RIVER (New Brunswick)
RISTIGOUCHE RIVER (Quebec)
Originated with the Micmac *Lustagooch* – the exact meaning has been lost; however, probably indicates "good river". Both spellings have been used from earliest times: Restigoch (*Jesuit Relations*, 1642); Ristigouche (Denys, 1672); Restigousche (Des Barres, 1778).

REVERSING FALLS   ·Descriptive. Created by the rise and fall of the Bay of Fundy tide and the flow of water from the Saint John River. Attributed by Rayburn to "Sir Charles G. D. Roberts, who wrote a description of its reversible character in 1882".

REXTON   First named for Kingston, Yorkshire, England. Name changed in 1901 to Rexton, thus avoiding confusion in the mails.

RICHIBUCTO   River, cape, and village. Traceable to Micmac sources: however, the exact form is unknown. May possibly mean "runs back bay place – a reference to Richibucto Harbour" (Rayburn). R. de Rechibouctou (Denys, 1672). Modern spelling from about 1755.

RIVERSIDE–ALBERT   A locational place name. Post office called Albert from 1875; River Side from 1875 to 1932; Riverside from 1932. Village incorporated in 1966. *See* Albert

RIVERVIEW   Descriptive name for a suburban Moncton community dating from 1947. Amalgamated with town of Coverdale in 1973. "Heights" dropped in 1974.

RIVIÈRE-VERTE   Descriptive. First known as Green River; name changed in 1935 to Rivière-Verte.

ROBERTVILLE   Honours Abbé François-Antoine Robert (1820–88), parish priest at Petit Rocher, who organized the local parish in 1884.

ROCKPORT   Descriptive: "A natural rock cove with a caliper of broken stone that kept out all but the worst of weather" (Collie).

ROGERSVILLE   After the Rev. James Rogers (1826–1903), first Catholic Bishop of Chatham.

ROTHESAY   For the Prince of Wales (Duke of Cornwall and Rothesay), later King Edward VII, who embarked from this location for Fredericton during the royal visit of 1860.

SACKVILLE   Name taken from the township established in 1772

honouring Lord Sackville (1716–85), who served as Colonial Secretary from 1775 to 1782. *See also* Sackville, Nova Scotia

ST. ANDREWS   Tradition suggests that a French missionary landed here on St. Andrew's Day, erected a cross, celebrated mass, and named the location St. André (St. Andrews). Known by this name prior to the Loyalist period (CPCGN files).

SAINT-ANTOINE   Traceable to an eighteenth-century French mission which may have been named for the Recollet Seminary at Saint-Antoine-de-Padoue, France.

ST. CROIX RIVER   Champlain wrote: "le lieu est nommé par le Sieur de Monts, l'isle Sainte-Croix" (1604). River takes its name from the island (now Dochets Island in the state of Maine). Figured prominently in boundary disputes between Britain and the United States; however, relics of the Champlain habitation were discovered on Dochets Island, thus verifying the British claim.

SAINT-FRANÇOIS-DE-MADAWASKA   Name probably suggested by the St. Francis River. Named Petite Rivière St. François by Bishop Jean-Baptiste St. Vallier (1653–1727), second Bishop of Quebec, who visited the area in 1686.

ST. GEORGE   "Suggested, no doubt by the presence nearby of the other names of saints, particularly St. Andrews" (Ganong).

SAINT JOHN   River and city. River named by Sieur de Monts (Rivière Saincte-Jean) for the date of its discovery, the feast of St. John the Baptist, June 24, 1604. The city, which was incorporated in 1785 by Royal Charter, is the oldest incorporated city in Canada.

SAINT-LÉONARD   After Leonard Reed Coombes, a magistrate who settled in this area in the mid nineteenth century.

ST. MARTINS   From the parish established in 1786, this name is possibly for St. Martins, Maryland.

ST. QUENTIN   Replaced Anderson Siding (1920) and commemorates the Battle of St. Quentin, France, March 21, 1918, a prominent engagement in the First World War.

ST. STEPHEN   Parish dates from 1786. The name may have been suggested by a surveyor for Stephen Pendleton, or merely adopted as a complement to nearby St. Andrews and St. George. There is no cartographical evidence to connect the name with Sir Charles St. Stephen, one of the Knights Baronet of Nova Scotia.

ST. STEPHEN–MILLTOWN   Incorporated in 1973 as a result of the amalgamation of the two towns. Milltown once had as many as twenty-one mills.

SALISBURY   Suggested by nearby Salisbury Cove, "to which when [the parish was] set off it nearly extended" (Ganong).

SEVOGLE   May be traced to the Micmac *Sewokulook*, "river of many cliffs". Present spelling on maps since 1826. Name officially approved on May 5, 1949. An unsuccessful campaign was launched in 1964 to change the name to Mount Kennedy.

SHEDIAC   Derived from the Micmac *Esedeiik*, "running far back", a reference to Shediac Bay.

SHEFFIELD   First applied to the parish in 1786. For the Earl of Sheffield (1735–1821).

SHEMOGUE   Derived from the Micmac *Simooaquik*, of uncertain meaning, but most probably descriptive of the local topography.

SHEPODY   Traceable to the Micmac *Esedabit*, "the bay that turns back on itself".

SHIPPEGAN   From the Micmac *Sepaguncheech*, "a duck road" or "a small passage through which ducks fly" (Ganong). First applied to Shippegan harbour, later extended to the island (now Île Lamèque) and bay. *See* Lamèque

SILVERWOOD   Descriptive – from the abundance of silver birch trees in the region. Amalgamated with Fredericton 1973.

SKEDADDLE RIDGE   A popular hideout for the first American "draft evaders" – those who were not in sympathy with the northern cause in the Civil War. Defined by Wentworth and Flexner as "a disorderly retreat" (1861).

STANLEY   Honours Lord Stanley (1799–1869), who served as Colonial Secretary from 1833 to 1834 and later as Earl of Derby. He was British Prime Minister in 1852, from 1858 to 1859, and from 1866 to 1868. Stanley served as president of the New Brunswick and Nova Scotia Land Company responsible for settlement in the area in 1833–4.

SUSSEX   Probably for the Duke of Sussex (1773–1843), son of King George III.

TABUSINTAC   Originated with the Micmac *Taboosimkik*, "a pair of them", a possible reference to the main river and French Cove. Tabochemkek (Jumeau, 1685); Taboquinquet (Bellin, 1744); Tabucintac (post office, 1871, and *Canadian Almanac*, 1896). Modern spelling from 1931 onward.

TANTRAMAR   River and marshes. A corruption of the French *Tintamarre*, "thundering noise" – a reference to the noise of the tide rushing up the river or to the noise of flocks of wild geese on the marsh.

TELEGRAPH HILL   Several locations so named in New Brunswick. For a semaphore telegraph established by the Duke of Kent in 1794. The purpose was to link Halifax and Fredericton for the speedy relay of messages.

TEMPERANCE VALE   Possibly attributable to the temperance movement, which reached its peak in New Brunswick during the mid nineteenth century. Town founded by the New Brunswick and Nova Scotia Land Company about 1860.

TIDNISH   *See* Nova Scotia *entry.*

TOBIQUE RIVER   Named for a Malecite chief, Noel Toubic, or Tobec, who lived at the mouth of the river.

TORMENTINE   *See* Cape Tormentine

TRACADIE   From the Micmac *Tulakadik*, "camping ground". Variations of the word appear on early maps: Tregate (Champlain, 1603); Tregatté (Champlain, 1613); Tracadi (Jumeau, 1685); Tracady (Franquelin, 1686). *See also* Tracadie, Nova Scotia

UPPER CHARLO   *See* Charlo

UPSALQUITCH RIVER   Derived from the Micmac *Apsetkwechk*, "little or small river" – "a reference to its size when compared with Restigouche River" (Rayburn).

UTOPIA, LAKE   A facetious reference to the granting of lands "running directly across the lake" to Captain Peter Clinch (February 20, 1784). A later plan of Clinch's land shows "a reserve to make good the deficiency caused by the Lake Eutopia" (Rayburn).

WESTCOCK   Not of English origin, but traceable to the Micmac *Oakshaak*, of unknown meaning. The word was adopted by the French and has gone through many spellings: Oua Koc, Wascok, Westcoup, and finally Westcock from 1792 onward.

WOODSTOCK   Ganong suggests the name "was probably suggested by its nearness to Northhampton, as in England". May possibly be for Woodstock, Maine. Post office from 1830.

WOOLASTOOK PARK A provincial park established in 1969. From the Malecite name for the Saint John River – *Woolahs took* or *Oolahstook*, "good river".

Newfoundland

Although Newfoundland is one of the oldest place names on the eastern seaboard, its evolution may be easily followed. It was the "new founde isle" of John Cabot who sailed westward from Bristol in 1497; although Norsemen, Basques, and Bretons (among others) had undoubtedly preceded him. By 1502 "New found launde" was being used in official English documents with the French version "Terre Neuve" appearing as early as 1510 – a clear indication of the acceptance of the designation. Giovanni da Verrazano used the term "Terra Nova" on his map of 1529. Newfoundland entered Confederation as the tenth province of Canada on March 31, 1949.

Labrador

There remains an element of uncertainty, but most authorities credit the origin of the name Labrador to João Fernandes, a Portuguese explorer and *lavrador*, or "landholder", in the Azores. It was probably first applied to a section of the coast of modern Greenland and later transferred by cartographers to the northeastern coast of the continent. The *Dictionary of Canadian Biography*, Volume I, quotes an inscription (near Greenland) on the Weimar map of 1530: ". . . And as the one who first gave notice of it was a labrador of the Azores [João Fernandes], they gave it the name."

ADMIRAL'S COVE   Also Admiral Island and Admiral's Beach. All three names are reminders of the title (Fishing Admiral) assigned to the captain of the first vessel to reach a particular harbour on the Newfoundland coast. The system lasted from the early seventeenth to the late eighteenth century.

AGUATHUNA   First known as Jack of Clubs Cove and briefly as Limeville, the name was changed as a result of a local petition in 1911. It is from a Beothuk word meaning "white rock" or "grindstone".

ALEXANDER BAY   Possibly a family name replacing the earlier Bloody Bay that marked a massacre of Beothuks at this location.

ANGUILLE MOUNTAINS   *See* Cape Anguille

ANNIEOPSQUOTCH MOUNTAINS   From the Micmac word for "rocky mountains".

AQUAFORTE   The name is an anglicized version of an earlier Portuguese name, ". . . from a pretty cascade where a brook shoots its waters over a cliff into the sea" (Jukes).

ARGENTIA   Originally known as Little Placentia, the community was renamed to mark the opening of a silver mine in the vicinity. From the Latin *argentum*, "silver".

ATIKONAK RIVER, LABRADOR   Derived from the Montagnais word meaning "whitefish".

AVALON PENINSULA   Name bestowed by Sir George Calvert (1580–1632) "on a plantation officially styled in imitation of old Avalon in Somersetshire" (*The Newfoundland Journal of Aaron Thomas*).

AVONDALE   The earlier name, Salmon Cove, was changed in 1906 by order of the Newfoundland Nomenclature Board. For

Avondale, County Wicklow, Ireland.

BACCALIEU ISLAND   The name is derived from the Spanish *bacalao* or the Basque *baccalaos*, for "codfish".

BADGER   Possibly after a family name rather than the animal (a member of the weasel family common in western Canada).

BAIE VERTE   A descriptive ("green bay") which dates from the period of French influence in Newfoundland.

BATTLE HARBOUR, LABRADOR   Located on Battle Island. The name appears on early maps as Batel, probably from the Portuguese for boat or canoe.

BAY BULLS   A very old settlement. The name may have originated with the bull bird or ice bird. Recorded as Bay of Bulls on the Thomas Hood manuscript map, 1592.

BAY D'ESPOIR
HEAD BAY D'ESPOIR   Derived from the French Baie d'Espoir (Bay of Hope); *c. d. Espera* on early maps. Ganong suggests that this location may be Cartier's "hable du Sainct Esperit", named by him on Whitsuntide, 1536.

BAY DE VERDE   Descriptive. The name is of Portuguese origin (*verde,* "green") and dates from the late sixteenth century. Rendered as Greene Bay by John Guy in 1612.

BAY ROBERTS   Originated with a French family name (Seary). Appears on Thornton map, 1689.

BELLE ISLE, STRAIT OF   A euphemistic name which was first applied to Bell or Belle Island (then Isle de la Grand Baye), and Belle Isle (Alfonse, 1544).

BELLEORAM   "Very euphonious but unintelligible" (Howley).

The name is of uncertain derivation.

BELL ISLAND (Conception Bay)   Descriptive, "from an immense rock in the form of an inverted bell" (Seary). *See also* Wabana

BISHOP'S FALLS   Commemorates a visit to Newfoundland by the Anglican Bishop John Inglis (1777–1850).

BLACK JOKE COVE   Possibly after a pirate ship of the same name.

BLAKETOWN   For Sir Henry Arthur Blake (1840–1918), who served as Governor of Newfoundland from 1887 to 1888.

BLOW ME DOWN   This unusual name occurs numerous times in Newfoundland and at least once in Labrador. It is ". . . no fanciful name, but describes the effect of a downrush of wind over an escarpment on a small vessel beneath it" (Seary). *See* Blomidon, Nova Scotia

BONAVISTA   Of possible Spanish, Portuguese, or French origin. Cap de Bonne Viste (Cartier, 1534). May have been bestowed by Gaspar Corte Real in 1500 after one of the Cape Verde islands – Boa Vista.

BONNE BAY   Descriptive. Traceable to Basque or French sources. The modern form dates from the Cook survey of 1767.

BOTWOOD   Marks the career of Archdeacon E. Botwood (1828–1901). The early form was Botwoodville.

BRIGUS   Has been attributed to Bridge or Brighouse, near Huddersfield, Yorkshire, England; however, it is more probably after the French family name Bregou (Seary).

BUCHANS   The name was transferred from Buchans Island in

Red Indian Lake. It honours David Buchan (1780–1838), a British naval officer who saw service in Newfoundland.

BURGEO   Applied first to the islands off the coast. Once Mill Virgines (Chaves-Oviedo, 1536), later Virgeo, and eventually Burgeo, the name was bestowed in commemoration of the eleven thousand virgins who, on return from Rome, are believed to have been killed by the Huns at Cologne in the fourth or fifth century.

BURIN   May be traceable to the French word for an engraving or carving tool, or may possibly be from a Gaelic word for "low, rocky place or promontory".

BURLINGTON   A variation of Bridlington, Yorkshire, England. *See* Burlington, Ontario

CAMPBELLTON   First known as Indian Arm, it was renamed in honour of a local mill owner.

CAPE ANGUILLE   From the French *anguille*, for "eel", the name was applied later to the Anguille mountains.

CAPE BROYLE   Derived from the old English *broile* or *brolle*, "to roar or sound loud", indicative of heavy seas. The name appears as C. Brolle and as Cabreuil on early maps.

CAPE CHIDLEY, LABRADOR   Assigned by the explorer John Davis (1550–1605) for "his neighbour Mr. John Chidley of Broad Clyst, near Exeter, Devonshire, England".

CAPE FREELS   A transfer name from the Portuguese Ilha de frey luis, "the island of Brother Louis" (Seary).

CAPE RACE   Perhaps named for Pointe du Raz in Brittany or for Capa Raso in Portugal. *See* Trepassey

CAPE ST. MARYS   Cabo de Sancta Marie, 1536, and Cap de

Saincte Marie, 1544. The cape was possibly first named by the Portuguese and has survived in translation.

CAPE SPEAR   Derived from the Portuguese (Cauo de la Spera – Olivieriana, 1505–8), "the cape of hope" or "waiting for fair winds".

CARBONEAR   Of uncertain origin. The name may have been suggested by: C. Carvoeiro on the coast of Portugal; Carboneras in southern Spain; Carbonnier, a French family name; or the site of a charcoal industry.

CARMANVILLE   Former name, Rocky Bay. Named by proclamation on June 18. 1906, after the Rev. Albert Carman (1833–1917), General Superintendent of the Methodist Church.
See Carman, Manitoba

CARTWRIGHT, LABRADOR   Honours Captain George Cartwright (1739–1819), author, trader, and explorer.

CATALINA   Referred to by Jacques Cartier as Havre Saincte-Katherine in 1534; however, the Spanish form, Cataluña, superseded the French and has survived.

CAT HARBOUR   *See* Lumsden

CHAMBERLAINS   Derived from an English family name.

CHANNEL–PORT AUX BASQUES   Formerly two separate communities now amalgamated as one town. Channel is a descriptive, while Port aux Basques predates Champlain (1612) and may be attributed to early Basque fishermen.

CHARLOTTETOWN   Originally Brown's Cove; the name was changed toward the end of the nineteenth century. It may have been suggested by Charlottetown, Prince Edward Island.

CHATEAU BAY, LABRADOR   "Owes its name to the very striking castle-like masses of basaltic rocks of Castle and Henley
islands at its entrance." (Ganong)

CHURCHILL RIVER
CHURCHILL FALLS, LABRADOR   Formerly Hamilton River,
the river and falls were renamed by Premier J. R. Smallwood on
February 4, 1965 (see the opening chapter). *See* Hamilton Inlet

CLARENVILLE   The name was adopted about 1900 for the amalgamated settlements of Lower Shoal Harbour, Dark Hole, Brook
Cove, and Red Beach. After Clarence Whiteway, son of Sir William Whiteway (1829–1908), once Prime Minister of Newfoundland. The community was first known as Clarenceville; the name
was later shortened to Clarenville.

CLARKE'S BEACH   From a family name common to the area.

CODROY   Valley and river. Both names are derived from the
French form for nearby Cape Ray – Cap de Roy or C. de Roy.

COLLIERS   The name is probably traceable to a common English family name.

COME BY CHANCE   The harbour may have been discovered
"by chance". Appears as Comby Chance in documents of the
eighteenth century.

CONCEPTION BAY   The name is from the Portuguese B. de
Comceica or B. de Conceicao (Conception) and was bestowed for
the Feast of the Conception, December 8. It appears erroneously
as Consumption Bay on some seventeenth-century maps.

CONCHE   May be named for the Abbey of Conches in Normandy, or possibly it is an early French descriptive which "seems
to have escaped the dictionaries, but may be an equivalence with
the English 'bight' or 'road' in its navigational sense" (Ganong).

COOK'S HARBOUR   Commemorates the work of James Cook (1728–79), English hydrographer and explorer, who charted portions of the Newfoundland coast in the 1760s.

CORMACK   Marks the career of William Epps Cormack (1796–1868), the first white man to cross Newfoundland from east to west (1822).

CORNER BROOK   For the Corner Brook (so named by Captain James Cook), which flows through the present-day city. Corner Brook was incorporated as a city in 1956 with the amalgamation of Corner Brook East, Corner Brook West, Humbermouth, and Curling.

CRESTON   "That the western section of Mortier Bay, extending from West's Point to Glendon (including Butler's Cove) be re-named Creston" (Proclamation, September 22, 1914). It has been facetiously suggested that the Protestant settlement was originally Christ's Town (as opposed to the Catholic Marystown) and that Creston is a variant of same (Seary).

CUPIDS   Originally named Cupers Cove, it was the site of a settlement by John Guy in 1610. The name is possibly traceable to Cooper family.

CURLING   For the Rev. J. J. Curling (1844–1906). *See also* Corner Brook

DANIEL'S HARBOUR   Possibly named for the explorer Captain Charles Daniel (?–1661).

DARK COVE   A local descriptive.

DEER LAKE   Descriptive. This part of Newfoundland is famous for its caribou herds.

DILDO   Of obscure derivation. The theories of origin include:

"a word used in the refrain of ballads"; "a cylindrical glass"; "phallus or penis substitute"; and "a local form of the doldrums". For a detailed discussion see Seary, *Place Names of the Avalon Peninsula*.

DOATING COVE   The name is derived from "doater", an obsolete word which meant an old seal. It is mentioned in Captain Cartwright's *Journal* (1792).

DUNVILLE   Possibly traceable to the River Dun, Ireland, or for the family name of early settlers – Dun or Dunn.

ECLIPSE ISLAND   One of the Burgeo Islands off the south coast. Here, Captain James Cook witnessed an eclipse of the sun, August 5, 1766.

ELLISTON   Formerly Bird Island Cove. The name was changed in 1892 to honour the Rev. William Ellis, who is credited with conducting the first Methodist service in the community in 1812.

ENGLEE   A corruption of the French word *anglais*.

EXPLOITS   Bay and river. Of unknown origin. The name has been attributed to the Buchan expedition of 1810, which was sent to the area to befriend the Beothuks. However, Howley traced the name as far back as Cook's maps and charts of 1774. It was known as B. de Kork or Cork on maps prior to that date.

FAIRHAVEN   A coined name adopted by the Newfoundland Nomenclature Board on June 29, 1940, to replace Famish Gut.

FERRYLAND   The name appears as Farilham or Port Farelhao (1529, Portuguese); Forillon (1547, French), and Ferriland (1627, English). The modern name is a distillation of all these early sources. Originally it was probably a descriptive, traceable to the Portuguese Farelhao – "steep rock or reef".

FOGO   This place name is also of Portuguese origin and is from *fuego*, for "fire". It may have been suggested by Fogo Island in the Cape Verdes. *See* Bonavista

FORTEAU, LABRADOR   The site of a succession of forts built by the French and the English. The first was erected about 1710 by Augustin Le Gardeur de Courtemanche (1663–1717).

FORTUNE   Bay and town. The name stems from the Portuguese *fortuna*, or "luck", and may refer to a now unknown incident in the seafaring history of Newfoundland. Town incorporated in 1946.

FOX HARBOUR   A transfer name from nearby Fox Island. Appears as I. du renard (Detcheverry, 1689).

FRESHWATER   A common descriptive place name in Newfoundland, which undoubtedly refers to the search by fishermen and mariners for "fresh water".

FUNK ISLAND   The name may be traced to a Norse or Icelandic word for "a small haycock", which the island is said to resemble.

GANDER   The lake, town, and air base take their name from Gander River, so named for the wild geese abundant in the vicinity. The transatlantic air base dates from 1935.

GAULTOIS   Descriptive. The name is from the Norman French *Galtas*, meaning "pinnacle" or "dormer".

GLOVERTOWN   The first name of the community, Flat Island, was changed in honour of Sir John Hawley Glover (1829–85), Governor of Newfoundland from 1875 to 1881. Also Glover Island in Grand Lake.

GOOSE BAY   The name was chosen in 1941 for the site of an air base to accommodate a shorter Atlantic air-ferry route to Britain. It "relates to a variety of goose found there". Happy Valley amalgamated with Goose Bay in 1975.

GOULDS   So called from a "gold or yellow flower which grows abundantly on the banks of some brooks" (Jukes). This may possibly be a reference to the marsh marigold.

GRAND BANK   Descriptive, and dates from the late seventeenth century. Refers to the hill or bank on the west side of the harbour.

GRAND FALLS, LABRADOR   Named by their discoverer in 1838, John McLean (1797–1890), an employee of the Hudson's Bay Company. Name changed to Churchill Falls on February 4, 1965.

GRAND FALLS, NEWFOUNDLAND   Descriptive for the falls on the Exploits River. Originally a company town established in 1909.

GREENS HARBOUR   Possibly stems from the family name of the first fishermen to settle the area.

GREENSPOND   Derived from the names of the first two families to settle in the district – Green and Pond. Appears as Greenspond (Moll, 1701).

GROS MORNE   Mountain and national park. From the French *gros*, "large", and *morne,* which refers to "a bluff or small hill". The word *morne* "may come from a West Indian modification of the Spanish 'morro' for mound" (Poirier, quoted by Rayburn).

HAMILTON INLET AND RIVER, LABRADOR
HAMILTON SOUND, NEWFOUNDLAND   The name was first applied to the inlet (river named after the inlet) in honour of Sir Charles Hamilton (1767–1849), Governor of Newfoundland from

1818 to 1824. Hamilton Sound was also named for Sir Charles. *See* Churchill River *and* Grand Falls (Labrador)

HANTS HARBOUR   Appears as L'ance Arbre or Ance Arbre in early French records. Hants Harbour is probably a variation of same.

HAPPY ADVENTURE   The name was suggested by that of a pirate ship.

HAPPY VALLEY, LABRADOR   Established in 1942 as a townsite for workers at Goose Bay and amalgamated with Goose Bay in 1975. A euphemistic name.

HARBOUR GRACE   Probably a transfer name from Havre de Grace, the name used for Le Havre, France, when it was founded in 1517.

HARBOUR MAIN   Attributed by Howley to "the harbour of St. Meen, a small town near St. Malo" and by Seary to "a French family name".

HARE BAY   "An allusion to the prevalence of the Arctic hare *Lepus americanus* which formerly abounded in Newfoundland" (Howley). The name dates from the seventeenth century and appears as B. aux Lievres on French charts of the period.

HEAD BAY D'ESPOIR   *See* Bay d'Espoir

HEART'S CONTENT
HEART'S DELIGHT
HEART'S DESIRE   These may be euphemistic names "bestowed with the idea of making a good impression"; however, Heart's Content is possibly traceable to the name of a ship.

HEBRON, LABRADOR   The name of a Moravian mission established in 1829–30. After the biblical city of Hebron. The name means "friendship" in Hebrew.

HERMITAGE BAY   An early rendezvous for fishermen from the Channel Islands. "...They saw in an island in the bay a resemblance to the Hermitage, off the port of St. Helier, Jersey." (Howley)

HOLYROOD   Probably after Holyrood House, Edinburgh, Scotland.

HOPEDALE, LABRADOR   In 1752 the ship *Hope* carried the first Moravian missionaries to Labrador. Settlement dates from 1782.

HOWE HARBOUR   Marks the career of Admiral Richard Howe (1726–99).

HUMBER RIVER   Suggested by the river of the same name in England.

IGLUKSOATULLIGARSUK ISLAND, LABRADOR   Of Inuit origin, the name may be translated as "a collection of sod houses".

ISLE AUX MORTS   "Deadman's" island. Undoubtedly refers to an incident in the early seafaring history of Newfoundland.

JERSEYSIDE   The name is an indication of the long association between Jersey (one of the Channel Islands) and Newfoundland.

JOE BATT'S ARM   Named for a Joseph, or John, Batt, "who was sentenced to receive fifteen lashes for stealing a pair of shoes and buckles valued at 7s 6p about 1754 at Bonavista" (Pedley).

KEPPEL HARBOUR   Name bestowed by Captain James Cook in honour of Augustus, first Viscount Keppel (1725–86), an admiral of the British navy.

KING GEORGE IV LAKE   Assigned by William Epps Cormack for King George IV (1762–1830).

KINGS COVE (Trinity Bay)   Originally known as Cannings Cove (for an early settler). Over the years local pronunciation "had a tendency toward elision" and the name Kings Cove resulted. It survived an attempted name change to Port Royal in 1901.

KIPPENS   This name may possibly be derived from an old English word for "a bundle of hides" or "an English family name not traced in Newfoundland" (Seary).

LABRADOR CITY, LABRADOR   For origin of Labrador see provincial entry. Labrador City, built by the Iron Ore Company of Canada, dates from 1962.

LAMALINE   The bay and ledges "may have been named for Belem near Lisbon" (Ganong); however, exact origin is uncertain.

LANCE COVE   The name may be derived from "lance", an implement used for spearing fish, or may simply be a variation of the French *l'anse*, "cove". Written as Lants Cove (Jukes, 1840).

L'ANSE AU LOUP, LABRADOR   Site of a fort erected by Augustin Le Gardeur de Courtemanche (1663–1717). The name undoubtedly refers to a long-forgotten incident involving a wolf.

L'ANSE AUX MEADOWS   Site of a pre-Columbian Viking settlement discovered and excavated (1961–8) by Norwegian explorer and archaeologist Helge Instad. It is a descriptive (French-English) name which may be translated as "the bay with the grasslands". It is also possibly a misspelling of an early French designation, L'Anse aux Meduses, "the bay of jellyfish".

LARK HARBOUR
LARK ISLAND   Named for H.M.S. *Lark*, a ship used in the coastal surveys conducted by Captain Cook in the 1760s.

LA SCIE   French for "saw", "so called from the appearance of the cliff" (Howley).

LAWN   Traced by Howley to the French *l'âne*, "the ass", a possible reference to the caribou. L'anse Sauvage (Wild Ass) on early maps.

LEWISPORTE   Originally Big Burnt Bay and later Marshallville, it was renamed for Lewis Miller and Company, a Scottish firm once engaged in lumbering in the area. *See* Millertown

LITTLE CATALINA   *See* Catalina

LOBSTICK LAKE, LABRADOR   For the lobstick, a type of marker used by the Montagnais-Naskapi people (among others). It was usually a conspicuous tree from which all but the topmost branches had been removed. Name possibly assigned by John McLean (1797–1890), an employee of the Hudson's Bay Company. It is now part of Smallwood Reservoir.

LOGY BAY   Derived from the Cornish *lugh-ogo*, for "cave calf or seal" (Seary). Lugy Bay on early maps.

LOURDES   Formerly known as Clam Bank Cove, the community was renamed for "Our Lady of Lourdes", one of the titles by which the Virgin Mary is venerated.

LUMSDEN   First known as Cat Harbour, denoting the presence of "cats", a term for young baby seals. It was renamed to mark the career of Rev. James Lumsden, a Methodist minister who was known as the "Skipper parson".

MARY MARCH BROOK   The name commemorates Demasduit (Mary March), wife of the Beothuk chief Nonosbawsut, who was captured and died in captivity on January 8, 1820. *See* Shanadithit Brook

MARYSTOWN   Originally Mortier Bay. Marystown was adopted "... for the sake of distinction as there is a few miles south another bay called by the French Mortier Bay" (Howley). *See* Creston

MECATINA RIVER, LABRADOR   Derived from a Montagnais word for "where there is a large mountain" (Lemoine).

MEELPAEG LAKE   May be translated from the Micmac as "lake of many bays or coves".

MELVILLE LAKE, LABRADOR   Honours Henry Dundas, first Viscount Melville (1742–1811), who served as Lord of the Admiralty from 1804 to 1805.

MICHIKAMAU LAKE, LABRADOR   Originates with Naskapi-Montagnais sources; the exact meaning is unknown. Now part of Smallwood Reservoir.

MILLERTOWN   Named for the Scottish firm of Lewis Miller and Company. *See* Lewisporte

MOUNT CORMACK   After William Epps Cormack (1796–1868), who in 1822 crossed Newfoundland from east to west.

MOUNT MISERY   Named by Cormack "in remembrance of an unpleasant night [October 16–17, 1822] snowbound at this location".

MOUNT PEARL   For Sir James Pearl, "a retired naval officer who was given by the Home Government . . . 600 acres of land ever since known as Mount Pearl" (Prowse).

MOUNT SYLVESTER   Named by Cormack in honour of his guide, Joseph Sylvester. *See* Cormack

MUSGRAVE HARBOUR
MUSGRAVETOWN   Originally known as Muddy Hole and Goose Bay, the communities were renamed by Sir Anthony Musgrave (1828–88), who served as Governor of Newfoundland from 1864 to 1869.

NASKAUPI RIVER, LABRADOR   Derived from the name of the Naskapi, or Naskaupi, tribe which inhabit this part of Labrador. The meaning of the name is uncertain.

NEW HARBOUR   Probably descriptive (in relation to an older settlement).

NEW PERLICAN   *See* Old Perlican

NEW WORLD ISLAND   Resulting from *Novus Mundus*, to be found on the Verrazano map of 1527.

NORRIS ARM   For James Norris, the first settler in the area. The name is mentioned in Cartwright's *A Sketch of the River Exploits*, 1768.

NORRIS POINT (Bonne Bay)   Traceable to a common family name.

NORTH WEST RIVER, LABRADOR   Descriptive. The community is on the site of Fort Smith (1836) and the name was changed in 1840 to North West River House. The present form dates from the late nineteenth century.

NOTRE DAME BAY   This name ("Our Lady Bay") was bestowed by the French mariners and dates from the sixteenth century.

OLD FORT BAY, LABRADOR   Once known as Vieux Fort, this was the site of a post erected in 1704 by Augustin Le Gardeur de Courtemanche (1663–1717).

PENETANGUISHENE   Assigned in the 1950s, the name is an "arbitrary imposition from Ontario" (Seary). *See* Penetanguishene, Ontario.

PERLICAN ISLAND
OLD PERLICAN
NEW PERLICAN   The place name may have originated with the island, I. du Perlican (Bellin, 1754), and is possibly traceable to the name of a ship (Prowse).

PETERS ARM   May possibly be derived from a local family name.

PETITSIKAPAU LAKE, LABRADOR   Originates with a Montagnais-Naskapi word meaning "willow-fringed".

PETTY HARBOUR   The name dates from the sixteenth century and is undoubtedly descriptive since the location is ". . . a small harbour compared with the great harbour of St. John's" (Seary).

PLACENTIA   Founded by the French in 1662 as "Plaisance . . . a sentinel on the flank of Cabot Strait"; the name is older and probably stems from Plasencia, a town in Salamanca, Spain.

POINT LEAMINGTON   After Leamington, Warwickshire, England. *See* Leamington, Ontario

PORT AU CHOIX   Appears as Portichoa (Detcheverry, 1689) and is probably Basque or French in origin. The harbour gave its name to the peninsula.

PORT AU PORT   Of Basque origin. Ophor portu (Detcheverry, 1689). Has been freely translated as "port of rest in time of storm".

PORT AUX BASQUES   *See* Channel–Port aux Basques

PORT BLANDFORD   The name was suggested by Blandford Forum, a municipal borough of North Dorsetshire.

PORT DE GRAVE   Traceable to the French *grève* or *grave* for "pebbly beach" or "sandy beach". Early French fishermen frequently dried cod on the shingle, or beaches.

PORT SAUNDERS   Honours Admiral Sir Charles Saunders (1713?–75), who served as Commodore and Commander-in-Chief of the Newfoundland station in 1752.

PORTUGAL COVE   Name dates from the early seventeenth century: B. of Portugal, 1610, and B. Portugall, 1625 (Ganong). It is evidence of Portugal's long connection with the Newfoundland fishery.

PORT UNION   Founded in 1914 by Sir William Coaker (1871–1938) as the headquarters for his Fishermen's Protective Union and the Union Trading Company.

POUCH COVE   Pouche Cove (Jukes, 1840). The name may have its origin in the French family name Pouche (Seary).

QUIDI VIDI   This is an "uncommon name of uncertain origin". Seary records twenty-five variations in spelling, from "Quilli widdi" to "Quidy Vidy". The phonetic rendering "Kitty Vitty" is common in early documents – e.g., "Colonel Amherst marched to Kitty Vitty and made himself master of that important post." (Dispatch of Rear Admiral Lord Colville, September 20, 1762.) The most plausible theory of origin is that given by Seary as "... a conjectural derivation from a French family name Quidville (Picardy) or Quetteville (Jersey)".

RAMEA ISLAND   The name is of probable French origin, from *rameau*, for "bushy". *La ramée* is used on the island of Guernsey to indicate vetch, a low, bushy plant.

RANDOM ISLAND From the old English "randon" or "ranted", this name refers "to some incident, or by metaphor [describes] turbulent weather or sea" (Seary).

RED INDIAN LAKE The name is evidence that the now-extinct Beothuks (who because of their attachment to red ochre gave their nickname to the native people of North America) once occupied this area.

RENEWS From the Portuguese *ronhoso* or the French *rogneux*, "scabby"; it is a possible reference to shell-covered rocks. Appears as *Rougnouse* in Cartier's narrative, July 19, 1536.

ROBERTS ARM The name is an association with a common Newfoundland family name.

ROCKY HARBOUR (Bonne Bay) Descriptive. Here the shoreline is bordered by rocky ledges. Appears on the Admiralty chart of 1897 as Roche or Rocky Harbour.

RODDICKTON Adopted in the 1930s in commemoration of the career of Sir Thomas George Roddick (1846–1923), who achieved fame as a surgeon.

ROMAINE RIVER, LABRADOR A corruption of the Amerindian *alimun*, translated as "difficult", a reference to the difficulty in navigating the lower section of the river in Quebec (Geographic Board of Canada Report, 1924).

ROSE BLANCHE A descriptive, which was assigned by the French for an outcropping of white or rose-white granite.

ST. ALBANS After St. Albans, Hertfordshire, England.

ST. ANTHONY Name bestowed by Cartier, June 13, 1534, on a harbour (on the mainland) which he entered on St. Anthony's

Day. The name was later transferred to a location on the north-west coast of Newfoundland.

ST. BRENDAN'S   For the Irish saint and hero of a legendary voyage across the Atlantic in a leather boat. The town is located on Cottel Island, which was the early settlement name. The voyage was re-enacted in 1977, giving credence to the legend.

ST. GEORGE'S BAY   The name is attributed to a parish of the same name in Guernsey.

ST. JOHN'S   Derived from the supposed date of discovery – on the Feast of St. John the Baptist, 1497. The name has survived through a series of translations from the Portuguese (S. Joham) to the French (b. de Saincte Jean) to St. John's.

SALVAGE   The name may refer to a marine incident or tragedy.

SANDRINGHAM   Named for Sandringham House, the country residence of the royal family in Norfolk.

SHANADITHIT BROOK   Named after Shanadithit, a Beothuk woman, captured in 1823, who died in 1829 and was reputedly the last survivor of her race. *See* Mary March Brook

SHEARSTOWN   First known as Spaniards Bay Pond, the town was renamed for the Rev. C. W. Shears, who served as Anglican rector in the area.

SIGNAL HILL   A prominent landmark in St. John's and once the location from which the approach of ships was signalled.

SMALLWOOD RESERVOIR, LABRADOR   Named for Joseph R. Smallwood, Premier of Newfoundland from 1949 to 1972. "It is the principal water storehouse for the Churchill Falls hydro-electric power development and is the third-largest man-made lake in the world." (Smallwood, *I Chose Canada*)

SPANIARD'S BAY   The name is testimony to the involvement of Spain in the Newfoundland fishery. Known as Spaniard's Bay Beech (Wix, 1836).

SPANISH ROOM   The name originated with the division of the shore among fishing crews, each nationality (e.g. Spanish) having his own "room" or area.

SPRINGDALE   The name is probably a descriptive.

STEPHENVILLE
STEPHENVILLE CROSSING   Name assigned by the Rev. Thomas Sears (?–1885), Catholic missionary, after the first child baptized in the community, Stephen Le Blanc (White).

TERRA NOVA NATIONAL PARK   Once a common designation (*Terra Nova*, "New Land") for Newfoundland (Verrazano, 1529), the name was adopted in 1957 for Canada's most easterly national park. It was officially opened in 1961.

TILT COVE (Green Bay)
TILTING (Fogo Island)   Both place names stem from the "tilts", small huts or cabins used by the early settlers. Tilting is a variation of Tilt Town.

TORBAY   Generally considered to be named after Tor Bay, Devonshire, England.

TREPASSEY   Derived from Baie des Trépassés near Pointe du Raz in Brittany. *See* Cape Race

TRINITY   Bay and town. Name possibly bestowed by Gaspar Corte Real, who reputedly entered the bay on Trinity Sunday, 1500.

TWILLINGATE   The name, of Breton origin, was adapted from Pointe de Toulinguet in Brittany.

VICTORIA   Once known as Victoria Village, the community was presumably named for Queen Victoria.

WABANA   The name is of Micmac origin and stems from *Wabunaki*, "east land", or *Wâban*, "the dawn" (Rand). It was applied to Bell Island. The name was revived in 1895 by Thomas Cantley, an official of the Nova Scotia Steel and Coal Company. *See* Bell Island

WABUSH LAKE, LABRADOR   Traceable to an Amerindian word, *Waboz*, which has been translated as "rabbit".

WESLEYVILLE   The settlement was first known as Coal Harbour but was renamed in 1884 in honour of John Wesley (1703–91), the founder of Methodism.

WHITBOURNE   Named for Sir Richard Whitbourne (fl. 1579–1628), merchant, colonizer, and governor of Sir William Vaughan's colony at Trepassey, Newfoundland, from 1618 to 1620.

WHITE BAY   The modern name is a translation of Baye Blanche, recorded in Champlain's map of 1612.

WINDSOR   Formerly Grand Falls Station, it may possibly have been named for the royal house of Windsor.

WINTERTON   The original name, Sille, or Scilly, Cove, was changed by the Newfoundland Nomenclature Board in honour of Sir James Spearman Winter (1845–1911), who was Prime Minister of Newfoundland from 1897 to 1900.

WITLESS BAY   The name may be a corruption of Whittle's Bay, from a common Dorsetshire family name, or perhaps it was "used metaphorically to describe the [crazy, lunatic] sea" (Seary).

Nova Scotia

 Although applied first on September 29, 1621, when Sir William Alexander (1567?–1640) received a grant of "the lands lying between New England and Newfoundland ... to be known as Nova Scotia, or New Scotland", the name did not become fixed on the map until after the signing of the Treaty of Utrecht in 1713.

Prior to this, the name *Acadia* was generally used by the French to denote the Maritime provinces along with adjacent portions of New England and Quebec. The origin of the word Acadia is in dispute. It is generally accepted to be from Archadia (Acadia), assigned by Giovanni da Verrazano in 1524 and suggested by the classical name for a land of rustic peace (Rayburn). The claim that it is of Micmac origin is probably coincidental. The Micmac word *Quoddy* or *Cady* was rendered by the French as *cadie* and meant "a piece of land or territory" (Clark).

ALDERSHOT   Named for Aldershot, Hampshire, England. Both are military bases.

AMET ISLAND   From the French Isle l'Ormet, so named because of its resemblance to the shape of a helmet. Also Amet Sound.

AMHERST   Commemorates the career of Lord Jeffrey Amherst (1717–97), commander-in-chief of the British forces in North America during the Seven Years War. On the surrender of Montreal in 1760, he became Governor General. *See* Amherstburg, Ontario

ANNAPOLIS ROYAL, ANNAPOLIS BASIN and **RIVER**   The area surrounding the basin was named Port Royal by Champlain in 1604. Following final capture by the British in 1710 "they strengthened the [fortifications] and gave it the name Annapolis Royal in honour of Queen Anne" (Haliburton).

ANTIGONISH   Town and country. Derived from the Micmac *Nalegitkoonechk*, which has been translated by Rand as "where branches are torn off". The spelling has varied over the years: Articougnesche (Denys, 1672); Artigonieche (Jumeau, 1685); Antigonich (Bellin, 1744). The modern spelling became commonly accepted from the late eighteenth century onward.

APPLE RIVER   The name is a direct translation of the original French name, Rivière aux Pommes.

ARICHAT   Settlement, cape, harbour, and head. The name is probably of Micmac or Micmac/French origin, but its exact meaning has been lost. Rendered on early maps as Nerichat or Nerichac, it was mentioned in the Morris survey of 1764 as ". . . the harbour of Grand Narishak, called by the French Port St. Mary's".

ARISAIG   Settled in the 1780s by families from Arisaig, Scotland, and named by them for their former home.

ARMDALE   The name may be traced to the estate of Sir Charles Tupper (1821–1915), located on the North West Arm of Halifax Harbour. Since 1941 it has been applied to a residential suburb of Halifax.

ASPY BAY   According to Ganong "all considerations point to Gaspa or Gaspé as the original form of Aspy". It was probably a Micmac word to denote the limits of their territory. Brown suggests that it may have been named by Basque sailors after Pic d'Aspe in the Pyrénées. *See* Gaspé, Quebec

AYLESFORD   After the fourth Earl of Aylesford, Lord of the Bedchamber to King George III. The township was established on October 6, 1786. The post office dates from 1835.

BACCARO   A variation of *bacculaos* or *bacalao*, "codfish". The name is probably of Basque or Spanish origin. *See* Baccalieu Island, Newfoundland

BADDECK   Village, bay, and river. "Without reasonable doubt [the name] is identical with Bedeque, Prince Edward Island, and is a corruption of the Micmac *Petekook*, the place that lies on the backward turn, a reference to the position of the Baddeck River in relation to Indian travel from Bras d'Or Lake." (Ganong)

BALMORAL MILLS   Site of a grist mill dating from 1830, the community was named for Balmoral Castle, Aberdeenshire, Scotland.

BARACHOIS   Derived from the French *barachoix* for "sand bar". "They give the name barachois to small ponds near the sea, from which they are separated only by a kind of causeway or sand bar." (Pichon, 1760) A common place name in Nova Scotia, New Brunswick, and Newfoundland.

BARRINGTON PASSAGE   Settled in the period from 1760 to 1763 by New England planters. Named in 1767 for William Wildman Barrington (1717–93), later Viscount Barrington, who served as Chancellor of the Exchequer from 1761 to 1762.

BEAR RIVER   Referred to as Rivière Hébert by Lescarbot in 1606, the stream was named for Louis Hébert, apothecary and a member of the Du Gua de Monts expedition to Acadia. The modern name is an English corruption of the original French.

BEDFORD   The name was first applied to Bedford Basin in honour of John Russell, fourth Duke of Bedford, Secretary of State (Southern Department) from 1748 to 1751.

BEINN BHREAGH   From the Gaelic for "beautiful mountain", the name was first applied to the summer home of Alexander Graham Bell (1847–1922).

BELLIVEAU COVE   Originated with the name of the first settler, Charles Belliveau, who returned to Nova Scotia following the Expulsion of 1755. The post office was established in 1856.

BELL LAKES   Formerly Baddeck Lakes, these features were renamed in 1974 to honour Alexander Graham Bell, inventor of the telephone. *See* Mount McCurdy

BERWICK   "One of our residents once travelling in the United States passed through [Berwick, Maine] and . . . pleased with its neat and tidy appearance, [he] suggested the name." (CPCGN files)

BIBLE HILL   Attributed to the piety of the Archibald family, early residents of the area.

BLOMIDON, CAPE   The name may be traced to "blow me down", a nautical phrase "used as a place name shortened apparently for cartological convenience" (Ganong). *See* Blow Me Down, Newfoundland

BOULARDERIE   Commemorates the career of Louis-Simon Le Poupet de la Boularderie (? – 1738), who served as commandant at Port d'Orléans, Île Royale (Cape Breton Island), from 1719 to 1738.

BRAS D'OR LAKE   The name is probably a variation of La Bras d'Or, which in turn is "... a corruption of the name *labrador* extended to Cape Breton and vicinity seemingly for geographical and political reasons in connection with the exploration of this region by the Portuguese Fagundes prior to 1521" (Ganong).

BRIDGEPORT   Named for a member of the London firm Rundell, Bridge and Rundell, an original supporter of the General Mining Association once active in the area. The Community was known briefly as Bridgeport Mines in the 1880s.

BRIDGETOWN   Originally known as Hicks Ferry, the descriptive name was adopted on January 24, 1824, "being undoubtedly chosen by reason of the appreciation of the residents of the new bridge".

BRIDGEWATER   Appropriately named "owing to its location near the bridge over the LaHave River" (Brown).

BRIER ISLAND   Of uncertain origin, the name appears as Bryer Island on the Des Barres chart of 1775; the modern spelling is consistent from 1864 onward.

BROOKFIELD (Colchester County)   The descriptive name was assigned in 1784 by the first settler, William Hamilton (1758–1838).

BROOKLYN (Queens County)   First known as Herring Cove, "the name was probably chosen because of a small stream running through the settlement." (Fergusson)

BRULE POINT (Colchester County)   Designated by the French

Pointe Brûlé because they found that the forest had been burned over. The anglicized version prevailed following the expulsion of the Acadians in 1755.

CAMBRIDGE (Kings County) Originally Sharpe's Brook, the name was changed because of close family ties with Cambridge, Massachusetts (CPCGN files).

CANNING Honours George Canning (1770–1827), British Prime Minister in 1827. The name was adopted by public vote to replace Apple Tree Landing. The post office dates from 1846.

CANSO The name is derived from the Micmac *Kamsok*, translated by Rand as "the place beyond the cliffs", a description of its position in relation to the line of cliffs along the south side of Chedabucto Bay.

CANSO, STRAIT OF Known to the French as the passage de Fronsac for a locality nearby named for Cardinal Richelieu, Duc de Fronsac (1585–1642). The title "Sieur de Fronsac" was later assumed by Richard Denys (1654–91). The Strait of Canceau, or Canso, became common in the early nineteenth century. The name was also adopted for the Canso Causeway, completed in 1955.

CAPE BRETON Of possible Basque or Breton origin, this is one of the oldest names on the Atlantic seaboard. The evidence points to its being named for the Basque Cap Breton, a location near the modern town of Bayonne. "Basque fishermen from Cap Breton gave their name to the island long before their northerly neighbours from Brittany ventured into these waters." (PAC, Johnson Papers) From 1784 to 1820 Cape Breton was a separate Crown colony.

CAPE SABLE ISLAND Listed as Cap de Sable by Champlain, the name is probably a French descriptive.

CARIBOU (Pictou County)   Originally Carriboo Harbour and Carriboo Island (on Arrowsmith map, 1838), the earlier spelling has persisted locally, although Caribou is the official designation. The name is said to have arisen from the presence of herds of deer, which were mistaken for caribou.

CHEDABUCTO BAY   The word is a corruption of the Micmac *Sedabooktook*, meaning "a bay running far back".

CHESTER   First known as Shoreham after Shoreham, Sussex; the area was settled by New England planters in the 1760s. Possibly named for Chester, Pennsylvania.

CHETICAMP   The name is of probable French origin and may have indicated a poor camping ground or encampment (Fergusson). From the French *chétif*, "poor" or "miserable".

CHEZZETCOOK   The name stems from the Micmac *Chesetkook* or *Sesetkook*, translated as "flowing rapidly in many channels". Fergusson lists an alternative French derivation – Chez les Coques, or "home of the sea birds".

CHIGNECTO   *See* New Brunswick *entry*

CHURCH POINT   The settlement (Point de l'Église) was founded in 1771. It was named for St. Mary's Church, which occupied a prominent location in the community. The post office was known as Port Acadie during the interval from 1863 to 1893.

CLARKS HARBOUR   "After one Captain Clark, who repeatedly made this harbour his headquarters while on a fishing expedition from New England in the middle of the nineteenth century." (CPCGN files)

CLEMENTSPORT   The early name, Moose River, was changed in 1851, and the new designation was derived from the township of Clements. The name of the latter is of uncertain origin.

COBEQUID   Bay and mountains. The name was spelled Coco-bequy in a land grant to Mathieu Martin in 1689 and as Gobetick by Abbé Le Loutre in 1738. It is of Micmac origin and may well be traced to *Wakobetquitk*, "end of flowing water", a reference to the tidal bore common to the rivers and streams of the area.

COXHEATH   The name originated with a grant of land to Captain William Cox in 1790. The post office (Cox Heath) was established in 1861.

DARTMOUTH   Although some doubt exists as to exact origin, the city was probably named for the Earl of Dartmouth (1672–1750), whose death occurred the year the settlement was founded.

DEBERT   The name dates from the French colonial period and is a variation of the original Ville de Bourq or Ville Burke.

DENMARK   "All the land here belonged to [Rt. Rev. Charles Inglis, Bishop of Nova Scotia] and his successors in office for a Dean and Chapter." The boundaries were indicated with the Dean's mark, which in time became Denmark (CPCGN files).

DIGBY   Named for Admiral Robert Digby (1732–1815), commander of H.M.S. *Atlanta*, flagship of the convoy which brought the Loyalist settlers to found the town in 1783.

DOMINION   First known as Dominion No. 1 (for a local mine shaft), the name of the town was changed to Dominion by provincial statute in 1906.

DONKIN   Named for Hiram Donkin, general manager of the Dominion Coal Company when the local coal mines were opened in 1904.

DUNMAGLASS   Founded by settlers from Dunmaglass, Inverness, Scotland, and named by them for their earlier home.

DUNVEGAN   This name (for Dunvegan Castle, Isle of Skye) was bestowed by statute in 1885 replacing Broad Cove Marsh.

EARLTOWN   The community was settled in 1817 by immigrants from the parishes of Brora and Rogart, Sutherlandshire, Scotland, and named Earlstown for the Earl of Dalhousie (1770–1838), who served as Lieutenant-Governor of Nova Scotia from 1816 to 1820. Shortened to Earltown about 1836.

ECONOMY   Derived from the Micmac *Kenomee,* translated as "long point jutting out into the sea" (Brown). The post office dates from 1836.

ECUM SECUM   This unusual name is of uncertain origin. It may be a corruption of an earlier Micmac designation. Early spellings were: Ekamsagen and Ekemsikam (Fergusson).

FALMOUTH   Generally considered to have been named for Edward Boscawen, Viscount Falmouth (1711–61). However, the name of the settlement (founded in 1760 by New England planters) may have been suggested by Falmouth, Massachusetts.

FLORENCE   Named after Florence McDonald, wife of D. D. MacKenzie (1859–1927), federal Liberal House Leader from 1917 to 1919.

GABARUS   This is a place name of "quite unknown origin" (Ganong). It is possibly a variation of a French family name; however, the suggestion that it might be a gallicized corruption of Cabot's Cross, indicating the landfall of Cabot, is "only speculation". Appears as Baye de Gabaru on the Bellin map of 1764.

GARDINER MINES   Formerly known as Sydney Road; the name was changed to mark the fact that coal was discovered on the farm of Margaret Gardiner (CPCGN files).

GEORGE, CAPE   Known to the French as Cap St. Louis, it was renamed in honour of St. George, patron saint of England. *See* St. Georges Bay

GLACE BAY   The *Plan de l'Isle Royalle* by Franquet (1751) shows B. de Glace; accordingly, the name dates from the French period and is undoubtedly a descriptive (*glace*, "ice").

GRAND PRÉ   Grand Pré, or "great meadow", is a French translation of an earlier Micmac descriptive *'mskegoo-a-kadik*, literally "grass at its occurence place" (Ganong). It was described by Paul Mascarene in 1720 thus: "a platt of meadow, part of which is damn'd in from the tide, and produces very good wheat and pease".

GUYSBOROUGH   Originally Chedabucto during the French period, the name was changed to Guy's Borough in honour of Sir Guy Carleton (1724–1808) and was officially approved as Guysborough by the Geographic Board of Canada, December 2, 1901.

HALIFAX   Founded June 21, 1749, and named for George Montagu Dunk, Earl of Halifax (1716–71), then President of the Board of Trade. Became the capital of Nova Scotia on July 14, 1749.

HAMMONDS PLAINS   The name marks the career of Sir Andrew Snape Hamond (1738–1828), Lieutenant-Governor of Nova Scotia from 1780 to 1782. The post office was known for a time as English Corner.

HANTSPORT   The name is derived from the abbreviation for Hampshire, England. It was adopted as a place name in 1849 "because the place had become the chief seaport in Hants County" (Fergusson).

HAVRE BOUCHER   Bishop Joseph-Octave Plessis visited the area in 1812 and reported that the place took its name from Captain François Boucher, "who had been overtaken by the winter of

1759 and had to stay there until spring".

HECTANOOGA   The name may be traced to Amerindian sources and is possibly a French corruption of the original. It is of unknown meaning.

HERRING COVE   The name may have been inspired by the fishing industry or may be for Thomas Herring, an early settler (Halifax County). Herring Cove in Queens County was known to Isaac de Razilly (1587–1635) as a fishing station.

HUBBARDS   The community, known first as Hubbards Cove takes its name from one of the first families to settle the area. The word "cove" was dropped in 1905.

IMPEROYAL   Site of an Imperial Oil refinery. The name was coined as a contraction of the company name. It is now part of the city of Dartmouth.

INGONISH   Originally the community was known as Niganiche or Inganiche, which may possibly be derived from Micmac sources. During the French colonial period it was known as Port d'Orléans, although the earlier name continued to be used and has survived as Ingonish.

INVERNESS   The name, for Inverness-shire, Scotland, was first applied to the county upon the suggestion of Sir William Young (1799–1887), who represented the area in the House of Assembly.

ISLE MADAME   The island was known as Île Ste. Marie to Nicolas Denys, and this was later transcribed by French cartographers to Isle Madame. It was the site of a French fishing station from the early eighteenth century onward. Isle Madame (not Madame Island) was adopted as an official designation on March 1, 1956 (CPCGN files).

JEDDORE   The name is believed to be a corruption of Theodore, since the area was referred to by Nicolas Denys in 1672 as Rivière de Théodore.

JOGGINS (Cumberland County)   Derived from the Micmac *Chegoggin*, the name has been translated as "a place of fish weirs". Joggins (Digby County) is descriptive of an inlet which "jogs in" from the sea.

JOLLIMORE   The place name may be traced to the family name that was originally spelled Jolimois, Jollymore, or Jollimore (part of the Montbéliard "Foreign Protestant" migration to Nova Scotia). The community is now incorporated with the city of Halifax.

JUDIQUE   The name is considered to be of French origin. During the early colonial period the harbour was frequently closed in by sand. "...Heavy northerly storms would close up the channel and after a little time it would break through. . . . This gave rise to the name playing channel," *Jou-jou-dique*, which eventually became shortened to Judique (CPCGN files).

KEJIMKUJIK NATIONAL PARK   The name was first applied to the lake and approved by the Geographic Board of Canada, March 18, 1909. Brown suggests that it may be traced to the Micmac *Koojumkoojik*, meaning "attempting to escape". The word may also mean "swelled private parts", caused by exertion in rowing across the lake (CPCGN files).

KENLOCH   The word originated with the Gaelic *Caennloch,* meaning "the head of the lake".

KENNETCOOK   The name is derived from Micmac sources and may possibly be traced to *Kunetkook*, which has been translated as "a place near or close at hand".

KENTVILLE   The original name, Horton Corner, was replaced by Kentville in 1826 in honour of the Duke of Kent (1767–1820).

KINGSTON   The name was suggested by its location within the boundaries of Kings County.

LA HAVE   Settlement, cape, island, and river. Cap de la Have was first applied to the cape by Pierre Du Gua de Monts (1558?–1628) and was suggested by Cap de la Hève, two miles north-northwest of the entrance to Le Havre, France.

LAKE AINSLIE   Named in honour of George Robert Ainslie (1776–1839), Lieutenant-Governor of Cape Breton from 1816 to 1820.

LAKE ROSSIGNOL   Named after Jean Rossignol, a French adventurer and trader, who is reputed to have been the first white man to visit the lake.

LAWRENCETOWN   Annapolis and Halifax counties. Both locations mark the career of Charles Lawrence (1709–60), who served as Governor of Nova Scotia from 1753 to 1760.

LIVERPOOL   Founded in 1760 and named for Liverpool, England, being at the mouth, as well, of the Mersey River.

LOCHABER   The name of the lake and later of the settlement was suggested by Lochaber, Inverness-shire, Scotland.

LOCKEPORT   Settled by New England planters and fishermen and named after Jonathan Locke, a native of Rhode Island. First known as Locke's Island, the name was changed on February 16, 1870.

LONDONDERRY   The first settlers (Ulster Scots) emigrated from both Northern Ireland and New Hampshire. The community was named for Londonderry, New Hampshire.

LOUISBOURG   First known as Havre à l'Anglois, it was founded on September 2, 1713, and named in honour of King Louis XIV of France. For a period of time the spelling Louisburg was used; however, the earlier spelling was officially adopted on June 6, 1966.

LUNENBURG   Designated in honour of the royal house of Brunswick-Lüneburg. In 1714 the elector of Hanover, Duke of Brunswick-Lüneburg, became King George I of England.

LYONS BROOK   Honours the Rev. James Lyon, a member of the Philadelphia Land Company, which sent the first settlers to Pictou in 1767.

MABOU   Derived from the Micmac *Malabokak* or *Malabo*. The origin of the word has become lost.

MACCAN   Site of a French settlement (Makan). The name may be traced to the Micmac *Maegan* or *Maakan*, "fishing place".

MAHONE BAY   The name dates from the French colonial period and refers to the "low built pirate ships that frequently used the bay" (Fergusson).

MALAGASH   The name originates with the Micmac *Malegawate*, which may refer to "a place of games".

MALIGNANT COVE   The name is the result of the wreck nearby of H.M.S. *Malignant*. The community survived an attempt to impose the Scottish place name, Barradale.

MARGAREE   Harbour, island, river, and valley. The area was first settled (about 1780) by the French, and church registers show Mâgré as the early spelling. The modern spelling is a corruption of the original French.

MARGARETSVILLE   Site of the summer residence of Sir Brenton Halliburton (1775–1860), and named for his wife, Margaret Inglis, eldest daughter of Bishop Charles Inglis.

MERSEY RIVER   Named for the River Mersey in England. Sometimes referred to as Liverpool River; however, Mersey was officially adopted on December 7, 1937.

METEGHAN   Derived from an Amerindian word meaning "blue stone". "The smooth stones along the shores . . . of St. Mary's Bay are of a remarkably blue tinge." (CPCGN files)

MIDDLETON   The name was chosen in the mid nineteenth century at a public meeting and denoted the fact that the town is midway between Annapolis Royal and Kentville and nearly in the centre of Wilmot township.

MILTON (Queens County)   Originally "the Falls", the new name was a corruption of Milltown and dates officially from the establishment of the post office in 1855. It is probable that the name was in common usage well before that time.

MINAS BASIN   Derived from the French name, Le Bassin des Mines, applied first by Champlain to indicate the discovery of copper mines at Cape d'Or.

MIRA   River, lake, bay, and village. This name, like many others of early origin, is a puzzle. La Bay de Miray (applied to the bay) appears on the Jumeau map of 1685 and is repeated as late as 1815 in the *Journal* of Bishop Plessis. The name Miré, to denote the settlement, is common in early ecclesiastical records. The explanations range from an Amerindian origin (Ganong) to the name of a French officer, Jean Miré (Bourinot); however, the exact origin is lost.

MISSIGUASH RIVER   *See* New Brunswick *entry*

MONASTERY   The name results from the establishment in 1825 of the Trappist monastery of Petit Claivaux.

MOUNT MC CURDY   Named in 1974 for aviation pioneer

J. A. D. McCurdy (1886–1961). He served as Lieutenant-Governor of Nova Scotia from 1947 to 1952.

MOUNT THOM   Named by Thomas Troop, who, with a companion, Ephraim Howard, walked through the woods from Truro to lend assistance to settlers from Philadelphia, who arrived in Pictou on June 10, 1767.

MOUNT UNIACKE   Commemorates the career of Richard John Uniacke (1753–1830), who served as Attorney General of Nova Scotia from 1797 to 1830.

MULGRAVE   First known as Port Mulgrave in honour of the Earl of Mulgrave (1819–90), who served as Lieutenant-Governor of Nova Scotia from 1858 to 1863.

MUSQUODOBOIT   The name is a French and English variant of the Micmac *Mooskudoboogwek*, which has been translated as "rolling out in foam" or "suddenly widening out after a narrow entrance at its mouth". Name assigned as Mouscoudobouet, a seigneurial or territorial grant to Mathieu des Groutins during the French colonial period.

NEILS HARBOUR   Named for an early settler, Neil McLennan.

NEW ANNAN   Name bestowed by John Bell, a native of Annandale, Dumfries-shire, Scotland, who settled the area around 1820. *See* New Annan, Prince Edward Island

NEW GERMANY   The first settlers in 1785 were of German origin, which gave rise to the name. Post office dates from 1854.

NEW GLASGOW   Named after Glasgow, Scotland, by William Fraser, who surveyed the townsite. In ". . . forecasting the future [he] saw in a vision another Clyde [the East River] and another Glasgow." (CPCGN files)

NEW MINAS   *See* Minas Basin

NEW WATERFORD   The name was suggested by J. J. Hinchey, one of the earliest settlers and a native of Waterford, Ireland.

NICTAUX   Derived from *Niktak*, a Micmac term which designated the forks of a river.

NORTH SYDNEY   *See* Sydney

OXFORD   Originally Head of the Tide, the name stems from a ford over the River Philip where oxen used to cross to pasture.

PARRSBORO   Marks the career of John Parr (1725–91), who served as Lieutenant-Governor of Nova Scotia from 1782 to 1791.

PEGGY'S COVE   Possibly named for the wife of an early settler, William Rodgers (Rogers).

PESIQUID LAKE   This name was adopted for the artificial lake created by the erection of a causeway across the Avon River in 1970–1. It is of Micmac origin and has been translated as "place where tidal flow forks". Approved on July 14, 1971.

PETIT-DE-GRAT   The name may be of Basque origin and is a descriptive meaning "small fishing station".

PICTOU   Derived from the Micmac *Piktook*, "an explosion" or "fire". Listed by Nicolas Denys in 1660 as La rivière de Pictou.

PICTOU ISLAND   The name was applied in the 1760s by J. F. W. Des Barres (1722–1824) to the island located near Pictou in the Northumberland Strait.

POINT TUPPER   Named for Ferdinand B. Tupper, who received a land grant in the area in 1823.

PORT HAWKESBURY   Honours Charles Jenkinson, first Baron Hawkesbury (1727–1808). *See* Hawkesbury, Ontario

PORT HOOD   Marks the career of Viscount Hood (1724–1816).

PORT MORIEN   Bay and cape. The name was applied first to the cape and may be of Portuguese origin, possibly a corruption of the Portuguese form of St. Martin (Brown). Called by the French in the 1770s Le Cap Mordienne and Bay de Mordienne.

PORT ROYAL (Annapolis County)   The modern community is part of the area designated Port Royal by Champlain in 1604 (*see* Annapolis). The name was officially adopted in 1949, replacing Lower Granville.

PORT WILLIAMS   The name was chosen in 1865 to honour Sir William Fenwick Williams (1800–83), a native Nova Scotian and the "hero of Kars" in the Crimean War (1854–5). *See also* Fenwick, Ontario

PUBNICO   Derived from the Micmac *Pogomkook*, which has been translated as "land from which the trees have been removed to fit it for cultivation" (Brown). The French form was Pombon-coup, from which the modern spelling has evolved.

PUGWASH   This name is traceable to Micmac sources. It is derived from *Pagweak*, "shallow water or shoal". A move was made in 1826 "to change its present uncouth name to Waterford"; however, the attempt failed.

RESERVE MINES   The name evolved from the fact that the General Mining Association held the coalfields "in reserve for future operations".

RIVER HEBERT   Possibly named for an early French settler.

RIVER JOHN   The name is of French origin and was possibly derived from Rivière Jaune. Designated "John" by Des Barres and applied to the river and nearby cape.

RIVER PHILIP   The name is mentioned in Haliburton's *History of Nova Scotia* and may be traced to an early settler "named Philip to whom with others a grant of land was made in 1785".

ROCKINGHAM   The name was bestowed by Sir John Wentworth (1737–1820), who served as Lieutenant-Governor of Nova Scotia from 1792 to 1808. It honours Charles Watson-Wentworth, second Marquess of Rockingham (1730–82).

SABLE ISLAND   The "graveyard of the Atlantic" has for centuries been a menace to mariners. The name is a French descriptive derived from *sablon*, "sand". In common usage from the sixteenth century onward.

SACKVILLE   Originally Fort Sackville, it was named for George Sackville Germain, first Viscount Sackville (1716–85). *See* Sackville, New Brunswick

ST. GEORGES BAY   The name was applied by J. F. W. Des Barres in honour of the patron saint of England. The location was known for a time as George Bay and Georges Bay. The present form was officially recognized on July 20, 1967.

ST. MARGARETS BAY   The name Le Porte Saincte Marguerite was bestowed by Samuel de Champlain in 1631. Gradually it became anglicized and was applied to the bay.

ST. MARYS BAY   Derived from the French form, La Baie Saincte Marie, applied by Pierre Du Gua de Monts (1558?–1628) in 1604.

ST. MARYS RIVER   The name originated with Fort Sainte Marie, established by the French adventurer Sieur de La Giraudière. The fort was captured by the English in 1669 and the name is now applied to the nearby river. *See* Sherbrooke

ST. PETERS   Founded as a Portuguese fishing station (San Pedro) in 1521, the name has survived in translation. From 1650 it was known as St-Pierre, until 1713, when the English form was imposed.

SALMON RIVER (Colchester County)   The name is possibly a translation of an earlier Micmac descriptive.

SCATARIE ISLAND   The name dates from the early eighteenth century and is probably a corruption of *secétere*, "dry land".

SCOTSBURN   The name was adopted in 1867 to replace Roger's Hill. It was suggested by Hugh Ross in honour of his birthplace in Ross-shire, Scotland.

SHEET HARBOUR   A descriptive which was assigned "because of a large white cliff at the harbour entrance which appeared like a sheet spread to dry".

SHELBURNE   Known to the French as Port Razoir, because the shape of the harbour reminded them of a partly folded razor, it became, in 1713, Port Roseway to the English. Later, on July 22, 1783, with the arrival of the Loyalists, the name was changed to honour the Earl of Shelburne (1737–1805), who served as British Prime Minister from 1782 to 1783.

SHERBROOKE   Named for Sir John Coape Sherbrooke (1764–1830), who served as Lieutenant-Governor of Nova Scotia from 1811 to 1816 and later from 1816 to 1818 as Governor General. Site of the French Fort Sainte-Marie. *See* St. Marys River

SHUBENACADIE   The name, of Micmac origin, may be traced to Segubunakadik, translated by Rand as "the place where ground nuts occur". An early spelling, Chicabenadadi, gradually evolved to the modern spelling.

SISSIBOO RIVER   The name is probably traceable to the Micmac *Cibou*, for "big", a reference to the river. The legend that it was derived from six owls (*six hiboux*) is undoubtedly apocryphal. *See* Weymouth

SKHIR DHU   The name is a Gaelic descriptive, "black rock" in translation.

SPRINGHILL   A descriptive; the hill on which the town developed once contained numerous springs. Incorporated as a town in 1889.

SPRYFIELD   Named for Captain William Spry, who saw service at the siege of Louisbourg in 1758. Now part of the city of Halifax.

STELLARTON   The original name, Albion Mines, was changed on February 1, 1870, to note the fact that Stella coal was found locally.

STEWIACKE   Applied first to the river, the name is a corruption of the Micmac *Esiktaweak*, translated by Rand as "whimpering or whining as it goes along".

SYDNEY
NORTH SYDNEY
SYDNEY MINES   Present-day Sydney was named for Thomas Townsend, first Viscount Sydney (1733–1800). During the years from 1784 to 1820, Sydney was the capital of the separate colony of Cape Breton. It was incorporated as a town in 1886 and as a city in 1904. The nearby towns of North Sydney (1885) and Sydney Mines (1889) derive their names from the same source.

TANGIER   The name of the settlement, harbour, island, and river, in all probability may be traced to the shipwreck in 1830 of the schooner *Tangier*.

TATAMAGOUCHE   In Micmac, Takamegootk was a descriptive place name meaning "barred across the entrance with sand" (Rand). The modern spelling has evolved from this early form. Variations are: Tahamigouche (LeLoutre, 1738); Tatmagouch (Morris, 1755); Tatmegouche (Des Barres, 1774); Tatamagouch (Haliburton, 1828); Tatamagouche (Plan of Des Barres Estate, 1837). In the early nineteenth century a Scottish settler, Wellwood Waugh (1741–1824), attempted unsuccessfully to impose the name Southampton. *See* Tatamagouche, Yukon

THORBURN   Formerly known as Vale Colliery. The present name was coined in 1886. It is derived from "Thor", god of thunder, and "burn", for brook (Brown).

THREE MILE PLAINS   A descriptive name for a community located three miles from Windsor.

TIDNISH   The name is possibly traceable to the Micmac *Tedeneche. See* Tignish, P.E.I.

TIMBERLEA   Assigned in 1922 to replace the earlier Bowser Station, the name is descriptive, meaning "a grassy field in timber land" (Fergusson).

TIVERTON   First known as Petit Passage. The new name was assigned in 1867 for Tiverton, Devonshire, England.

TOBEATIC   Lake and game sanctuary. The name originated with the Micmac *Toobeadoogook*, of unknown meaning.

TRACADIE   This place name appears in all three Maritime provinces and may be derived from Micmac sources. (*See* New Brunswick *entry.*) There is a folk tradition that Tracadie, Nova Scotia, was named for Joseph Tracady, "the Captain of the crew who in early times called in the harbour for the purpose of buying cordwood". It may also be a modification of Acadia with the prefix "Tr" added. All these locations are Acadian settlements, and the spelling Tracady was common in eighteenth-century documents.

TRENTON   Name proposed by Harvey Graham in 1882 when the town was laid out. Named for Trenton, New Jersey.

TRURO   On the location of the French settlement of Cobequid. The new name was suggested in 1759 upon the resettlement of the area by New Englanders and Ulster Scots. Named for Truro in Cornwall, England.

TUSKET   The name is derived from the Micmac *Neketaouksit*, meaning "the great forked tidal river".

WALLACE   This name, for Michael Wallace (1747–1831), long-time provincial treasurer of Nova Scotia, was assigned in 1810, replacing the Micmac name, Ramsheg.

WALTON   The name was proposed in 1837 in honour of James Walton Nutting, a landholder in the district.

WATERVILLE   A local descriptive, adopted by a vote of the inhabitants on November 21, 1871.

WAVERLEY   The name originated with "Waverley", a cottage built by Charles P. Allen, and was assigned for the Waverley novels of Sir Walter Scott (1771–1832).

WEDGEPORT   First recorded as "The Wedge" or "Tusket Wedge", the form Wedgeport gradually evolved and was in common usage from the mid nineteenth century onward.

WENTWORTH (Cumberland County)   Honours Sir John Wentworth (1737–1820), who served as Lieutenant-Governor of Nova Scotia from 1792 to 1808.

WESTCHESTER   The name was chosen by Loyalists from Westchester County, New York, who settled in the area in 1784.

WESTMOUNT   A descriptive, derived from its location being on the west side of Sydney River.

WESTPORT   Originally Brier Island Settlement, the new name, a descriptive, was adopted in 1839, the date of the establishment of the post office.

WESTVILLE   The early name, Acadia Village, was replaced on February 25, 1868, "probably because it was the westernmost of the East River mining towns" (Fergusson).

WEYMOUTH   Once known by the name of the river on which it is situated (Sissiboo), the town changed its name in 1823 because it "sounded too uncouth and savage to the ears of the inhabitants" (Haliburton). A Loyalist settlement, it was renamed for Weymouth, Massachusetts.

WHYCOCOMAGH   The name stems from the Micmac *Wakogumaah*, translated by Rand as "beside the sea". Other meanings have been given: "the head of the water", "the end of the bay".

WINDSOR   Adopted on December 24, 1764, for Windsor, England, replacing Pisiquid or Pesiquid, the Micmac and Acadian name for the area. *See* Pesiquid Lake

WOLFVILLE   Named in 1829 for Elisha De Wolf, postmaster and member of a prominent local family. The early name was Mud Creek. Incorporated as a town in 1893.

WOODS HARBOUR   Originally the community was known as *Cockouquit*, from a Micmac word for a species of duck. The new name was adopted in 1772 in honour of Rev. Samuel Wood, an early settler. The first name survives in Cockerwit Passage, officially adopted in July 1953.

YARMOUTH   Designated Port Fourchu or Forked Harbour (a translation of the Micmac *Maligeak*) by Champlain, the new name was transferred from Yarmouth, Massachusetts, by New England planters and fishermen in the mid eighteenth century.

Ontario

 The name was first applied to the lake (1641) and is traceable to Amerindian sources. It may be a corruption of *Onitariio*, meaning "beautiful lake" (Johnson Papers, PAC), or *Kanadario*, variously translated as "sparkling" or "beautiful" water. Later European settlers gave the name to the land along the lakeshore and then to an ever extending area. "Old Ontario" was a term sometimes loosely applied to the southern portion of the province. Entered Confederation as the province of Ontario, 1867.

ABITIBI Lake and river; an Amerindian word meaning "half-way water", derived from *abitah*, which may be translated as "middle" or "halfway", and *nipi*, "water". Originally used by the French to designate a band of Algonquin Indians who lived near the lake, the name was descriptive of their location halfway between the trading posts on Hudson Bay and those on the Ottawa River.

ACTON First settled in the 1820s and previously called Adamsville after Zenas, Rufus, and Ezra Adams, early residents. Name changed in 1844 to Acton, after the borough of Acton, Middlesex, England. *See* Halton Hills

AGINCOURT *See* Scarborough

AILSA CRAIG Name taken from an island in the Firth of Clyde, Scotland. The town was founded as a result of development by the Grand Trunk Railway in 1858.

AJAX Of twentieth-century origin, the town was established in 1941 as the site of a munitions factory. The name honours one of the British cruisers involved in a naval engagement with the German battleship *Graf Spee* off Montevideo in 1939. The town of Ajax, the village of Pickering, and part of the Township of Pickering (as of January 1, 1974) formed the town of Ajax.

ALBANY RIVER From Fort Albany, a trading post established in 1684. Name originated with a title of King James II – Duke of Albany.

ALEXANDRIA Area was settled by disbanded soldiers from the Glengarry Fencibles in 1804. The townsite was first known as Priest's Mills, marking the residence of the Rev. Alexander Macdonnell (1762–1840), chaplain of the regiment and later designated Roman Catholic bishop of Kingston, the first such appointment in the province. In 1819 the name was changed to Alexandria, an adaptation of Father Macdonnell's Christian name.

ALFRED Name taken from the Township of Alfred, which was named in honour of Prince Alfred, infant son of George III (1780–2). Post office established in 1842. Incorporated as a village in 1952.

ALGOMA District in northern Ontario, village in Long Township, Algoma District, Ontario. Post office – Algoma Mills as of 1882. Name created by an American ethnologist, Henry Rowe Schoolcraft (1793–1864), who was appointed Indian agent to the Ojibway in Sault Ste. Marie region in 1822. "Al" is derived from *Algonquin*, while "goma" is a variant of *gomee*, meaning lake or water. The Ojibway, a branch of the Algonquin family, were the first residents of the area. Schoolcraft married the daughter of a local Ojibway chief and was considered an authority on Amerindian lore.

ALGONQUIN PROVINCIAL PARK Origin of this name, originally denoting a number of scattered bands of Amerindians, is uncertain. Formerly thought to have been contracted from *Algomequin*, loosely translated as "those on the other side", but now generally believed to be derived from the Micmac *Algoomaking*, signifying "at the place of spearing fish and eels". The park, a wilderness area of 1,754,240 acres on the height of land between the Ottawa River and Lake Huron, was recommended in a report drafted by James Dickson in 1884 and set aside as a park by the Ontario legislature in 1893.

ALLISTON Named in 1848 by William Fletcher, the first settler, in honour of his native village in Yorkshire, England. Incorporated as a village in 1874 and as a town in 1891.

ALMONTE Originally known in 1819 as Sheppard's Fall for an early settler, David Sheppard, the area experienced numerous name changes in the early nineteenth century. In 1856, upon the suggestion of Lieutenant-Colonel J. A. Gemmill, Almonte (for

General Juan Almonte, 1804–69, a military figure in Mexico) was adopted.

ALVINSTON   A corruption of the place name "Alverstone" on the Isle of Wight, England. Former names of the community were: Gardner's Mills for Archibald Gardner, the first settler; Brooke Mills; and Brannen.

AMHERSTBURG   Town in Essex County, Ontario, south of Windsor.
AMHERST ISLAND   Frontenac County
AMHERSTVIEW   Town in Lennox and Addington County, Ontario, west of Kingston.
A common place name found in many parts of Canada and commemorating Lord Jeffrey Amherst (1717–97), Field-Marshal of the British Army, Commander-in-Chief in North America, and Governor General of British North America from 1760 to 1763.
    Amherstburg, on the site of the Bois Blanc Mission, established in 1747, and of Fort Malden, built in 1784, was a centre of activity during the War of 1812. It was incorporated as a village in 1851 and as a town in 1878.
    The name Amherstview is descriptive of that town's location, looking toward Amherst Island in Lake Ontario.

ANCASTER   Named after the Township of Ancaster, formed in 1792, which, in turn, was named for a town in Lincolnshire, England. Post office established in 1825.

ANGUS   The first post office was opened in 1856 and named in honour of Angus Morrison, then Member of the Legislative Assembly for Simcoe North.

ANSONVILLE   Founded in 1921 and named after James Anson, a director of the Abitibi Power and Paper Company. Amalgamated with the town of Iroquois Falls, January 1, 1971.

ARKONA   Probably for Cape Arkona on the Baltic coast of

Germany; however, the name may be a misspelling of Akron, Ohio. Formerly Bosanquet.

ARNPRIOR   Named by Archibald McNab, last laird of the Clan McNab, in honour of the ancestral home ("Arnpryor", Scotland) of his associates Andrew and George Buchanan. The settlement, begun in 1823, was incorporated as a village in 1862 and as a town in 1892.

ARTHUR   Located in Arthur Township, which was named after Arthur Wellesley, first Duke of Wellington (1769–1852). Post office established in 1841.

ATHENS   This town was first settled by United Empire Loyalists in 1784. The original name, Farmersville, was coined to mark an agricultural emphasis in the area. Later, when the community became an educational centre, the name Athens was adopted. Post office named in 1890.

ATIKOKAN   Derived from the Ojibway word for "caribou bone".

ATTAWAPISKAT RIVER   From the Amerindian *atawabiskat,* which has been translated as "rock bottom" (CPCGN files).

ATWOOD   Originally Newry Station, founded in 1875 with the opening of the Wellington, Grey and Bruce Railway, the new name was coined in 1883 as a compromise when local factions took sides over the renaming of the community.

AURORA   Settled in 1804 and named Machell's Corners for one of the first residents; name changed to Aurora, after the goddess of the morning, in 1854; incorporated as a town in 1888.

AUSABLE RIVER   A corruption of the French for "sand river". Sometimes referred to as "Little River aux sables" on early maps.

AVON RIVER   For the River Avon in England, on which the renowned Stratford-on-Avon is located. *See also* Stratford

AYLMER   First called Troy for Troy, New York. Name changed
just before the Rebellion of 1837 to Aylmer for Lord Aylmer,
Governor General of Canada from 1831 to 1835.

AYR   After Ayr, Scotland, this name marks the fact that many
of the first settlers were of Scottish origin. Post office designated
in 1840. Incorporated as a village in 1884. *See* Nith River

BADEN   Founded and named about 1850 by Jacob Beck, a native of Baden, Germany. Post office dates from 1854.

BANCROFT   Earlier names were York River, York Mills, York
Branch, or The Branch. Name changed in 1878 at the instigation
of Senator Billa Flint (1805–94) for his wife, Phoebe Bancroft
Flint. The choice was unpopular, though gradually accepted by
local residents.

BARRIE   There are two possibilities for the origin of this name:
(1) Honours Commodore Robert Barrie, a British naval officer,
     who served as Acting Commissioner of the Navy at Kingston;
     or
(2) For Captain A. Barry, who commanded the 15th Regiment of
     York. The regiment travelled through this area while trans-
     porting stores to Penetanguishene.

BARRY'S BAY   Commemorates the Barry family, early settlers
in this region. One family settled on an island in Kamaniskeg
Lake, giving rise to the early name "Barry's Camp on the Bay".
Post office established in 1876.

BATAWA   A company town established by the Bata Company
(a Czechoslovakian shoe firm) in 1939. The ending "wa" was added to their trade name to conform to a frequent place-name ending in Canada.

BATH   A United Empire Loyalist settlement in Ernestown Township, first known as Ernestown (for Prince Ernest, Duke of Cumberland, 1771–1851); name changed to Bath in 1812 after the English city. Post office designated in 1819.

BAY OF QUINTE   *See* Quinte

BEACHVILLE   Named for the owner of an early grist mill – Andrew Beach.

BEAMSVILLE   Founded by Jacob Beam in 1790. Post office established in 1832. *See* Lincoln

BEARDMORE   A family name. This appears first on the Geological Survey map of 1836.

BEAVERTON   Named originally in 1835 after the Beaver River. The name Beaver River was changed to Beaverton in 1928 by the G.B.C.

BEETON   So named for a local apiary. Formerly known as Clarksville for Robert Clark, an early settler; name changed to Beeton in 1878.

BELLE RIVER   From the French descriptive term, *belle rivière*. Early names Woodslee and Rochester. Called Belle River after 1874.

BELLEVILLE   Named by Governor Francis Gore (1769–1852) for his wife, "Belle" – Annabella Wentworth. Wentworth County also designated by Gore. *See* Halton Hills

BELLS CORNERS   Honours Hugh Bell, innkeeper and first assessor of Nepean Township. Post office opened in 1851.

BLACK BAY   On north shore of Lake Superior. Origin of name unknown. Appears on an 1804 map of American and British territories. Possibly a descriptive term.

BLENHEIM   Formerly called Rondeau, this town was renamed for Blenheim Palace, seat of the Duke of Marlborough.

BLIND RIVER   Descriptive name; the mouth of the river is "not discernible from the lake". Post office established in 1877 (CPCGN files).

BLOOMFIELD   Possibly a descriptive name, since the vicinity is noted for wild flowers; more probably after Captain A. Bloomfield. Name chosen at a public meeting in 1833.

BLYTH   Originally Blythe; the "e" was dropped July 1, 1862. For an early landowner, James Blythe.

BOBCAYGEON   From the Amerindian *Abobkajewun*, variously translated as "the narrow place between rocks" or "where the water comes through".

BOLTON   Name originated with the first settlers, James and George Bolton, who established a grist mill in the area in 1824. Became part of the town of Caledon on January 1, 1974.

BONFIELD   After James Bonfield (1825–1900), one-time M.P.P. for South Renfrew in the Ontario legislature. Town and neighbouring township were amalgamated on January 1, 1975.

BOTHWELL   Named by George Brown of the Toronto *Globe* about 1856 for Bothwell, a town in Lanarkshire, Scotland.

BOURGET   Honours Bishop Ignace Bourget (1799–1885), who died about the time of the founding of the settlement.

BOWMANVILLE   For Charles Bowman, an early landowner. Incorporated as a town in 1858. Became part of Newcastle on January 1, 1974. *See* Newcastle

BRACEBRIDGE   Taken from Washington Irving's (1783–1859)

Bracebridge Hall. Also the name of a parish in Lincolnshire, England. *See* Gravenhurst. The name was assigned by W. D. Le Sueur (1840–1917) (CPCGN files).

BRADFORD   For Bradford, Yorkshire, England, home of the Robinson family, early settlers in the district. Recognized by the Post Office Department in 1850.

BRAMPTON   After Brampton, a town in Cumberland, England, birthplace of John Elliott, one of the first settlers.

BRANTFORD   Brant County and the city of Brantford were both named for Joseph Brant (1742–1807), a Mohawk Indian chief.

BRIDGENORTH   The community once possessed a "floating bridge" over Chemung Lake – hence the name. Post office dates from 1854.

BRIDGEPORT   Descriptive; for the bridge which crossed the Grand River at this point. Amalgamated with Kitchener on January 1, 1973.

BRIGHTON   Possibly for John Bright (1811–89), British statesman, but more probably after Brighton, England. The local landscape is said to be similar to that of the English city (Gardiner).

BRIGHTS GROVE   Originally known as Maxwell, for the home of Robert Owen, British socialist and pioneer in the co-operative movement (an unsuccessful socialist community experiment was launched here in 1829–30). Name changed to Brights Grove in 1935 (OGNB files).

BROCKVILLE   Formerly Elizabethtown, for Princess Elizabeth, third daughter of King George III. Renamed by General Isaac Brock (1769–1812) shortly before his death.

BRONTE   After one of the titles of Lord Nelson (Duke of Bronte). Post office dates from 1851. The community is now part of Oakville.

BROOKLIN   First known as Winchester, it is now part of the town of Whitby. Probably a descriptive name.

BRUNETVILLE   From the Brunet family, a name common in the district. This name was officially approved on April 9, 1969.

BRUSSELS   For Brussels, Belgium, this name was officially adopted in 1872.

BURFORD   After Burford Township, which in turn was named for Burford, Oxfordshire, England. The post office dates from 1819.

BURK'S FALLS   Commemorates David Francis Burk, an early settler.

BURLINGTON   The name is a corruption of Bridlington, Yorkshire, England. Burlington Bay as a name dates from about 1792. The site of the city was first called Wellington Square. Upon petition the name Burlington was applied to the post office in 1876.

BURNHAMTHORPE   Named for a village in Norfolk, England, the birthplace of Lord Nelson.

BYRON   For the poet George Noël Gordon, Lord Byron (1788–1824). The area is now part of the city of London. Before 1857 the community was known as Hall's Mills, for Charles Hall, postmaster.

CABOT HEAD   Name bestowed by John Graves Simcoe (1752–1806) to mark the career of the explorer John Cabot. The lighthouse dates from 1896.

CACHE BAY   After the nearby water feature on a "hidden bay" of Lake Nipissing. The post office was established in 1889.

CALEDON   From a shortened form of Caledonia, the Roman name for North Britain. The townships of Albion and Caledon, along with the villages of Bolton and Caledon East, were amalgamated as the town of Caledon, effective January 1, 1974.

CALEDONIA   *See above*. Became part of the town of Haldimand on April 1, 1974.

CALLANDER   Probably for Callander House, seat of the Earls of Linlithgow and Callendar, Stirlingshire, Scotland; or for the birthplace in Scotland of the first postmaster, George Morrison (OGNB files).

CAMBRIDGE   Officially adopted (as a result of a plebiscite) as the name for the amalgamated city of Galt–Preston–Hespeler. Proclaimed January 1, 1973. The original name of Preston (prior to 1830) was Cambridge Mills, for Cambridge, England. *See* Galt, Preston, *and* Hespeler

CAMPBELLFORD   Founded and named by Major Robert Campbell about 1829. First known as Campbell's Ford. Incorporated as a town in 1906 and new spelling officially adopted (OGNB files).

CANNINGTON   After the parish of Cannington, Somerset, England. Post office from 1849.

CAPE CROKER   Honours one-time Secretary-General of the Admiralty, John Wilson Croker (1780–1857).

CAPREOL   For Frederick Chase Capreol (1803–86), financier and railway promoter. Founded in 1911, incorporated as a town in 1918.

CARADOC   *See* Mount Brydges

CARDINAL   The name appears on early maps as Pointe au Cardinal. It may have been assigned in honour of Cardinal Richelieu.

CARLETON PLACE   Named by early settlers for Carlton Place, a square in Glasgow, Scotland. Because it is near Carleton County, it is often erroneously ascribed to Sir Guy Carleton, Lord Dorchester (1742–1808) (CPCGN files).

CASSELMAN   Named for Martin Casselman, an early landowner and sawmill operator. The post office was established in 1857.

CATARAQUI   Of Amerindian origin and variously translated as: "place where one hides", "impregnable", and "rocks drenched with water" (CPCGN files).

CATFISH CREEK   The name or its French equivalent, Rivière à la Barbeau, dates back to 1721, when it was assigned by Pierre-François Xavier de Charlevoix (1682–1761). Survived an attempt at name-changing in 1948; the suggested alternatives were Charles River, Tansy River, or River Silvern.

CAYUGA   Named for the Cayuga tribe of the Six Nations Indians, the community became part of the town of Haldimand on April 1, 1974. *See* Haldimand

CHALK RIVER   The exact origin of this name is unknown. Possibly poplar and alder (plentiful in the area) were gathered and charred for chalking or marking square timber. It may also be that the colour of the water gave rise to the name (Rayburn).

CHAPLEAU   Honours Sir Joseph Adolphe Chapleau (1840–98), Premier of Quebec from 1879 to 1882; federal Cabinet Minister from 1882 to 1892; Lieutenant-Governor of Quebec from 1892 to 1898.

CHATHAM   Name bestowed by John Graves Simcoe for Chatham, England. Earlier names were Raleigh and McGregors Mills, but the city was called Chatham consistently after 1852.

CHELMSFORD   For a town in Essex, England. The post office dates from 1888. It is now part of the town of Rayside-Balfour.

CHENAIL ESCARTÉ   This name stems from the French-Canadian *chenail* or *chenail écarté* and refers to a secondary outlet of a river, or a side channel which bypasses a falls or rapids. The Snye River, on which the town is situated, is part of the St. Clair system and "splits off from it" (OGNB files).

CHESLEY   The first name, Sconeville, was replaced in 1868 to mark the career of Solomon Chesley, an official in the Indian Office.

CHESTERVILLE   Named for Chester Casselman, a prominent local landowner.

CHIPPAWA   Sometimes spelled Chippewa on early maps, for the Amerindian tribe also known as Ojibway. The name has been translated as "people without moccasins". Chippawa was amalgamated with the city of Niagara Falls on January 1, 1970.

CHRISTIAN ISLAND   The name dates from 1649 when the island was a place of refuge for the Jesuits and the Christianized Hurons fleeing from the Iroquois who captured and razed the mission Sainte-Marie-des-Hurons.

CLARK POINT   Derived from the community of Clarkes Church, which was named after William Clark, an immigrant from Edinburgh, who settled in the area. He later became treasurer and clerk of Greenock Township.

CLINTON   Originally known as The Corners for the intersection of the London and Huron roads. The name was changed in

1844 by William Rattenbury in honour of Lord Clinton, on whose Devonshire estate Rattenbury's father was a tenant farmer.

COBALT   Assigned in 1904 by Provincial Geologist Dr. Willet G. Miller, who "was impressed by the presence. . .of the mineral cobalt in the local silver ore". First known as Cobalt Station (OGNB files).

COBDEN   Named for Richard Cobden (1804–65), British statesman. The post office dates from 1851.

COBOURG   Name bestowed in 1819 to mark the marriage of Princess Charlotte to Prince Leopold of Saxe-Coburg.

COCHRANE   For Francis Cochrane (1852–1919), Ontario Minister of Lands, Forests and Mines and later federal Minister of Railways from 1911 to 1917.

COCKBURN ISLAND
(1) St. Lawrence River – after Vice-Admiral Sir George Cockburn (1772–1853).
(2) Manitoulin District – for Colonel Francis Cockburn (1779–1854), Deputy Quartermaster-General, who accompanied Lord Dalhousie on an inspection of the area in 1821.

COLBORNE   For Sir John Colborne, Lord Seaton (1778–1863), Lieutenant-Governor of Upper Canada from 1828 to 1835. *See also* Port Colborne

COLDWATER   A descriptive term, the name is a translation of the local Amerindian word for Coldwater River.

COLLINGWOOD   Named for Collingwood Township, which in turn commemorates Admiral Collingwood (1750–1810), Nelson's second-in-command at Trafalgar.

COMBER   Possibly for Comber in County Down, Northern Ireland.

COMBERMERE   Named for Sir Stapleton Cotton, Viscount Combermere (1773–1865).

CONESTOGO RIVER   Name assigned in 1806 by local residents because of this river's resemblance to the Conestoga River in Pennsylvania. From the Conestoga Amerindian tribe.

CONISTON   *See* Nickel Centre

COOKSTOWN   The community dates from 1831 and the name honours an early pioneer, Thomas Cook. The post office was established in 1847.

COOKSVILLE   Named for Joseph Cook, one of the first settlers. It is now part of the city of Mississauga.

COPPERCLIFF   A descriptive name. This community is at the centre of a copper-producing region. The post office was established in 1890. Now part of the city of Sudbury.

CORNWALL   The city is located in Cornwall Township, the name of which may be traced to the title of the Duke of Cornwall, eldest son of King George III. The original name was New Johnston for Sir John Johnston (1763–1828). This was changed to Cornwall in 1797. Incorporated in 1834.

CORUNNA   For the Battle of Corunna in Wellington's Peninsular Campaign of 1809.

COUCHICHING, LAKE   The name is of Amerindian extraction, although the exact origin is in dispute. It was rendered on early maps as: Cougichin (1859) and Couchouching (1862). The name may possibly be a translation of a word, interpreted as "pinery" or "a group of pine trees" or more probably as "outlet", which was applied first to a stream and later to the lake.

COURTRIGHT   Named after Milton Courtright, once president of the Canada Southern Railroad.

CREEMORE   The name was assigned by Senator Sir James Robert Gowan (1815–1909). The first part may be a corruption of the Gaelic *cridhe* for "heart".

CREIGHTON   For David Creighton, one-time member for North Bay in the Ontario legislature. Now part of the town of Walden.

CRYSTAL BEACH   The name is descriptive and arises from the clear water and sandy beach found locally. The community amalgamated with the town of Fort Erie on January 1, 1970.

DEEP RIVER   The stretch of the Ottawa River from High View to Des Joachims was designated La Rivière Creuse by French voyageurs, and appears as such on early maps. The descriptive name Deep River was applied to a new townsite, established in 1945.

DELHI   The post office was Middleton until immediately after the Great Indian Mutiny of 1857–8 when Delhi (for the city in India) replaced the earlier name.

DESERONTO   Marks the career of John Deserontyou, a Mohawk chief. The town went through numerous name changes in the nineteenth century and was incorporated as Deseronto in 1889.

DETROIT RIVER   From the French word meaning "strait" or "narrows".

DIXIE   Named for Dr. A. Dixie (?–1896), a medical practitioner in the district during the 1840s. It is now part of Mississauga.

DON RIVER   Suggested by Elizabeth Gwillim, the wife of Lieutenant-Governor John Graves Simcoe, for the River Don in Yorkshire, England.

DORCHESTER   Applied first to the township, the name honours Sir Guy Carleton, Lord Dorchester (1724–1808). It was changed from Dorchester Station on May 3, 1961.

DOUGLAS POINT   Appears first on 1852 map of Province of Canada. Replaced in 1862 by MacPherson's Point (for Malcolm MacPherson, 1854–93, reeve of Kincardine Township). The name Douglas Point was reapplied and officially approved on April 7, 1902. Exact origin unknown.

DRAYTON   After the English residence of Sir Robert Peel (1788 –1850), Drayton Manor.

DRESDEN   In 1872 Dresden, which was named for the city in Germany, and Fairport, at the head of navigation on the Sydenham River, were united as the village of Dresden. Post office established in 1852.

DRYDEN   Marks the career of John Dryden, M.P.P. for South Ontario from 1879 to 1905, Minister of Agriculture from 1890 to 1905.

DUNDALK   For Dundalk, County Louth, Ireland, the native town of an early settler, Elias Gray.

DUNDAS   For Henry Dundas (1742–1811), prominent British Cabinet Minister around the turn of the nineteenth century.

DUNNVILLE   First settled in 1829 and named for John Henry Dunn (?–1854), who served as Receiver General of Upper Canada.

DURHAM (Grey County)   Originally Bentinck; renamed in 1866 in honour of the English city and county. Durham Regional Municipality east of Toronto is derived from Durham County, which was named in 1792 for the English county.

EARLTON   Established in 1903 by settlers from Trois-Rivières. Name from that of the first child born in the settlement, Earl Brasher.

EASTVIEW   *See* Vanier

EGANVILLE   For a pioneer farmer and lumberman, John Egan. Post office dates from 1852.

EKWAN RIVER   Appears as *Equam* on Bellin map of 1744. Of Cree origin, meaning "the river far up the coast".

ELGIN   For James Bruce, eighth Earl of Elgin (1811–63), Governor General from 1847 to 1854.

ELK LAKE   Originally a Hudson's Bay Company post, it was named after the animal.

ELLIOT LAKE   The town takes its name from the lake. There is no official record of origin of name; the earliest appearance is on the Dominion map of 1901. The townsite name was approved on August 14, 1952.

ELMIRA   Probably named for Elmira in New York State. The post office was established in 1867.

ELMVALE   This descriptive dates from the mid nineteenth century, when the community was named for the abundance of elms.

ELORA   Founded in 1832 by William Gilkerson; the name was bestowed for the ship *Elora*, owned by his brother, Captain John Gilkerson.

EMBRUN   Named in 1856 by Rev. Father François Coopman after Embrun, in the Département de Hautes-Alpes, France.

EMO   Named for a river in Ireland. The post office, Emo River, dates from 1887 (CPCGN files).

ENGLEHART   Marks the career of Jacob Lewis Englehart (1847–1921), one-time chairman of the Temiskaming and Northern Ontario Railway Board. Incorporated in 1908.

ENGLISH RIVER   Formed part of the early trade route "down which the English came to Hudson's Bay" (G.B.C. Report, 1924).

ERIE, LAKE   Named after the Erie tribe of Amerindians, who once inhabited the south shore of the lake. This name comes from the Huron word meaning "long tailed" and refers to the panther or wildcat (CPCGN files).

ERIN   The poetic name for Ireland. Erin Township was first named with the neighbouring townships of Albion and Caledon (after England and Scotland respectively). The community was later named for the township of Erin.

ESPANOLA   Derived from the English pronunciation of the French word for Spaniard – *l'Espagnol. See* Spanish River

ESSEX   After the county name which was bestowed by Lieutenant-Governor John Graves Simcoe for the English county.

ETOBICOKE   Of Amerindian origin, the name may mean in translation "a place where the alders grow".

EXETER   Named by William McConnell, early settler, after Exeter, Devonshire, England.

FAIRPORT
FAIRPORT BEACH   A descriptive name used because of the presence of favourable physical features.

FALCONBRIDGE   Named for Falconbridge Township, which

honours Sir William Glenholme Falconbridge (1846–1920), Chief Justice of the King's Bench in Ontario from 1900 to 1920. It is now part of Nickel Centre.

FENELON FALLS   Fenelon Township was named in commemoration of the career of Abbé François de Salignac de la Mothe-Fénelon (1641–79), a Sulpician missionary sent by Bishop Laval to serve the Iroquois north of Lake Ontario.

FENWICK   Possibly named for Sir William Fenwick Williams (1800–83), a hero of the Crimean War (1854–5). The post office dates from 1862. *See* Port Williams, Nova Scotia

FERGUS   From the name of its founder (1834), Adam Fergusson, a Scottish immigrant. Post office established in 1836.

FIELD   Name originated with the township. The township was named for C. C. Field, who served as a member of the legislature for Northumberland West from 1886 to 1890.

FLOWERPOT ISLAND   From the presence of a flowerpot-shaped rock standing about fifty feet in height. Part of Georgian Bay Islands National Park.

FOLEYET   Probably named for Foley Bros., railway contractors involved in building the Canadian Northern Railway from Sudbury. According to a story told by railroaders in the area, Sir Donald Mann (1853–1934) wanted to name the station Foley but met with opposition. He is reputed to have said, "I'll have it named Foley yet." (CPCGN files)

FONTHILL   There are two possibilities as to the origin of this name: 1) for Fonthill Abbey, Wiltshire, England; or 2) after a public drinking fountain erected on a local hillside. The post office dates from 1856.

FOREST   A descriptive resulting from a heavy stand of timber.

The post office was established in 1859.

FORT ERIE   *See* Erie

FORT FRANCES   Located on the site of Fort St. Pierre, erected by Pierre de La Vérendrye (1685–1749) in 1731. A later Hudson's Bay post on this spot, Fort Frances, took its name from Lady Frances Ramsay Simpson, wife of Sir George Simpson (1792–1860), governor of the company.

FORT WILLIAM   Named for William McGillivray (1764?–1825), president of the North West Company. It was first known as Fort Camenestigoyan (1678) and later as Fort Kaminestiquia (1833). *See* Kaministiquia River *and* Thunder Bay

FRANKFORD   Sometimes rendered as Frankfort on early maps. The name is attributed to Sir Francis Bond Head (1793–1875), who visited the area while Lieutenant-Governor in 1836.

GALT   Originally Shades Mill for Absalom Shade, an early settler, the name was changed in 1827 to honour John Galt (1779–1839). Amalgamated with Hespeler and Preston in 1973 to form the city of Cambridge. *See* Cambridge *and* Goderich

GANANOQUE   Derived from an Amerindian word said to signify "rocks rising out of the water", a possible reference to the "marble rock which rises above the surface . . . in the middle of the river" (Armstrong).

GARSON MINE   This community's name is taken from the township, which was named after William Garson, one-time member of the Ontario legislature for Lincoln. Became part of Nickel Centre in the regional municipality of Sudbury.

GEORGETOWN   Has been attributed to George Kennedy, an early settler and land surveyor. The original name was Hungry Hollow, due to "hard times locally" (OGNB files). The new name may have been inspired by the death of King George III in 1820, the date when Kennedy settled in the area.

GEORGIAN BAY   Named as part of Captain H. W. Bayfield's Admiralty Survey (1819–22) in honour of the reigning monarch, King George IV.

GERALDTON   The result of a combination of Fitz*Gerald* and Erring*ton* – for the two financiers prominent in the early development of the gold-mining industry.

GLENCOE   Suggested by A. P. Macdonald, surveyor, for Glencoe, Scotland.

GODERICH   Founded in 1827 by John Galt, Commissioner for the Canada Company. Honours Viscount Goderich (1782–1859), who served as Secretary for the Colonies from 1837 to 1838.

GOGAMA   Of Amerindian origin. Possibly from *Gogaam gigo,* translated as "The fish leap up over the surface of the water." (Baraga)

GORE BAY   Probably for Francis Gore (1769–1852), Lieutenant-Governor of Upper Canada from 1806 to 1817; or after the steamer *Gore*, which ran between Sault Ste. Marie and Collingwood from 1860 to 1870.

GRAND BEND   First known as Eaux Croches, a name bestowed in 1845 by settlers from Quebec who were "impressed by the twisting course" of the Auxsables River. Became Grand Bend in 1860 "for the abrupt swing of the river channel".

GRAND RIVER   Appears on early maps as Rivière Rapide "because of the violence of the current"; later called Urfe River for Abbé François-Saturnin Lascaris d'Urfé (1641–1701), a Sulpician missionary; eventually, through popular usage, became La Grande Rivière. John Graves Simcoe unsuccessfully attempted to change the name (by royal proclamation, July 16, 1792) to Ouse, for a river of that name in England.

GRAND VALLEY   Takes it name from the Grand River, which flows through the valley. *See above*

GRAVENHURST   Assigned by the Department of the Postmaster General. Probably for a fictional place name in Washington Irving's *Bracebridge Hall*. The name was assigned by W. D. Le Sueur (1840–1917) (CPCGN files). *See* Bracebridge

GRIMSBY
GRIMSBY BEACH   After Grimsby, Lincolnshire, England. Post office established in 1816.

GROUNDHOG RIVER   A translation of the Algonquin *Akskwidjie Kipi*, "ground hog".

GUELPH   Chosen by John Galt (1779–1839), Commissioner for the Canada Company, on St. George's Day, 1827, "in compliment to the Royal Family whose baptismal name was Guelph". *See* Goderich, Galt, *and* Cambridge

HAGERSVILLE   Settled in 1842 by David and Charles Hager. Post office dates from 1852. Became part of the town of Haldimand, April 1, 1974. *See* Haldimand

HAILEYBURY   Name conferred in 1873 by C. C. Farr, a graduate of Haileybury College in England (CPCGN files).

HALDIMAND   Town of Caledonia, villages of Cayuga and Hagersville, townships of North Cayuga, Oneida, Seneca, and South Cayuga, plus portions of the townships of Rainham and Walpole united to form the town of Haldimand, April 1, 1974. Honours Sir Frederick Haldimand (1718–91), who served as Governor from 1778 to 1786. Haldimand County was also named for Sir Frederick.

HALIBURTON   Marks the career of Thomas Chandler Haliburton (1796–1865), humorist, historian, jurist, member of the British Parliament and Chairman of the Canadian Land and Emigration Company.

HALTON HILLS   Effective January 1, 1974, the towns of Acton and Georgetown, along with parts of the township of Esquesing and the town of Oakville, amalgamated to form the town of Halton Hills. For Major William Halton, secretary to Sir Francis Gore, Lieutenant-Governor of Upper Canada from 1806 to 1817. *See* Belleville

HAMILTON   Formerly Burlington Bay, renamed in 1813 after George Hamilton (1787–1835), son of Robert Hamilton. Became a town in 1833 and achieved city status in 1846. *See* St. Catharines

HANOVER   First called Buck's Crossing and later Buck's Bridge after innkeeper Abraham Buck. Name changed to honour the German city in the mid nineteenth century.

HARRISTON   Founded by the Harrison family in 1854–5 and named for Archibald Harrison. First sawmill erected by George Harrison in 1854. Became a town in 1874.

HARROW   Assigned by John O'Connor (1824–87) possibly during his term as Postmaster General from 1880 to 1881. For Harrow-on-the-Hill, Middlesex, England.

HASTINGS   Originally Crook's Rapids after grist-mill owner James Crooks, it was renamed in 1847 in honour of the wife of the first Marquess of Hastings.

HAVELOCK   Commemorates the career of Sir Henry Havelock (1795–1857), a hero of the Indian Mutiny of 1857.

HAWKESBURY   The name was taken from the township which was named for Charles Jenkinson, Baron Hawkesbury and Earl of

Liverpool (1727–1808). First known as LeChenal, Hamilton's Mills, and Hawkesbury Mills. It was incorporated as a town in 1896.

HEARST   Marks the career of Ontario Premier Sir William Howard Hearst (1864–1941).

HENRIETTA MARIA, CAPE   Designated in 1631 by explorer Captain Thomas James (1593–1635?). James, part of a survey party in this area, sailed on the ship *Henrietta Maria*, which was named in honour of the wife of Charles I.

HENSALL   Founded in 1854 by George and James Petty and named for their native village in Yorkshire, England.

HESPELER   The early name, Bergytown after Michael Bergy, was changed to Hespeler in 1858 for Jacob Hespeler, a miller and distiller. Incorporated as a village in 1858, and as a town in 1901, it was amalgamated with Galt and Preston in 1973 to form the city of Cambridge.

HOLLAND LANDING   Located on the east branch of the Holland River, which was named for Samuel Holland (1728–1801), noted surveyor. The name of the nearby Holland Marsh is derived from the same source.

HORNEPAYNE   After R. M. Horne-Payne, one-time financial representative of the Canadian Northern Railroad Company in Britain.

HUDSON BAY   *See* Manitoba *entry*

HUMBER RIVER   Bestowed by John Graves Simcoe for the River Humber, England. Known briefly as Toronto River.

HUNTSVILLE   For George Hunt, first settler, who arrived in the area in 1858.

HURD, CAPE   After Captain Thomas Hurd (1757–1823), appointed hydrographer to the British Admiralty in 1808.

HURON, LAKE   Derived from the French *hure*, "shock of hair". A French soldier is reputed to have spotted a party of Indians "with their hair cropped and silver coloured and dubbed them – hurons" (Armstrong). Lake was discovered by the Recollet missionary Joseph LeCaron, who called it Mer Douce. Later referred to as Lac d'Orléans. Appears as Lac des Hurons on De l'Isle map of 1790 and in common usage thereafter.

INGERSOLL   Named by Colonel Charles Ingersoll, in memory of his father, Major Thomas Ingersoll, a United Empire Loyalist, who came to the area from Massachusetts in 1793.

IROQUOIS   Named for the Amerindian tribe. The original location of the village was a favourite camping ground. It was entirely relocated during construction of the St. Lawrence Seaway.

IROQUOIS FALLS   Stems from a legend that "Iroquois Indians once raided a Huron tribe near this location, killed the braves, took the women prisoners. They then curled up to sleep in their canoes tied to the river bank. Some Huron women escaped, cut the canoes loose and the Iroquois were swept over the falls to their deaths." (OGNB files)

JAMES BAY   *See* Quebec *entry*

JAMESTOWN   *See* Wawa

JARVIS   Named by Lieut.-Col. A. Jarvis, aide-de-camp to Governor John Graves Simcoe. Post office dates from 1851. Amalgamated with adjoining municipalities to form city of Nanticoke, January 1, 1974.

JERSEYVILLE   Founded in 1785 by the United Empire Loyalists from New Jersey and named for their former home.

KAMINISTIQUIA RIVER   Traceable to Amerindian sources, it is usually translated as "island's river" or "where there are islands in the river". Early spellings: Caministigoyan (DeLhut, 1678), Kaministiqouya (De l'Isle, 1762), Kaministiquioh (Palliser, 1857), Kaministiquia (Dept. of Interior, 1883). Approved by the G.B.C. in 1902 as Kaministikwia; the current form was approved on June 23, 1975.

KANATA   Of Amerindian origin, it is derived from the name for "a cluster or collection of huts".

KAPISKAU RIVER   River and lake. The name was first applied to Kapiskau Lake and is derived from the Amerindian word for "obstructed" or "blocked up".

KAPUSKASING   A local Amerindian term which was probably first assigned to the branch in the river. The Kapuskasing River is a branch of the Mattagami.

KEARNS   Settled in 1937 and first known as Chesterville. It was renamed in 1966 for William Kearns, aerial observer and photographer with the Ontario Forestry Service (OGBN files).

KEMPTVILLE   Name chosen by public meeting about 1830 in honour of Sir James Kempt (1764–1854), who was administrator of the government of Canada at that time. Post office established in 1831.

KENORA   First known as Rat Portage, the community was renamed by Act of Parliament in 1905 as Kenora, a coined word formed from the first two letters of *Ke*ewatin, *No*rman (a nearby community), and *Ra*t Portage.

KILLALOE   Named for the parish and town in County Clare, Ireland. It was incorporated as a village in 1908.

KINCARDINE   Originally Penetangore for "clay bluff" or "sand dune" in Ojibway. The name was changed upon the town's incorporation in 1858 in honour of the Earl of Elgin and Kincardine (1811–63), Governor General of British North America from 1847 to 1854.

KING   The township was possibly named after John King, who served as permanent undersecretary (Home Department) in the British government in 1792. The name King City, in use since 1932, is now part of the municipal township of King.

KINGSTON   Occupies the site of the Amerindian village of Cataraqui and later of Fort Frontenac, which was erected in the 1670s. Renamed in 1783 in honour of King George III. Incorporated as a town in 1838 and as a city in 1846.

KINGSVILLE   For Colonel James King, a prominent early resident of the district.

KIRKLAND LAKE   The lake was named in 1907 for Winnifred Kirkland, a secretary in the Lands Branch, Ontario Department of Mines. The town dates from the discovery of gold in 1911.

KITCHENER   Early names: Sand Hill and Ebytown (after Mennonite Bishop Benjamin Eby). The name was changed to Berlin in 1824 in deference to the local immigration from Germany. Renamed for Lord Kitchener (1850–1916) during the First World War.

KOMOKA   Of Amerindian origin (possibly Muncey), the name has been translated as "where the dead lie"(OGNB files). Another version suggests that it is the Amerindian name for "junction", for the junction of the Sarnia and Windsor branches of the Grand Trunk Railway.

LAC DES MILLE LACS   An early name which appears in the records of the North West Company, 1802, and the David Thompson map of 1813–14. Arrowsmith renders it as Thousand Islands

Lake in 1854 and, in 1865, as Lac des Milles Lacs. Descriptive, since the lake is studded with small islands containing ponds and small lakes.

LAC SEUL   First applied by French voyageurs in the eighteenth century. Later adopted as the name of a trading post (Fort Lac Seul), established about 1815. Appears in translation as Lonely Lake in the *Surveyors Report of Northern Ontario, 1900.*

LAKEFIELD   First known as Herriott's Falls for an early settler. Name changed in 1874 as a reflection of the nearby physical features.

LAKE OF THE WOODS   The islands in the lake are wooded; however, the name is probably a mistranslation of an Amerindian word meaning "the inland lake of the hills" for the range of sandy hills along the shore. Lac du Bois on early maps and gazetteers (PAC Johnson Papers).

LAKE ST. JOSEPH   *See* St. Joseph

LAMBETH   After Lambeth, a borough of the city of London, England. Post office dates from 1857.

LANARK   Settled in 1820 by emigrants from the Scottish counties of Lanark and Renfrew – hence the name. Post office established in 1823. *See* Renfrew

LANCASTER   From the township name, which in turn was bestowed in honour of King George III, one of whose titles was Duke of Lancaster.

LANGSTAFF   Suggested by the family name of an early (about 1800) settler.

LANSDOWNE   First spelling Lansdown; final "e" added after 1872. Not for the third Marquess of Lansdowne, Governor General from 1833 to 1888, but probably honours an earlier member of the family. Sir Frederick Haldimand (1718–91) sent reports on Canadian affairs to the second marquess.

LARDER LAKE A variation on the translation of the Amerindian for "hanging storehouse", applied to the lake because supplies were stored here. First gold in northern Ontario discovered here in 1905.

LA SALLE Commemorates the career of René-Robert Cavelier, Sieur de La Salle (1643–87), whose explorations took him to this area from 1679 to 1680. It is now part of the township of Sandwich West.

LEAMINGTON After a town in Warwickshire, England. Has had a post office since June 1854; it was incorporated as a town in 1890.

LEASIDE Part of the borough of East York since January 1, 1967. The name is derived from the Lea family who settled the area in the early 1800s. Name was assigned by William Lea about 1850.

LEVACK Named for Mary Levack, Mrs. John Mowat, mother of Sir Oliver Mowat (1820–1903), Premier of Ontario from 1872 until 1896. *See* Onaping Falls

LINCOLN In Lincoln County, which was named in 1792 for Lincolnshire, England. The town of Beamsville and the township of Clinton were amalgamated January 1, 1970, to form the town of Lincoln.

LINDSAY The township (Bruce County) dates from 1856 and the name was suggested by Lord Bury, Earl of Albemarle (1832–94), in honour of his mother's family. He served as Superintendent of Indian Affairs from 1854 to 1857.

Town (Victoria County). "The original survey of this site was made (in 1834) by John Huston, who had as an assistant a man named Lindsay. He died following an accidental shooting and the circumstances of his death led to the bestowal of the name." (Armstrong)

LION'S HEAD   Descriptive. A limestone cliff at the entrance to the harbour has a projection at the top resembling a lion's head.

LISTOWEL   Conferred by the Post Office Department in 1856 to supersede Mapleton and Windham (former names). For Listowel, County Kerry, Ireland.

LITTLE CURRENT   Descriptive. Heavy winds cause a slight current through a narrow channel. In use from 1865 onward (CPCGN files).

LIVELY   (Now part of Walden) Inco townsite between Copper Cliff and Creighton. Named in 1950 for Charles Lively, a native of Rawdon, Nova Scotia, an Inco employee for thirty-five years.

LONDON   In 1793 John Graves Simcoe selected "the Forks of the Thames" as his choice for a future capital of the province. The name was applied first (1799) to the District (after London, England). The present location was selected as the administrative centre for the region January 30, 1826. Appears as New London on 1793 Map of the River Tranche, now the Thames. Survived an attempt at being renamed Georgina on the Thames. Became an incorporated town in 1840 and achieved city status on January 1, 1855.

LONGLAC   Descriptive. A fur-trading post since the early 1800s. Incorporated on an improvement district 1952, changed to a township municipality on January 1, 1964.

LONG POINT   A "long point" of land on Lake Erie. Post office from 1816.

L'ORIGNAL   The town takes its name from Pointe à l'Orignal, which extends into the Ottawa River. From the French for "moose", denoting that the location was once a common crossing-place.

LUCAN   After Lucan, in Leinster, near Dublin, Ireland. Post office established in 1857.

LUCKNOW   The date of the original survey coincided with the Indian Mutiny 1857.

MADOC   For a legendary Welsh prince reputed to have discovered America about 1170. Post office dates from 1836.

MAITLAND   Named for Sir Peregrine Maitland (1777–1854), who served as Lieutenant-Governor of Upper Canada from 1820 to 1828.

MAITLAND RIVER   Renamed in honour of Sir Peregrine Maitland (*see above*). Originally known as Menesatung River – Amerindian for healing waters.

MALTON   Suggested by Malton, Yorkshire, England. Now part of the city of Mississauga.

MANITOULIN ISLAND   A corruption of *Manitowin* (from Manitou), applied by the Algonquins "to any supernatural object calling for their fear or worship". *See* Manitou, Manitoba

MAPLE   Uncertain origin – probably attributable to the maple tree; however, it is also a family name and might be traced to an early settler.

MARATHON   Carleton County and Cochrane District for Marathon, Greece. Marathon (Thunder Bay District) is after the Marathon Paper Mills Company.

MARKDALE   Name chosen in honour of Mark Armstrong, an early settler. Post office established in 1869.

MARKHAM   Commemorates the career of the Rev. William Markham (1720–1806), Bishop of Chester and later Archbishop of York (England). The township dates from 1792.

MARMORA   Singular *marmor*, plural *marmora* – the Latin word for marble. There are marble quarries in the district, hence the name. The township was named in 1820.

MATACHEWAN   The name is derived from the Cree word for "meeting of the currents".

MATHESON   First known as McDougall's Chute after an early trapper. Renamed for Arthur J. Matheson (1842–1913), provincial Treasurer and M.P.P. for South Lanark. Became part of Timmins on January 1, 1973.

MATTAGAMI   River and lake. Of Amerindian origin, it is one of the dozens of place names translated as "where the waters meet".

MATTAWA   A local Algonquin term variously spelled as Matawa, Mattawan, and Mattawin. It means "where a river flows into another body of water", or "confluence".

MAXVILLE   Derived from the predominance of "Mac's" among early Scottish settlers.

MEAFORD   Early names: Peggy's Landing and Stephenson's Landing. Renamed by surveyors after Meaford Hall, Staffordshire, England, the country seat of Admiral Sir John Jarvis, Earl St. Vincent. Once part of township of St. Vincent.

MERLIN   Name bestowed by Post Office Department in 1868 after a village near Edinburgh, Scotland.

MERRICKVILLE   For William Merrick, an early Loyalist settler.

MERRITTON   Honours William Hamilton Merritt (1793–1862), promoter of the Welland Canal.

MICHIPICOTEN   Island, bay, river, and village. From an Algonquin tribe, Mishibigwadunk, whose name meant "place of bold promontories".

MIDLAND   Derived from the Midland Railway, which arrived from Port Hope via Beaverton in 1872.

MILDMAY   Possibly after "the place in England where the famous Mildmay Evangelical Meetings were held". Post office dates from 1868 (CPCGN files).

MILLBROOK   From the presence in pioneer days of sawmills and a grist mill. Settled in 1812.

MILTON   Most probably a corruption of Milltown for Martin Mills, an early settler. Appears as Milltown on early maps. Post office (Milton) from 1836 onward.

MILVERTON   Adopted by public meeting in 1871 to replace first name, West's Corner (for Andrew West, an early settler). Suggested by Milverton, Somersetshire, England.

MIMICO   Of Amerindian origin, this name means "the place of the wild pigeon". Amalgamated with the borough of Etobicoke on January 1, 1967.

MINDEN   Named for the Battle of Minden, 1759, an important engagement in the Seven Years War. Settlement dates from 1863.

MISSINAIBI RIVER   River and lake. Name derived from an Amerindian word, *Missinaibie,* translated as "pictures on the water", a reference to Indian pictographs reflected on water (CPCGN files).

MISSISSAUGA   City on Lake Ontario named after an Amerindian tribe. The name is descriptive of the mouth of a river – *michi* or *missi,* meaning "large", and *saki,* "outlet", a river having several outlets. Early spellings include: Messasague, Mississaga, and Massassauga. The city was incorporated on January 1, 1968, amalgamating the municipal township of Toronto, the town of Port Credit, and the town of Streetsville.

MITCHELL   For a black settler of the same name who built a small shanty on the nearby Thames River. "Perhaps the only place name in Ontario named for a negro" (OGNB files). Post office opened in 1842.

MONTROCK   Descriptive – after a nearby rocky hill. Part of the town of Iroquois Falls.

MORRISBURG   Honours James Morris (1798–1865), member for Leeds County in the Assembly of Upper Canada. He served as Postmaster General from 1851 to 1853, when the village was named.

MOUNT BRYDGES   For C. J. Brydges (1827–89), general manager of the Grand Trunk Railway from 1861 to 1874. The earlier name, Carradoc, was replaced in 1856. The latter remains as a township name (Caradoc) for a village in Shropshire, England.

MOUNT FOREST   Chosen by William McDonald, first postmaster. After Forest Town, Ireland. Post office established 1853.

MOUNT PLEASANT (Brant County)   Named by Henry Ellis, one of the first settlers, after his home in Wales. Known briefly (1862–75) as Mohawk; however, earlier name prevailed.

MUSKOKA   Lake and river. Probably a corruption of the name of *Misquuckkey*, an Indian chief whose name appears on two treaties for the surrender of land, bearing the dates 17 and 18 November 1815 (CPCGN files). Lake Muskoka appears on some French maps as Petit Lac des Hurons.

NANTICOKE   A local Amerindian descriptive word meaning "crooked or winding", applied to a creek. The village of Jarvis, town of Port Dover, town of Waterford, and parts of adjacent townships were amalgamated to form the City of Nanticoke, April 1, 1974.

NAPANEE   Town takes its name from river; early spelling *Appanea*. Of unknown Amerindian origin. No basis for suggestion that it is a Mississaugan synonym for flour.

NEWBURGH   Name assigned in 1839 by Dr. Isaac Aylesworth because of the town's physical resemblance to Newburgh-on-the-Hudson in New York State.

NEWCASTLE   Name originated with a desire of early settlers to honour their home town in England. The town of Bowmanville, the village of Newcastle, and the townships of Clarke and Darlington amalgamated on January 1, 1974, to form the town of Newcastle.

NEW HAMBURG   First settlers were German and they assigned the name Hamburg for the city in Germany. Name later changed to New Hamburg. Post office dates from 1851.

NEW LISKEARD   For the town of Liskeard in Cornwall, England. The post office dates from 1903 when "New" was added to the name to avoid confusion with Leskard in southern Ontario.

NEWMARKET   Founded in 1780 and called Beman's Corners until 1806. Name changed about 1810 in honour of Newmarket, Suffolk, England. The post office was opened in 1826, and until 1890 the name was spelled New Market.

NIAGARA   River and falls. The name is of undoubted Amerindian origin, possibly from the Huron word meaning "thunder of waters" or "resounding with great noise". The name of the town at the falls was Clifton until 1881, when it became Niagara Falls. It was incorporated as a city in 1904.

NIAGARA ISLAND (St. Lawrence River, Leeds County)   Appears on an Admiralty chart of 1828. It was named after the vessel *Niagara*, launched at Kingston on July 13, 1809.

NIAGARA-ON-THE-LAKE   Located at the mouth of the Niagara River, it was settled in the 1780s and known as Niagara. Renamed Newark by John Graves Simcoe in 1792. The name was later restored to Niagara and then changed to Niagara-on-the-Lake in 1906 to avoid confusion with Niagara Falls.

NICKEL CENTRE   Descriptive name for a company town founded by International Nickel Company. It was established in 1973 as part of the Regional Municipality of Sudbury by amalgamating the town of Coniston and the townships of Neelon, Garson, Falconbridge, Dryden, and Maclennan. Coniston was established by the Mond Nickel Company (later INCO) in 1910 and became a town in 1934.

NIPIGON   Lake, river, and bay. The name is said to be derived from the Ojibway word *Animi-bee-go-ong*, translated as "continuous water", a reference to the route to the lake by way of the Nipigon River. Variations: Nemipigon (La Hontan, 1703); Alimipigon and Alimipegon (Bellin, 1755) (Rayburn).

NIPISSING   Lake and district. The name originates with the Amerindian descriptive *Nipisisinan,* for the "little body of water". It was so called because Lake Nipissing "though of considerable extent is much smaller than any of the Great Lakes" (CPCGN files).

NITH RIVER   After the River Nith, Dumfries-shire, Scotland, the name was bestowed by James Jackson, a founder of the village of Ayr.

NORTH BAY   Descriptive. In 1882 the C.P.R. "selected the flat shore of the north bay of Lake Nipissing for railway yards" (*Encyclopedia Canadiana*). Incorporated as a city in 1925.

NORWICH   The township and village were named for Norwich, Norfolk, England. The post office dates from 1829 onward. It was incorporated as a village in 1876.

NORWOOD   Prior to 1838 the community was known as Keeler's Mills after Joseph A. Keeler, grist-mill owner and early settler. The change was suggested by Miss Harriet Keeler, "who was reading a book descriptive of Norwood, a suburb of London, England" (CPCGN files).

NOTTAWASAGA   Bay and river. Originates with the Algonquin *Nahdoway* or *Nahdowa,* which was their designation for "Iroquois", and *saga* or *saghi,* meaning "outlet of river". The Iroquois used this river when on the warpath against the Algonquins (*Smith's Gazetteer,* 1846). *See* Nottawa River, Quebec. *Note also* Stayner *and* Wasaga Beach, Ontario

OAKVILLE   The settlement dates from 1805; it was incorporated as a town in 1857. The community was named by R. B. Sullivan, Commissioner of Crown Lands, because it was the centre of an oak-stave industry.

ODESSA   Name assigned by the Post Office Department in 1854 for the Russian port which was the scene of an engagement during the Crimean War.

OGOKI RIVER   Lake and a river that is a tributary of Albany River. Derived from a local Cree term, *mekowikew,* meaning "he is swift", for the "swift river".

OMEMEE   Name suggested by the Cree or Ojibway word for pigeon or dove. Incorporated in 1874.

ONAPING   River and lake (Sudbury District). From the Cree *Onumunaning,* meaning red paint or vermilion. (Onaman Lake and Wunnumin Lake have a similar meaning.)

ONAPING FALLS   A new town as of January 1, 1973, resulting from an amalgamation of the township of Dowling with the town of Levack, the township of Levack, and the improvement district of Onaping.

ONTARIO, LAKE   The name was applied to the lake as early as 1641; for origin see provincial entry.

ORANGEVILLE   Honours Orange Lawrence, who settled in this area in 1844 and established a mill. The post office dates from 1851.

ORILLIA   The name was probably assigned to the township by Sir Peregrine Maitland (1777–1854), Lieutenant-Governor from 1818 to 1828. It is derived from the Spanish for "margin" or "bank" of river (Maitland served in the British Army in Spain). A less plausible theory suggests an Amerindian origin – for *orelia,* a red berry (OGNB files).

ORLEANS   Named by Msgr. Ebrard in the late 1850s for the city of the same name in France. According to CPCGN files he applied for establishment of a post office "plus tard en 1859". It was granted in 1860.

ORONO   Originated with the town of Orono, Maine, U.S.A. "A stranger who dropped in suggested the name after his home in Maine." (CPCGN files) Originally for Joseph Orono, an Amerindian chief. Name may be of French origin (Stewart).

OSHAWA   From Amerindian (Seneca) sources, it may mean "crossing of a stream" or "carrying place". Incorporated as a village in 1850, a town in 1879, and a city in 1924.

OTOSKWIN RIVER   An Amerindian descriptive term, translated as "elbow". For the shape of the river.

OTTAWA   Called Bytown until 1855 after Colonel John By
(1781–1836) of the Royal Engineers, to whom the British government entrusted the construction of the Rideau Canal. Derived
from the Algonquin term *adawe*, "to trade", the name given to the
tribe which controlled the trade of the river. The name was applied first to the river. The French form is *Outaouais*.

OWEN SOUND   First assigned to the bay on which the town is
situated, the name commemorates the career of Admiral Sir Edward William Campbell Rich Owen (1771–1849). It has been assumed that Owen Sound was named after the Admiral's brother,
Captain William Fitzwilliam Owen (1774–1857), but local features such as Cape Commodore, Point William, Campbell Bluff,
and Point Rich "practically demonstrate the accuracy of the
above observation" (OGNB files). The town was originally called
Sydenham for Lord Sydenham (1799–1841), Governor General
from 1839 to 1841. The name was changed to Owen Sound upon
incorporation in 1857.

PAISLEY   Originally called Mud River, the town was renamed
in 1856 after a town in Renfrewshire, Scotland.

PAKENHAM   For Sir Edward Pakenham, brother-in-law of the
Duke of Wellington. Township named in 1823.

PALMERSTON   The town (1854) and township (1822) both
mark the career of Henry John Temple, Viscount Palmerston
(1784–1865), who served as Prime Minister of Great Britain from
1855 to 1858 and from 1859 to 1865.

PARIS   The settlement was called "The Forks of the Grand
River" until 1836 when the new name was selected by a public

meeting, "both for convenience and for the crude plaster of paris in the locality" (OGNB files).

PARKHILL   Probably named for a community in Ross-shire, Scotland. It was sometimes spelled Park Hill on early maps. The settlement dates from 1860.

PARRY SOUND   Assigned by Captain H. W. Bayfield (1795–1885) to honour Arctic explorer Sir William Edward Parry (1790–1855). The post office was established in 1865.

PELEE ISLAND   Island and township. The name is descriptive and was chosen by early French voyageurs. It is from the French *pelé*, "bare or bald", because the east side of the point "consisted largely of sand dunes and no trees". Point Pelé (*Smith's Gazetteer*, 1846).

PELHAM   Probably suggested by the career of Henry Pelham, fifth Duke of Newcastle (1811–64), who served as Secretary of State for the colonies in the mid nineteenth century.

PEMBROKE   For Sidney Herbert, son of the Earl of Pembroke (1810–61), Secretary of the Admiralty in 1843 when the name was adopted.

PENETANGUISHENE   From an Amerindian descriptive translated as "the place of white falling sands". *See also* Penetanguishene, Newfoundland

PERTH   After the city of Perth on the River Tay, Perthshire, Scotland. Perth-upon-Tay in some early gazetteers. Perth County may also be named for the Scottish city or by settlers from the Ontario town.

PETAWAWA   River, township, and village. A corruption of the Amerindian word *pitawewe*, meaning "where one hears the noise of water far away". Early spellings: *Pittoiwais* (Hawkins, 1839), *Petawawauwe* (Bouchette, 1846).

PETERBOROUGH   Derived from the name of Colonel Peter Robinson (1785–1838), who was responsible for settling some two thousand Irish immigrants in the area in the 1820s.

PETROLIA   Applied in 1861 by the first postmaster, Patrick Barclay, and is derived from *petroleum*, "the production of which is the staple industry of the place" (Armstrong). The name was spelled Petrolea for a number of years.

PICKERING   From Pickering, Yorkshire, England. Pickering Township was named in 1790. In 1794 the town of Pickering was established. The former village of Pickering was amalgamated with Ajax in the 1970s to form the town of Ajax.

PICTON   In memory of Major-General Sir Thomas Picton (1758–1815), who fell in action at the Battle of Waterloo, June 18, 1815.

PIE ISLAND   Designated Île Pâté by French voyageurs from its resemblance in profile to a pie. Pie Island (Bayfield, 1828).

PIGEON RIVER   On Ontario-Minnesota boundary. Also bay, falls, and point in the United States. Appears as Rivière aux Tortues on early French maps, possibly for pigeons mistaken for turtle doves. The first translation was Dove River; Pigeon River became the common name in early nineteenth century.

PINE GROVE   Listed in Lowell's *Gazetteer*, 1881. A descriptive term.

PLANTAGENET   From the royal house established by King Henry II. Settled in 1811–12. Post office from 1838.

POINT EDWARD   Formerly called Huron, it was renamed in 1860 to mark the visit by the then Prince of Wales, later Edward VII. Incorporated 1879.

PORCUPINE   From an island in the nearby river reputed to "be shaped like a porcupine". The settlement is now part of the city of Timmins.

PORT ARTHUR   Formerly known as Prince Arthur's Landing (1870) after Prince Arthur, Duke of Connaught (1850–1942). The name was changed at the instigation of the C.P.R. in 1882 to Port Arthur. *See* Thunder Bay

PORT BURWELL   Founded by Mahlon Burwell (1783–1846), surveyor for the government of Upper Canada from 1809 to 1840. The post office was established in 1829.

PORT CARLING   Named in 1865 for Sir John Carling (1828–1911), a long-time member of the House of Commons, who served as Postmaster-General and Minister of Agriculture in the Cabinet of Sir John A. Macdonald.

PORT COLBORNE   Selected by William Hamilton Merritt to honour Sir John Colborne (1778–1863), who was Governor in 1839. *See also* Colborne

PORT CREDIT   During the fur-trading era, traders meeting with the Amerindians "at the mouth of the river frequently extended credit for supplies". The town was amalgamated with city of Mississauga on January 1, 1974.

PORT DOVER   After Dover, Kent, England. Part of the city of Nanticoke.

PORT ELGIN   Early name, Normanton, was changed to honour Lord Elgin (1811–63), who served as Governor General from 1847 to 1854.

PORT HOPE   Selected at a public meeting in 1817 to mark the career of Colonel Henry Hope and replace the former name, the prosaic Smith's Creek (for Peter Smith, an early trader). Post office from 1820.

PORT MC NICOLL   Founded in 1909 by the Canadian Pacific Railway and named for railway executive David McNicoll (1852–1916).

PORT PERRY   First known as Scugog Village (from Lake Scugog), it was renamed in 1852 for Peter Perry (1793–1851), a member of the Upper Canadian legislature.

PORT ROBINSON   Honours Sir John Beverley Robinson (1791–1863), who became Chief Justice of Upper Canada in 1829, retiring in 1862. Post office from 1835 onward.

PORT ROWAN   Assigned by the Post Office Department in 1839 for Captain William Rowan, secretary to Governor Sir John Colborne.

PORT STANLEY   Surveyed and named in 1818 by Colonel John Bostwick for Lord Stanley (father of Lord Stanley, Governor General from 1888 to 1893), "who visited Colonel Thomas Talbot about the time the place was named" (CPCGN files).

POWASSAN   Of Ojibway origin and variously translated as "the bend" or "big bend", this name is possibly a descriptive for a nearby bend in the South River. Prior to 1891 the community was known as Powassan Station.

PRESCOTT   A reminder of the career of Major General Robert Prescott (1725–1815), Governor General from 1796 to 1799. Incorporated as a town, 1851.

PRESQU'ILE   Bay, peninsula, and point. Descriptive name – the bay and point take their name from the peninsula (presqu'île). Presque Isle (*Smith's Gazetteer,* 1813).

PRESTON   Named for Preston, Lancashire, England. *See* Cambridge

PUNKEYDOODLES CORNERS   Located at a point where the counties of Perth, Oxford, and Waterloo meet. The name has given rise to numerous apocryphal stories. The most plausible credits John Zurbuchen, an early pioneer, with a mispronunciation of his favourite song, "Yankee Doodle" (OGNB files).

QUEENSTON   Attributed to John Graves Simcoe because the Queen's Rangers were once stationed there. In a letter of November 4, 1792, he wrote, "The Queen's Rangers are hutted by great exertions at the Niagara Landing, now Queenston." (CPCGN files)

QUETICO PROVINCIAL PARK   Most probably a combination of the first letters of: *Que*bec *Ti*mber *Co*mpany. The park was established by order-in-council in 1913.

QUINTE, BAY OF   From the name of an Amerindian settlement *Kinte* or *Kantay*, probably a descriptive referring to a meadow at the west end of the bay. Site of a Sulpician mission during the French period.

RAINY RIVER   From Rainy Lake, derived from the French Lac la Pluie (Lake of Rain). Appears as Rain Lake in 1813 *Gazetteer*. Post office (Rainy River) established in 1886.

RAYSIDE-BALFOUR   Established on January 1, 1973, through the amalgamation of the townships of Rayside, Balfour, and parts of Snider and Creighton. It also includes the communities of Chelmsford and Azilda.

RED LAKE   Probably an early descriptive, the name appears on the Bouchette map of 1875. Officially approved on December 7, 1909.

RENFREW   County and town. Named for Renfrewshire, Scotland. No doubt suggested as a logical partner to Lanark. Town first known as Second Chute; name later changed to Renfrewville. Renfrew after 1848.

RICE LAKE   Descriptive – for the wild rice that grows in profusion along the shore of the lake. The earlier Amerindian name was *Pemecoutayang* or "Lake of the Burning Plains", a reference to "the plain on the south west end of lake which was burnt over every spring to allow the grass to grow more quickly" (CPCGN files, James White).

RICHMOND   In honour of the Duke of Richmond (1764–1819), who served as Governor from 1818 to 1819. Village incorporated 1850. *See also* Richmond, Quebec

RICHMOND HILL   Also named for the Duke of Richmond. "On July 13, 1819, the Duke stopped there for dinner and attended the raising of the Presbyterian Church, the village was immediately renamed in his honour." (CPCGN files) Earlier name: Mount Pleasant.

RIDEAU   Samuel de Champlain stood on the banks of the Ottawa River in 1613 and described the waterfall where the Rideau empties into the Ottawa as "a pair of curtains covering the landscape" (CPCGN files). The name was subsequently transferred to the river, to a group of lakes near Smiths Falls, to the residence of the Governor General (Rideau Hall), and, in 1972, to the municipal township of Rideau.

RIDGETOWN   Named for the ridge where the town is located. The ridge divides the north and south watersheds of the area. Post office dates from 1853.

RIDGEWAY   For its location on the Ridge Road, site of a battle on May 31, 1860, during the Fenian Raids.

ROCKCLIFFE PARK   Named by T. C. Keefer (1821–1915), a civil engineer, from the local landscape.

ROCKLAND   Possibly for the local topography. Post office dates from 1869.

ROCKWOOD   First known as Brotherstown; renamed about 1848. Descriptive – "the village and immediate vicinity is quite rocky and the land heavily timbered with wood" (CPCGN files).

RODNEY   Marks the career of Admiral Lord Rodney (1718–92) of the Royal Navy. Name assigned by the Post Office Department in 1875.

ST. CATHARINES   Named in 1809 in honour of Catharine Askin Hamilton, first wife of Robert Hamilton (*see* Hamilton). Post office dates from 1817. Sometimes spelled St. Catherines in early records and postmarks and still today frequently misspelled St. Catherines.

ST. CLAIR, LAKE   On August 16, 1679 (date of the feast of Ste. Claire), La Salle reached the lake. "Time with its effacing finger has rubbed out the final 'e' in both words" (Johnson Papers, PAC).

ST. GEORGE   After the first postmaster, Colonel George Stanton. Sometimes designated St. George–Brant in early listings.

ST. JACOBS   After Jacob Snider, early sawmill and grist-mill owner.

ST. JOSEPH ISLAND   Assigned in the seventeenth century by Jesuit missionaries.

ST. MARY RIVER   Named Rivière Sainte-Marie after the Virgin Mary by French missionaries.

ST. MARYS   For Mary Strachan Jones, daughter of Bishop John Strachan and wife of Thomas Mercer Jones, Commissioner of the

Canada Company. Mrs. Jones was present at the naming ceremony and "suggested her own as a good name in default of a better . . . Mrs. Mary Jones was canonized on the spot." (OGNB files)

ST. THOMAS   First named Kettle Creek Village for its location, the new name commemorates the career of Thomas Talbot (1771 –1853). Incorporated as a village in 1852, as a town in 1861, and as a city in 1881.

SANDY LAKE   Descriptive. Survived an attempt at renaming in the 1930s (the proposed name was McInnis Lake for Dr. William McInnis, a director of the Geological Survey). The original name was restored on December 12, 1939.

SARNIA   The name, Port Sarnia, was suggested by Sir John Colborne, who visited the area in 1839 (during his term as Lieutenant-Governor). Sarnia was the Roman name for the island of Guernsey.

SAUBLE BEACH   A corruption of the French *sable*, "sand". Descriptive of the local sand dunes.

SAUGEEN RIVER   Derived from the Ojibway *saging*, translated as "at the mouth" (of a river), early name for the Bruce Peninsula (*Smith's Gazetteer*, 1846).

SAULT STE. MARIE   First known as Sault de Gaston for a brother of King Louis XIII, it was renamed when a Jesuit mission was established here in the mid seventeenth century. Sainte Marie du Sault, or Saint Mary of the Rapids, was an early designation.

SCARBOROUGH   After the town of Scarborough, Yorkshire, England. The "craggy cliffs" to be found in both locations suggested the name to the wife of John Graves Simcoe.

SCHREIBER   Marks the career of Sir Collingwood Schreiber (1831–1918), a civil engineer and later Deputy Minister in the Department of Railways and Canals.

SCHUMACHER   Name taken from the Schumacher Mine. Now part of the city of Timmins.

SCUGOG   Township, lake, island, and river. From an Amerindian designation for "muddy bottom" or "submerged land" (CPCGN files).

SEAFORTH   Possibly for the Earl of Seaforth or for a loch in Inverness-shire, Scotland. Incorporated as a village in 1868 and as a town in 1874.

SEVERN RIVER   Named by the explorer Captain Thomas James (1593–1635?) after the River Severn, England. First known as the New Severn. *See* James Bay, Quebec

SHARBOT LAKE   After the Sharbot family, who were local residents. Appears in *Lowell's Gazetteer,* 1874.

SHELBURNE   Originally Jellys Corners for William Jelly, an early settler. Name changed in 1865 to mark the career of Lord Shelburne (1737–1805).

SIMCOE   County, town, lake, and island. The county and town were named for John Graves Simcoe (1752–1806), who served as Lieutenant-Governor from 1791 to 1799. Earlier, Governor Simcoe had named the lake after his father, Captain John Simcoe, R.N. Simcoe Island (Frontenac County) was also named after Captain Simcoe.

SIOUX LOOKOUT   The "precipitous hill" where the Ojibway "kept watch up and down the waterways for raiding Sioux" (CPCGN files).

SMITHS FALLS   For Major Thomas Smyth, a United Empire Loyalist, who received a grant of land in the area on September

21, 1804. Originally called Smith's Falls; an act of the Ontario legislature was required to remove the apostrophe.

SMITHVILLE   The early name was Griffintown after Richard Griffin, a United Empire Loyalist; renamed by his son, Smith Griffin, "in memory of his mother's maiden name".

SMOOTH ROCK FALLS   Descriptive – the building of a dam in 1915 caused water to flow over a huge smooth rock. Incorporated 1929.

SNYE RIVER   *See* Chenail Écarté

SOUTHAMPTON   The earlier name Saugeen was changed in 1895 in honour of Southampton, England.

SOUTH PORCUPINE   *See* Porcupine

SPANISH RIVER   First called the Spaniard's River for an early Spanish or Mexican settler who married the daughter of an Amerindian chief. He was referred to as "L'Espagneul". *See also* Espanola (OGNB files).

STAMFORD   Name assigned in 1792 by John Graves Simcoe for Stamford, Lincolnshire, England. Now part of the city of Niagara Falls.

STAYNER   Listed as Nottawasage on early maps and later called Dingwall. Renamed for Sutherland Stayner, a prominent local landowner. Name dates from 1862. *See* Nottawasaga

STIRLING   For Stirling, Scotland, "because the first settlers thought that the surrounding countryside resembled Stirlingshire" (CPCGN files). Post office dates from 1852.

STITTSVILLE   Settled in 1818 by Jackson Stitt. Post office established 1854. Incorporated 1961. Now part of the municipal township of Goulbourn.

STONEY CREEK   Not a descriptive, but named for Edmund Stoney, an early settler.

STOUFFVILLE   After Abraham Stouffer, who moved to the area from Pennsylvania in 1806. On January 1, 1971, it became part of the town of Whitchurch–Stouffville.

STRATFORD   From Stratford-on-Avon, England. Originally Little Thames, the name was changed in 1835.

STRATHROY   Derived from the Gaelic *strathan*, "a valley", and *ruadh*, "reddish". Incorporated as a town in 1870. Originally Strath Valley or Red Valley, it was named about 1832 by John Stewart Buchanan for Strathroy, County Antrim, Northern Ireland.

STREETSVILLE   Founded by Timothy Street and named in his honour. Amalgamated with Mississauga on January 1, 1974.

STURGEON FALLS   First known as Barrier Falls, the town was renamed for the river, which in turn was named for the fish.

SUDBURY   Name given to the town by James Worthington, one-time superintendent of construction of the C.P.R. main line. After Sudbury, Suffolk, England, the birthplace of his wife.

SUNDERLAND   For Sunderland, Durham, England. First post office was known as Brock. Name changed in 1868 to Sunderland.

SUNDRIDGE   For Sundridge, a parish in Kent, England. The post office dates from 1879.

SUPERIOR, LAKE   Called by the Amerindians *Kitchigami*, "great water". On Jesuit maps of 1670–1 it is designated Lac Tracy ou Supérieur (for the Marquis de Tracy, 1603–70). Gradually Superior became the accepted name for the "upper one of the chain of great lakes because it is superior to any of the others in size" (Johnson Papers, PAC).

SUTTON   After Sutton parish, Yorkshire, England, it is now within the municipal township of Georgina.

SWANSEA   For Swansea, Wales. Now a part of the city of Toronto.

SWASTIKA   Included in present-day Kirkland Lake. Survived a determined effort to have name changed to Winston (for Winston Churchill) during the Second World War. "Called Swastika after the good luck charm on a lady's necklace" (OGNB files). Dates from 1906.

SYDENHAM   After Lord Sydenham (1799–1841), Governor General from 1839 to 1841.

TAVISTOCK   Name assigned by postal authorities in 1857. For Tavistock, Devonshire, England.

TECUMSEH   Derived from the Tecumseh road, "which was used by the famous Indian chief [Tecumseh] as a pathway" (CPCGN files).

TEESWATER   Named by an early survey party for the River Tees in England. Post office dates from 1855.

THAMESFORD   First called St. Andrews, the town changed its name in the mid nineteenth century because of its location on the Thames River. *See above*

THAMES RIVER   Name changed by proclamation from La Tranche on July 16, 1792. Another example of John Graves Simcoe's interest in assigning English place names to Canadian locations.

THAMESVILLE For the River Thames (*see above*). Post office established in 1832.

THEDFORD Traceable to Thetford, Vermont; however, a "misinterpretation of handwriting made it Thedford". Name changed in 1859 from the earlier Widder Station.

THESSALON Appears on early maps as Tessalon (Galinee, 1670), and later as Pointe aux Thessalons (Bellin, 1775). A corruption of an earlier Amerindian descriptive *Neyashewun*, meaning "a point of land".

THISTLETOWN Renamed in 1847 because the original name, St. Andrews, caused confusion with St. Andrews, New Brunswick. Honours Dr. J. A. Thistle, a local physician.

THORNBURY Probably after Thornbury, Somersetshire, England. Post office from 1854 onward.

THORNHILL Marks the career of one of the first merchants in the district, Benjamin Thorne, who settled there in 1822.

THOROLD After Sir John Thorold (1734–1815), a member of the British Parliament when the township was established in 1788. Incorporated as a town in 1875.

THUNDER BAY District and city. A translation of an Amerindian descriptive *Animikie Wekwed*, meaning "thunder bay". In folklore the thunderbird is the common personification or cause of thunder in many ancient legends. Adopted January 1, 1970, as the new name for the amalgamation of the cities of Fort William and Port Arthur, and the townships of McIntyre and Neebing. *See also* Fort William *and* Port Arthur

TILBURY Taken from Tilbury, Essex, England, it was originally Tilbury Centre; however, the word "centre" was dropped in 1895.

TILLSONBURG   Honours George Tillson (1782–1864), founder and one of the first settlers. For a time known as Tilsonburg. Name changed back to Tillsonburg on March 17, 1902, by an act of the Ontario legislature.

TIMAGAMI, LAKE   Of Amerindian origin, the probable meaning is "deep water" or "deep lake".

TIMMINS   After Noah A. Timmins (1867–1936), President of the Hollinger Consolidated Gold Mine Ltd. Mine claim staked in 1909.

TORONTO   Details surrounding exact origin are uncertain. Usually thought to be a Huron word translated as "a place of meeting". Listed as *Tarantou* (Sanson, 1656). Fort Rouillé (Fort Toronto) was built on the site by the French in 1749. In 1793, Governor John Graves Simcoe moved the capital from Newark (Niagara) to Toronto Bay and renamed it York. In 1834 the city was incorporated as Toronto.

TOTTENHAM   For John Totten, an early settler, and Alexander Totten, the first postmaster (1858).

TRENTON   The first name, Trent Port or Trent Town, was abbreviated to Trenton. The town is situated at the mouth of the Trent River, which in turn was named for the River Trent in England.

TWEED   From the River Tweed, Scotland. The post office was established in 1852.

UNIONVILLE   Possibly selected as a compromise name by early residents. The settlement dates from the early 1830s.

UXBRIDGE   Named by its founder, Joseph Gould, after Uxbridge, Middlesex, England. A local legend suggests that the town was nicknamed Oxbridge and the name was later changed to Uxbridge; however, the story cannot be authenticated. On January 1, 1974, the town of Uxbridge and the townships of Scott and Uxbridge became the township of Uxbridge in the regional municipality of Durham.

VAL ALBERT Name taken from that of an early settler and assigned by postal authorities on October 7, 1936, "to correspond with the village known as [Val] Albert" (CPCGN files). Annexed by Kapuskasing on January 1, 1974.

VALLEY FROST A descriptive name. The town was established on January 1, 1973, in the regional municipality of Sudbury.

VANIER Replaced the earlier name "Eastview" on January 1, 1969. Commemorates the career of Governor General Georges P. Vanier (1888–1967). *See* Vanier, Quebec

VANKLEEK HILL Traceable to the name of the first settler, Simeon Van Kleek, a United Empire Loyalist from Dutchess County in New York State.

VAUGHAN Named for Benjamin Vaughan, one of the British negotiators at the Treaty of Paris, 1783. Vaughan Township was established in 1792. On January 1, 1971, the town of Vaughan was created.

VERNER From the family name of the wife of A. Baker, one-time general superintendent of the Canadian Pacific Railway.

VINELAND Descriptive – because of its location in the fruit belt of the Niagara peninsula. Post office established 1894.

VIRGIL Chosen to replace the earlier name, Cross Roads. For the Roman poet.

VIRGINIATOWN After Virginia, wife of George B. Webster, an executive in the local Kerr-Addison gold mine.

WALDEN   Established on January 1, 1973, as a result of an amalgamation of the town of Lively and surrounding townships. The name is an acronym formed from *Wa*ters, *L*ively, and *Den*ison.

WALKERTON   Named for Joseph Walker, who settled in the area in 1850 and helped develop the town.

WALKERVILLE   First known as Walker Town and after 1858 as Walkerville. It was named for Hiram Walker (1816–99), a pioneer distiller. Annexed to Windsor, July 1, 1935.

WALLACEBURG   In all probability a tribute to Sir William Wallace, "the great champion of Scottish independence". Area largely settled by Scots.

WASAGA BEACH   Derived from the name Nottawasaga, translated as "outlet of invaders [Iroquois]". *See* Nottawasaga. Incorporated as a town on January 1, 1974.

WATERDOWN   A descriptive – this town was the location of an early mill. The post office dates from 1840.

WATERFORD   Named either for the city and county in Ireland or for a similar place in New York State. Founded as a result of the Loyalist migration; now part of the city of Nanticoke.

WATERLOO   In commemoration of the Battle of Waterloo, 1815. The township was named in 1817; Waterloo County in 1849. The community became a village in 1857 and a town in 1876, and achieved city status in 1948.

WATFORD   Named after Watford in Hertfordshire, England.

WAWA   The name is Ojibway for "goose" or "wild goose". Survived an attempt at being renamed Jamestown for Sir James Dunn in the 1950s. *See* p. 11

WELLAND The town was first known as The Aqueduct because of a wooden aqueduct built to divert the river; later the name was changed to Merrittsville for William Hamilton Merritt. The county, town, and river all take their name from the Welland River, Lincolnshire, England.

WELLESLEY The township name honours Richard Wellesley (1760–1842), eldest brother of the Duke of Wellington. The village was named after the township. On January 1, 1973, the village and township of Wellesley were amalgamated to form the municipal township of Wellesley.

WELLINGTON Village in Prince Edward County. Named for Arthur Wellesley, Duke of Wellington (1769–1852). The name was suggested to postal authorities by John Young, a resident of the district.

WEST LORNE Sometimes listed on nineteenth-century maps as Bismarck-Lorne. The present name was adopted in 1903 and is taken from "one of the titles of the Duke of Argyll" (CPCGN files).

WESTPORT Name chosen in 1845 to describe the location by Aaron Chambers and Louis Cameron, local businessmen. The post office dates from 1845.

WHEATLEY Named for one of the first settlers, Richard Wheatley (?–1837). The post office was established in 1864.

WHITBY The name, taken from the seaport town of Whitby, Yorkshire, England, was adopted in 1855 to replace Perry's Corners.

WHITE RIVER A descriptive for the white water on the river. Reputed to have the coldest recorded temperatures in Ontario.

WHITNEY Named for E. C. Whitney, managing director of the St. Anthony Lumber Company (Johnson Papers, PAC).

WIARTON From Wiarton Place, near Maidstone, Kent, England, birthplace of Sir Edmund Walker Head (1805–68), who was serving as Governor General at the time of the original survey.

WINCHESTER Applied first to the township in 1798 for the city of Winchester, England.

WINDMILL POINT Site of a windmill near Prescott which figured in an invasion from the United States, November 1838.

WINDSOR Named in 1834 for Windsor, England. Incorporated as a village in 1854, and as a town in 1858; achieved city status in 1935.

WINGHAM After Wingham parish and village, Kent, England. The post office dates from 1862.

WINISK Lake and river. The name may be translated from the Cree as "groundhog" or "woodchuck"; *Winiskisis* means "little woodchuck river".

WOLFE ISLAND Honours General James Wolfe (1725–59), killed at the battle of the Plains of Abraham in 1759. The name was changed by proclamation in 1792 from the earlier Grande Isle (once part of La Salle's seigniory).

WOODBRIDGE Adopted in 1854 to prevent confusion over original name, Burwick, which was chosen in 1837 for Rowland Burr. Probably descriptive. Amalgamated with the town of Vaughan on January 1, 1971.

WOODSTOCK Originally named Oxford by Governor Simcoe after Oxfordshire, England. The location was also known as Town Plot until about 1833, when it was renamed for Woodstock, England.

WUNNUMMIN LAKE Of Amerindian origin, the name may

be translated as "red paint". It is probably a corruption of an Amerindian descriptive. *See also* Onaping

WYOMING   From the town and valley of the same name in Pennsylvania, the name was assigned by railway officials in 1856.

ZURICH   Settled by German immigrants and named for the city in Switzerland.

Prince Edward Island

 The island appears under the name Île de Saint Jean in Champlain's narrative (1604) and on his map (1632); however, according to Ganong, the name is of earlier origin. After its acquisition by the British in 1759 the island was known as St. John's Island until the name was changed in 1798 to honour Prince Edward, Duke of Kent (1767–1820), father of Queen Victoria, then in command of the British forces at Halifax. Separated from Nova Scotia in 1769, Prince Edward Island entered Confederation on July 1, 1873.

ABEGWEIT PASSAGE   Derived from the original Amerindian name for Prince Edward Island. It is traceable to the Micmac *Abahquit*, "lying parallel with the land", or *Epegweit*, "to be lying in the water". Applied in 1962 to the passage between New Brunswick and Prince Edward Island traversed by M.V. *Abegweit*, a C.N.R. car ferry.

ABRAMS VILLAGE   May be traced to an early settler, Abraham Arsenault. Formerly rendered as Abraham's village.

ALBERTON   For Albert Edward, Prince of Wales, later King Edward VII (1841–1910), who visited Prince Edward Island in 1860.

ANNANDALE   Named in 1868 by James Johnston, an early settler, who emigrated from Annandale, Dumfries-shire, Scotland, in 1840. *See entries for* New Annan, P.E.I. *and* N.S.

BASIN HEAD   Descriptive. The name evolved from the shape of Basin Head Harbour.

BAY FORTUNE   *See* Fortune River

BEDEQUE   The name is said to originate with the Micmac *Petekook*, "the place that lies on the backward turn" (Ganong). Appeared as Bedek on early maps, "a token of French influence" (Douglas). *See* Baddeck, Nova Scotia

BELFAST   Name assigned in the 1770s by Captain James Smith for Belfast, Ireland. The post office was established in 1832.

BELLE RIVER   A descriptive which is traceable to the French period. Belle Rivière (Franquet, 1751).

BIDEFORD   The area was settled by "Westcountrymen" who named the district for their home town in Devonshire, England. Dates from 1818.

BORDEN   The ferry terminal was established in 1917 and named for Sir Robert Borden (1854–1937), the Prime Minister.

BRACKLEY   Bay, point, and beach. Named after A. Brackley (?–1776), who served as clerk of the Legislative Council from 1772 to 1776.

BRUDENELL POINT   Takes its name from Brudenell (*see below*). In 1731 Jean-Pierre Roma (fl. 1715–57), together with three associates, was granted all the land drained by the three rivers now known as Brudenell, Montague, and Cardigan. His settlement, Trois-Rivières, was located on present-day Brudenell Point.

BRUDENELL RIVER   The name was assigned by Captain Samuel Holland in honour of George Brudenell, Earl of Cardigan (1712–90). *See* Cardigan *and* Brudenell Point

CAPE TRAVERSE   The name dates from the French period – Rivière de la Traverse (de la Roque, 1752) – and was later applied to the nearby cape. This was a reference to the cape as the nearest point to the mainland. The name is now applied to the settlement, while the cape is known as Bells Point.

CARDIGAN   From Cardigan Bay and River, named for George Brudenell, Earl of Cardigan (1712–90). *See* Brudenell *and* Montague

CASCUMPEC BAY   Of Amerindian origin, the name may be traced to the Micmac word *Kaskamkek* for "sandy shore". The earlier spelling, Cascumpeque, was changed in 1966.

CAVENDISH   Name bestowed by Captain William Winter, a local landholder, in honour of his patron, Field-Marshal Lord Frederick Cavendish (1729–1803). The post office was established in 1833.

CHARLOTTETOWN   Listed as Charlotte Town on the Holland

Survey map of 1765, the city was named for Queen Charlotte (1744–1818), the consort of King George III. Incorporated as a town in 1855 and as a city in 1875.

CHERRY VALLEY   Possibly named for "an abundant growth of wild cherries" (CPCGN files), or for a place of the same name in Devonshire, or for Cherry Valley in New York State (Rayburn).

COLVILLE BAY   Assigned by Samuel Holland for Lord Colville (1717–70).

CRAPAUD   The name was originally applied to the river by the French – *rivière aux crapauds*, or "river of toads". Spelled Crappaux in a memorial dated February 20, 1818. A community name since 1857.

DESABLE   From the French *rivière de sable* or "sand river".

DEVILS PUNCHBOWL PROVINCIAL PARK   Named by John Hawkins for an incident in the pioneer period when reputedly "the devil ordered him to cut loose a cargo of rum . . . a story which met with considerable doubt" (Public Archives P.E.I.).

DUNK RIVER   Named by Captain Samuel Holland for George Montague Dunk (1716–71), Earl of Halifax. *See* Halifax, Nova Scotia

EGMONT BAY   Also named by Holland (*see above*) for John Perceval, Earl of Egmont (1711–70), who developed "a feudal fantasy [of landholding] which would have made the island a museum of mediaeval society" (Clark). Although the idea was rejected, it may have inspired the later land-allocation scheme which was to complicate Island history for a century.

FORT AMHERST NATIONAL HISTORIC PARK   Originally the location was known as Fort La Joie and was a French settlement. It was captured in 1758 and a new fort was erected on the site.

On October 10, 1758, Lord Rollo reported the completion of Fort Amherst, named for his superior, Major-General Jeffrey Amherst (1717–97). *See* Rollo Bay

FORTUNE RIVER   The name appears as Rivière à la Fortune (de la Roque, 1752). It was later applied to Bay Fortune at the mouth of the river.

GEORGETOWN   Assigned by Samuel Holland in honour of King George III (1738–1820). Incorporated as a town in 1912.

GOVERNORS ISLAND   For Robert-David Gotteville de Belile (fl. 1696–1724), who served as "commandant de l'Île Saint-Jean" from 1719 to 1722.

GREEN GABLES   Post office at Cavendish since 1953. Derived from the name of a nearby house made famous by Lucy Maud Montgomery (1874–1942) in the "Anne" series of books.

GREEN PARK   A provincial park that centres around the residence of James Yeo (1832–1916), built in 1865. A descriptive coined by Yeo for his property.

HAZELGROVE   Originally the name of an inn which was kept by Richard Bagnall. The name dates from about 1813 (Rayburn).

HILLSBOROUGH BAY
HILLSBOROUGH RIVER   Named for Wills Hill (1718–93), Earl of Hillsborough.

HUNTER RIVER   Honours Thomas Orby Hunter, who served as Lord of the Admiralty in 1761.

KENSINGTON   Previous to the opening of the Prince Edward Island Railway the community was known as Barretts Cross after an early tavernkeeper, Mrs. Barrett. The new name (after Kensington, London, England) was adopted at a public meeting in the early 1870s.

LENNOX ISLAND   For Charles Lennox, third Duke of Richmond (1735–1806).

MALPEQUE BAY   This name is a French variation of the Micmac *Makpaak* for "large bay".

MISCOUCHE   The name is derived from the Micmac *Menisgotjg* for "little marshy place" (Father Pacifique). It may also be a corruption of the Micmac *Manuskooch*, "little grassy island", which was first applied to Miscouche Island (Douglas).

MONTAGUE   Name bestowed in 1765 by Captain Samuel Holland for George Brudenell (1712–90), Earl of Cardigan, who was later created Duke of Montague. Rayburn suggests the name may "also have been given in honour of Montague Wilmot, governor of Nova Scotia from 1763 to 1766, which then included Prince Edward Island".

MORELL   The name originates with Jean-François Morel, whose family resided in the area in 1752.

MOUNT STEWART   Honours John Stewart (1758–1834), who emigrated from Scotland in 1778. He served as Speaker of the House of Assembly and published in 1806 *An Account of Prince Edward Island.*

MURRAY HARBOUR
MURRAY RIVER   Commemorates the career of James Murray (1719–94), who served as Governor of Quebec from 1763 to 1768.

NEW ANNAN   Named by William "Squire" Jamieson, who emigrated to this area from Annan, Dumfries-shire, Scotland, in the 1820s. *See* Annandale *and* New Annan, Nova Scotia

NEW GLASGOW   The settlement was established in 1819 by William Epps Cormack (1796–1868) and named for Glasgow, Scotland. *See* Cormack *and* Mount Cormack, Newfoundland

NORTHUMBERLAND STRAIT   The exact origin is uncertain, but probably it was assigned by J. F. W. Des Barres in 1764 for H.M.S. *Northumberland*, flagship of Lord Colville. Originally named Baie de Saint Lunario by Cartier, who entered the northern end of the strait on July 1, 1534, the day of St. Lunarius. *See* the opening chapter. The southern end was referred to as the Red Sea (Morris, 1749). According to Holland "the sea betwixt the island and [the mainland] is frequently of a red hue . . . by many people called the 'Red Sea'."

O'LEARY   Named after Michael O'Leary, an early settler; it was known first as O'Leary Road. The post office dates from 1877.

ORWELL   Bay, cove, and river. All three names are traceable to Lord Orwell, who served as Lord Commissioner of Trade and Plantations from 1762 to 1765. Orwell Corner is now the site of a restored nineteenth-century village.

POINT PRIM   A corruption of "prime", the first or south point of the compass. "Pte du Sud ou de prime" (Franquet, 1851). Point Prim has been in common usage since the early nineteenth century.

PORT HILL   Named by the "Westcountrymen" for the residence of A. S. Willet, near Bideford, Devonshire, England.

ROLLO BAY   Commemorates the career of Lieutenant-Colonel Andrew Rollo, fifth Baron Rollo (1703–65), British army officer who served at Louisbourg (1758) and later arranged for the capitulation of Île Saint-Jean and the removal of its inhabitants. *See* Fort Amherst

ROYALTY   When Charlottetown was surveyed in 1765, certain lands in the immediate vicinity were reserved for the Crown and termed "royalty". The word has persisted as a place name, e.g. West Royalty and Royalty Junction.

RUSTICO After René Rassicot, who emigrated to Île Saint-Jean in 1724 from Avanches, Normandy.

ST. ELEANORS For Eleanor Sanskey, daughter of Colonel Harold Compton, an officer in the Prince Edward Island Militia. The post office was established in 1833.

ST. PETERS BAY The settlement dates from the French period, and was named by Louis Denys de la Ronde Havre St. Pierre for Comte de St. Pierre, equerry to the Duchess of Orléans.

SEACOW HEAD (LOT 26) A promontory at the entrance to Summerside Harbour, so designated because early settlers found tusks of the seacow, or walrus, on the shore. Also Sea Cow Pond (Lot 1): "Walrus were once common in this locality. A number came ashore [in the 1840s] about two miles from North Cape." (CPCGN files)

SOURIS In the eighteenth century, "periodically the area was infested by mice, which came seemingly all at once ... not field mice not yet the house mice, but something between" (CPCGN files). The name dates from the French period, Havre à la Souris, for Colville Bay (Bellin, 1744). The name is possibly a corruption of Havre à l'Echoverie, "barred harbour", with the incorrect name, Havre à la Souris, becoming fixed as a result of the numerous plagues of mice (Rayburn). *See* Souris, Manitoba

STRATHGARTNEY PARK A provincial park which was once the estate of Robert Bruce Stewart. It was named after a valley in Perthshire, Scotland.

SUMMERSIDE For Summerside House, a licensed inn, which was established in 1840. Incorporated as a town in 1877.

TIGNISH   The name is derived from Micmac sources and is probably a variation of *Tedeneche*, "straight across", a reference to the straight entrance to the river (Rayburn).

TRAVELLERS REST   Originally the name of an inn or public house. Dates from the early 1800s.

TRYON   Assigned by Captain Samuel Holland for William Tryon (1725–88), who served as Governor of North Carolina in 1765 and of New York in 1771.

VERNON RIVER   Also named by Holland (*see above*) for Sir Edward Vernon (1723–94), an admiral of the British Navy.

WOOD ISLANDS   Descriptive. Originally known as Isles à Bois (Franquet, 1751).

Québec

 The name was applied first to the region of the modern city and the word is of undoubted Algonquin origin. Early spellings: Quebecq (Levasseur, 1601); Kébec (Lescarbot, 1609); Quebec (Champlain, 1613). Champlain wrote of the location in 1632: "It . . . is a strait of the river, so called by the Indians" – a reference to the Algonquin word for "narrow passage" or "strait" to indicate the narrowing of the river at Cape Diamond. The term is common to the Algonquin, Cree, and Micmac languages and signifies the same in each dialect.

ABBOTSFORD   Originally Yamaska Mountain, the name was changed in 1829 upon the suggestion of Bishop Jacob Mountain. For the Rev. Joseph Abbott (1789–1863), the first Anglican clergyman in the district and father of Sir John J. C. Abbott, third Prime Minister of Canada. The municipality is Saint-Paul-d'Abbotsford. *See* Abbotsford, British Columbia

ABITIBI   *See* Ontario *entry*

ACTON VALE   The community was founded in 1859 and takes its name from one of nine Actons in England. Most probably for Acton, Middlesex.

AHUNTSIC   Named for an Amerindian, who on June 25, 1625, witnessed the assassination of Abbé Nicolas Viel at a place now called Sault-au-Récollet.

ALBANEL   Honours the Rev. Charles Albanel (1616–96), Jesuit missionary and explorer.

ALENÇON   Possibly for Alençon, a city in the Department of Orne, France.

ALLUMETTE ISLAND   The French word for "match", indicating that the reeds which grew in quantity on the island were once used for matches.

ALMA   The name marks the Battle of Alma in the Crimean War (1854). Alma Island (east end of Lac-Saint-Jean) is also named for the same battle, which coincided with the original survey of the island by J. Duberger.

AMOS   Named for Lady Alice Gouin (née Amos), wife of Sir Lomer Gouin, Premier of Québec from 1905 to 1920.

AMQUI   An adaption of a Micmac place name, meaning "playground" or "place of amusement". The parish dates from

1881. *See also* Saint-Léon-le-Grand.

ANCIENNE-LORETTE   Named by Abbé Pierre-Joseph-Marie Chaumonot (1611–93), who lived for a time near Loreto, Italy. Incorporated as a town in 1967. Previously known as Notre-Dame-de-Lorette.

ANDRÉVILLE   The community was placed under the patronage of St. André in honour of André Fraser, an early settler in the district. Post office is Saint-André-de-Kamouraska.

ANGE-GARDIEN   The name originated with the church erected in 1670. A painting of the guardian angel was placed over the main altar.

ANGERS   For Angers, a city in the Department of Maine-et-Loire in France.

ANSE-AU-GRIFFON   The name appears on the Bellin map of 1744. It is probably derived from the name of a ship, the *Griffon*.

ANTICOSTI   Ganong suggests that *Natistco(s)ti*, of very early origin, in its first known map form is traceable to the sixteenth century and "is another of the fine native names preserved for us by Cartier". The word is undoubtedly of Amerindian (Huron, Iroquois, or Montagnais) derivation and is said to mean "hunting ground of the bear". There is no evidence to prove a possible Spanish origin: *ante*, "before" or "beyond", and *costa*, for "coast".

ARMAGH   After Armagh, a city and county in Ulster, Northern Ireland.

ARTHABASKA   The name is derived from the Cree *Ayabaskaw*, meaning "a place obstructed by reeds and grass".

ARUNDEL   For a town in Sussex, England.

ARVIDA   A coined name taken from the first two letters of each of *Ar*thur *Vi*ning *Da*vis, an official of the Aluminum Company of Canada.

ASBESTOS   The name originated with the discovery of asbestos deposits in the vicinity.

ATHELSTAN   A variation of Athelstaneford, a village near Haddington, East Lothian, Scotland.

AUDET   Probably for an early settler of this name.

AYER'S CLIFF   After Thomas Ayer, one of the first settlers in the area. The name was changed from Ayers Flat to Ayers Cliff in 1904.

AYLMER   First known as Symnes Landing for Charles Symnes, it was renamed in 1847 to honour Lord Aylmer (1755–1850), who served as Governor General of Canada from 1831 to 1835.

BAGOTVILLE   After Sir Charles Bagot (1781–1843), who served as Governor General during the years from 1841 to 1843. The settlement dates from 1839.

BAIE-COMEAU   Honours Napoléon Alexandre Comeau, a prominent local resident. The town was founded in 1936.

BAIE-DE-SHAWINIGAN   *See* Shawinigan

BAIE-DES-SABLES   A descriptive. Originally Sandy Beach; later, as settlement became French-speaking, the name was changed to Baie-des-Sables. The parish was established in 1850.

BAIE-D'URFÉ   Named for François-Saturnin Lascaris d'Urfé (1641–1701), a Sulpician missionary who served the area from 1667 to 1687.

BAIE-SAINT-PAUL The name is taken from the local parish, which dates from 1681 (Charlevoix County).

BAIEVILLE A descriptive indicating its location on a bay (a part of Lac-Saint-Pierre). Originally Baie-du-Febvre. The nearby seigniory of Baie-Saint-Antoine was granted in 1683 to Sieur Jacques Le Febvre.

BARRAUTE Named for Jean-Pierre Bachois, Sieur de Barraute, who served as an officer under Montcalm. The village was established in 1916.

BARVILLE Formerly known as Val-Laflamme, the present name was coined in 1954 from Barview Mines, a major industry in the area. The town was founded in 1950 and incorporated in 1953.

BASKATONG Of Algonquin origin, the name is translated in the 18th *Annual Report* of the G.B.C. as "where the water is [contracted] by sand", a possible reference to the narrows of the lake.

BATISCAN River and parish. Dates from 1639; parish established in 1684. This name is a Montagnais word translated by Father Arnaud as "light mist", for the mist frequently encountered at the mouth of the river.

BEACONSFIELD In commemoration of Benjamin Disraeli (1804–81), first Earl of Beaconsfield, British Prime Minister in 1868, and from 1874 to 1880. *See also* Disraeli

BEAUCEVILLE Named for the region of Beauce in northern France. The settlement of Beauce County also dates from the early eighteenth century. Beauceville-Est was once part of the town of Beauceville.

BEAUHARNOIS Honours Marquis Charles de Beauharnois de

la Boische (1670–1749), Governor General of New France from 1726 to 1746.

BEAUMONT From the seigniory of Beaumont, which was granted in 1672 to Charles Couillard, Sieur des Ilets. The parish was established in 1714.

BEAUPORT Two theories as to origin of this name:
1. from Robert Giffard (1587–1668), Sieur de Beauport, the seigniory, after the river, taking its name from the "beau port" at the river's mouth;
2. may have been named for a bay of the same name in Brittany.
The community dates from 1634.

BEAUPRÉ The name is possibly a descriptive, *beau pré*, or "beautiful meadow"; or for Viscount de Beaupré, who accompanied Cartier on his explorations in 1641.

BÉCANCOUR Town and river. Honours Pierre Robineau, Sieur de Bécancour (1654–1729), Chief Road Commissioner of New France from 1689 to 1729.

BEDFORD Formerly known as Stanbridge Falls, the town was renamed after Bedford, England. Founded in 1817; incorporated in 1890.

BEEBE PLAIN The name originated with the founders of the settlement in 1798, David and Calvin Beebe.

BELLECHASSE Island, bay, and county. The islands were designated on Champlain's map in 1629 as Îles-de-Chasse, the general name suggested by the excellence of local hunting conditions.

BELLETERRE The name is derived from the Belleterre Mining Company, which opened gold and silver mines in the district in 1936.

BELOEIL   The seigniory was established in 1694. It was possibly named for Beloeil, a town in Belgium near the French border, or is more simply a descriptive used in place of Bellevue to indicate a beautiful sight.

BERNIERVILLE   Honours Abbé M. Bernier, who served some thirty-six years as parish priest. Incorporated in 1898.

BERTHIER
BERTHIERVILLE   After Isaac Berthier (1638–1708), called Alexandre after 1665, captain in the Régiment de l'Allier de Carignan, who purchased the seigniory in 1673 from the original grantee, Sieur de Randin.

BETSIAMITES   River and town. The name is of Montagnais origin. The Betsiamites were a Montagnais tribe that originally inhabited the area. The name has been interpreted as designating "the area where there are lampreys".

BIC   The name originated with Champlain (1603) and is a corruption of *pic*, "peak". A portion of the seigniory of Bic was granted in 1675 to Charles Denys de Vitré (1645–1703), member of the Sovereign Council. Appears as Bic on the Bellin map of 1744. Also Île du Bic (opposite the village), originally Île du Massacre, for the seventeenth-century massacre by the Iroquois of a group of Micmacs (Ganong).

BIENVILLE, LAC   For Jean Baptiste le Moyne, Sieur de Bienville (1680–1767), who participated in a successful attack on Fort Nelson, Hudson Bay, in 1697. He was later Governor of Louisiana.

BIZARD ISLAND (ÎLE-BIZARD)   Named for Jacques Bizard (1642–92), who served as town-major of Montréal from 1677 to 1692. Bizard was granted the island in 1678 as a seigniory. Formerly Île-Bonaventure.

BLACK LAKE   A descriptive assigned because of the shadows cast by nearby mountains. Incorporated in 1906.

BLAINVILLE Derived from the married name of Anne-Marie-Thérèse Piot de Langloiserie, whose husband was Jean-Baptiste Celeron de Blainville. *See also* Sainte-Thérèse

BLANC SABLON A descriptive name meaning "white sand", dating from the narrative of Jacques Cartier. It may have been suggested by a similar place name in Brittany.

BOISBRIAND Possibly named for an old fief on Montreal island called Boisbriant (Rayburn).

BOIS-DES-FILION The name originated with the Fillion family, early settlers in the region. The town was incorporated in 1949.

BONAVENTURE ISLAND Probably named by Cartier as Bonne Aventure; less likely for the *Bonaventure*, a ship owned by Count de Pré-Ravillon et de Grandpré, discoverer of the walrus fishery in the Gulf of St. Lawrence.

BONSECOURS After the local seigniory of Bonsecours. Parish dates from 1679.

BOUCHERVILLE Honours Pierre Boucher, Sieur de Grosbois (?–1717), founder of the seigniory and Governor of Trois-Rivières from 1663 to 1665.

BOURLAMAQUE Established in 1920 and named for François-Charles de Bourlamaque (1716–64), a French army officer and aide-de-camp to Montcalm.

BRION ISLAND Named by Cartier in 1534 after the patron of his expedition, Admiral Philippe de Chabot, Sieur de Brion.

BROMONT Formerly West Shefford, the name was changed to

Bromont (a coined word, from Mont-Brome in Brome County) by order-in-council of July 20, 1966. The village of Adamsville amalgamated with Bromont on December 20, 1972.

BROMPTONVILLE   The village was established in 1804 and first became known as Brompton Falls, after Brompton in England – either the district in the city of London or the town in Yorkshire.

BROSSARD   The original name was Brosseau Station; it was changed in 1958 to avoid confusion with similar names.

BROWNSBURG   Named for its founder, George Brown, who established a sawmill in the area in 1818.

BRYSON   Earlier names: Hargreaves and Havelock. The latter was changed in 1873 in honour of George Bryson (1813–1900), member of the Quebec Legislative Council and prominent lumberman in the district.

BUCKINGHAM   The first settlers came from Buckinghamshire, England, in 1827. The town was named for its English counterpart.

BURY   Named in 1803 for the village of Bury, in Lancashire, England.

CABANO   From Lake Cabano, which is surrounded by steep-sided hills, giving the appearance of the walls of a cabin. Parish dates from 1905.

CACOUNA   Originally formed part of the seigniory of Rivière-du-Loup, or Kakouna. The word is from the Cree *kakouna*, which may be translated as "home of the porcupine". Founded in 1806.

CADILLAC   Settled in the 1930s and named for an officer in the Berry regiment of Montcalm's army. Incorporated on December 21, 1940.

CALUMET   Town, river, and island. The name is of French origin: *le calumet de paix*, after the "pipe of peace" frequently used in Amerindian ceremonies.

CAMPBELL'S BAY   Named for Donald Campbell, industrialist.

CANDIAC   "The name recalls the estate where the Montcalm family possessed a château, which is situated in Languedoc, the place of Montcalm's birth." (Beauregard)

CAP-À-L'AIGLE   Name bestowed by Champlain in 1608 because of the numerous eagles found on the cape.

CAP-AUX-MEULES   Island and village. The name is a descriptive, so called because two of the hills on the island resemble grindstones, translated in French as *meules*.

CAP CHAT   Probably named by Champlain for Commander Aymar de Chaste, under whose auspices he made his voyage in 1603. Corrupted spelling appears on Bellin map of 1744.

CAP-DE-GASPÉ   *See* Gaspé

CAP-DE-LA-MADELEINE   Originally Cap-des-Trois-Rivières, the location was renamed Cap-de-la-Madeleine by Abbé La Ferté (of Sainte-Marie-Madeleine-de-Châteaudun, diocese of Rouen, France), to whom the seigniory was granted in 1636 and who donated the land to the Jesuits in 1682. Incorporated as a town in 1918; became a city in 1923.

CAP-D'ESPOIR   Cape and settlement. Appears on Champlain's *Carte de la Nouvelle France*, 1632, and may be translated as "cape hope".

CAP-DES-ROSIERS   Also dates from Champlain's map of 1632. For the abundance of wild rose bushes located on the cape.

CAP-SAINT-IGNACE   The parish was established about 1700, taking the name of the cape which honours St. Ignace Loyola, founder of the Jesuit order. The first missionaries in the district were Jesuits.

CAP-TOURMENTE   Name assigned by Champlain. He wrote: "We named the cape [thus] because . . . in this place the water begins to be calm."

CAP-TRINITÉ   Descriptive. This cape is in reality three capes, equal in height and elevation.

CARIGNAN   Named in 1965 when the parish of Saint-Joseph-de-Chambly was incorporated as a town. Probably for the regiment (Carignan–Salières) in which Jacques de Chambly (?–1687) was a captain.

CARILLON   The name originated with a land grant to Philippe de Carrion in 1670. By an error in transcription the name became Carillon.

CARLETON   First called Tracadigetche (Micmac for "place of many herons"). The settlement, founded by Acadians, dates from 1756. It was renamed for Sir Guy Carleton (1724–1808), Governor General of Canada from 1768 to 1778 and from 1786 to 1796.

CAUGHNAWAGA   From the Iroquois *kahnawake*, which may be translated as "a rapid". An Iroquois mission was established in 1667 at this location.

CAUSCAPSCAL   River and town. The name is derived from the Micmac *casupscul*, signifying "rapid water".

CHAMBLY   After Jacques de Chambly (?–1687), captain in the Carignan–Salières Regiment, who was granted the seigniory of

Chambly on October 29, 1673. *See also* Fort Chambly

CHAMBORD   Commemorates Henry of Bourbon, Comte de Chambord (1820–83), pretender to the throne of France. Settled in 1855; incorporated on April 16, 1932.

CHAMPLAIN   The town and county were named for Samuel de Champlain (1567?–1635), explorer and founder of Québec. Settlement dates from 1679.

CHANDLER   Detached from the parish of Sainte-Adelaide-de-Pabos in 1914 and named in honour of an American industrialist responsible for locating a pulp mill in the area.

CHAPAIS   For Senator Thomas Chapais (1858–1946).

CHAPEAU   Descriptive. For a hat-shaped rock in the nearby Chenal-de-la-Culbute.

CHARLEMAGNE   For Romuald-Charlemagne Laurier (1852–1906), nephew of Sir Wilfrid Laurier and Member of Parliament for L'Assomption from 1900 to 1906.

CHARLESBOURG   Name transferred from Charlesbourg-Royal, a fort built by Cartier at Cap-Rouge and named after Charles IX, King of France. It was later shortened to Charlesbourg. Incorporated as a village in 1914 and as a town in 1949; achieved the status of a city in 1960.

CHARNY   After Charles de Charny, son of Jean de Lauzon, Governor of New France.

CHÂTEAU-D'EAU   Descriptive. A building that was located on a dam was referred to locally as a "château d'eau". On February 2, 1965, the town was annexed to Loretteville.

CHÂTEAUGUAY
CHÂTEAUGUAY CENTRE
CHÂTEAUGUAY HEIGHTS   Dates from 1672 when Charles le Moyne de Longueuil received the grant of a seigniory, which he named after Châteauguay, France.

CHÂTEAU-RICHER   Founded in 1678 and possibly named for a priory in France. A legend suggests that one Nestor Richer's house or hut was referred to locally as Château-Richer.

CHAUDIÈRE   River and falls. Descriptive. The name is a French rendering of an Algonquin word meaning "kettle" or "cauldron".

CHAUVEAU   Honours P. J. O. Chauveau (1820–90), who served as Premier of Québec from 1867 to 1873.

CHELSEA   Named for Chelsea, the Vermont home of an early settler, Thomas Brigham Prentiss. Dates from 1830.

CHÉNÉVILLE   First known as Sévigné; the name was changed in 1885 for Hercule Chéné, the first postmaster.

CHIBOUGAMAU   Lake and town. An Amerindian place name which in translation means "where the water is shut in", indicating the narrow outlet of the lake.

CHICOUTIMI   Of Montagnais origin, the name is traceable to *shkoutimeou*, meaning "the end of the deep water". Incorporated as a village in 1863 and as a town in 1879; achieved the status of a city in 1930.

CHOMEDEY   Created in 1961 through an amalgamation of the communities of Saint-Martin, Renaud, and L'Abord-à-Plouffe, for Paul de Chomedey (1612–76), first Governor of the island of Montréal. Amalgamated in 1965 with all municipalities on Île-Jésus to form the city of Laval.

CHUTE-AUX-OUTARDES   A descriptive for the rapids or falls and the fact that *outardes*, or "wild geese", frequent the area of the Outardes River.

CLARKE CITY   For Clarke Brothers, an American publishing firm that established a pulp-and-paper industry in the region.

CLERMONT   Named for an officer in Montcalm's army.

COATICOOK   River and town. From *koakiteku*, an Abenaki descriptive meaning "river of the pine land", or, less likely, *khwaktakwak*, translated as "something crooked which straightens itself", a reference to the crooks in the river.

COLERAINE   For Coleraine, a seaport town in County Londonderry, Northern Ireland.

COMO-EST   The name is derived from a physical resemblance of the area to Lake Como, Italy.

CONTRECOEUR   After Antoine Pecaudy de Contrecoeur (1596–1688), an officer in the Carignan–Salières Regiment and the first seignior of Contrecoeur. The seigniory was granted on October 29, 1672.

COOKSHIRE   Founded in 1799 by settlers from New Hampshire and Vermont and named for one of their number, John Cook. Incorporated as a town in 1892.

COTEAU-DU-LAC   A descriptive. The name is probably for a small hill (*coteau*) on the portage around the rapids in the St. Lawrence River.

CÔTE-ST.-LUC   Possibly for Joseph Marie La Corne de Chaptes de St. Luc (1714–99), priest and diplomat, who negotiated the appointment of Jean Olivier Briand as first Bishop of Québec after the conquest. Incorporated as a town in 1951 and a city in 1958. Replaced the earlier name, Côte-Notre-Dame-de-Liesse.

COULONGE   Lake and river. Honours the Ailleboust family, from Coulonge-la-Madeleine in France. Louis d'Ailleboust de Coulonge served as Governor of New France from 1648 to 1651.

COURVILLE   After Charles Cadieu de Courville, an early settler of the district.

COWANSVILLE   For Peter Cowan, the first postmaster, replacing the earlier name of Nelsonville on January 1, 1876.

CRABTREE   Probably for Edwin Crabtree, an early settler, who established a paper mill in the district. Earlier name was Crabtree Mills.

DANVILLE   For Danville, Vermont, which in turn was named for Jean Baptiste d'Anville (1679–1782), famous French geographer. Founded by settlers from Vermont in 1801.

DAVELUYVILLE   Founded in 1888 and named after Adolphe Daveluy, a prominent local merchant.

DÉGELIS   Named because a rapid in the adjacent river does not freeze (*geler*, "to freeze"). Incorporated as Sainte-Rose-du-Dégelé in 1915 and assigned present name in 1969.

DELSON   A coined word marking the railway junction of the Delaware and Hudson Railway.

DESCHAILLONS
DESCHAILLONS-SUR-SAINT-LAURENT   Originally the name of the seigniory granted to the St. Ours family in 1752. May be traced to the name of the St. Ours estate in France.

DESCHAMBAULT   For Jacques-Alexis Fleury d'Eschambault (1642–1715), the local seignior. D'Eschambault gained title to the land through marriage to Marguerite de Chavigny in 1764. Parish established in 1712.

DESCHÊNES   Amalgamated with Aylmer in 1976. Formerly a village at Deschênes Rapids where the Ottawa River flows east. The name means "oaks".

DES PRAIRIES   From a channel of the Ottawa River which separates the island of Montréal from Jésus Island. Possibly for Jean Desprairies, reputed to be the first white man to ascend the Ottawa River. *See also* Rivière-des-Prairies

DEUX-MONTAGNES   Town and lake. Descriptive; the two mountains are a short distance from the Ottawa River and gave rise to the name.

DEUX-RIVIÈRES   Also a descriptive name for the location at the merging of the Des Envies and Batiscan rivers. Changed to Saint-Stanislas on April 22, 1962.

DISRAELI   After Benjamin Disraeli (1804–81). *See* Beaconsfield

DOLBEAU   Commemorates the career of Jean Dolbeau (1586–1652), a Recollet priest who served the Montagnais mission at Tadoussac.

DOLLARD-DES-ORMEAUX   For Adam Dollard des Ormeaux (1635–60), commandant at Ville-Marie (Montréal), who, in the spring of 1660, led a party up the Ottawa River. About May 25 the "hero of the Long Sault" and his companions met death at the hands of the Iroquois. A résumé of the controversy surrounding the event may be found in the *Dictionary of Canadian Biography*, I, pp. 266–75.

DONNACONA   Name derived from the Donnacona Paper Company, a major industry in the town. The name is traceable to Donnacona, the Amerindian chief of Stadacona, who was taken to France in 1536. The settlement was detached from the parish of Les Écureuils in 1915 and became a town in 1920.

DORION   After Sir Antoine-Aimé Dorion (1818–91), politician and jurist. Incorporated in 1891.

DORVAL   For Jean-Baptiste Bouchard dit d'Orval, who was a prominent landholder in the area during the French regime. The ecclesiastical parish was named La-Présentation-de-la-Vièrge, because it was here that the Sulpicians built Fort-de-la-Présentation in 1668. Achieved status of a town in 1903 and became a city in 1956.

DOUGLASTOWN   Probably for Rear-Admiral Sir Charles Douglas, who was responsible for the relief of Québec in 1776.

DRUMMONDVILLE   For Sir Gordon Drummond (1771–1854), who took a prominent part in the War of 1812 and later served as administrator of Lower Canada. It was incorporated as a town in 1888 and as a city in 1938.

DUNHAM   For Thomas Dunn (1729–1818), once administrator of Lower Canada and a judge of the Court of King's Bench.

DUPARQUET   Named after Captain J. Duparquet, who served as an officer in the La Sarre Regiment under Montcalm.

EARDLEY   Possibly for a village of the same name in Staffordshire, England.

EAST ANGUS   Either for Angus (Forfarshire), Scotland, or for William Angus, a Montreal industrialist responsible for the building of a paper mill in the area in 1822.

EAST BROUGHTON
EAST BROUGHTON STATION   Undoubtedly for one of the several Broughtons in England.

EASTMAN   After Ezray Eastman, wife of an early settler in the district. Incorporated in 1888.

ESCOUMAINS (LES ESCOUMAINS)   River and bay. The name is derived from an Amerindian word, possibly translated as "where there are many red berries" (cranberries). Champlain's spelling was Lesquemain.

ESCUMINAC   The name is from the Micmac *escomenag*, "an observation post", referring to the hill behind the town.

ÉTANG-DU-NORD   A descriptive to distinguish among several ponds or pools (*étangs*) in the area.

EVAIN   Honours Abbé Isidore Evain.

FALARDEAU   Marks the career of Antoine Sébastien Falardeau (1823–89), a prominent Québec artist. The parish was organized in 1937.

FARNHAM   Named after a town in Surrey, England; it became a city in 1956.

FATHER POINT   *See* Pointe-au-Père

FERME-NEUVE   A descriptive name that traces its origin to a "new farm", established by Montréal interests to attract settlers to the region.

FONTAINEBLEAU   For a town in northern France, capital of an arrondissement in the Department of Seine-et-Marne.

FORESTVILLE   Originally Sault-au-Cochon, this town was renamed in 1941 as an indicator of the importance of the forest industry.

FORILLON   The name was first applied to a rock (which has since disappeared) off the Gaspé coast. It is from the French *pharillon* or *forillon*, indicating the pan in which fishermen made a light to attract fish at night.

FORT CHAMBLY   The fort, otherwise known as Saint-Louis, was built in 1665 by Jacques de Chambly (?–1687), a captain in the Carignan–Salières Regiment and later Governor of Acadia. In 1672 he was granted a seigniory on the site of present-day Chambly.

FORT CHIMO   Existed first as a Hudson's Bay Company post on the bank of the Koksoak River near its outlet in Ungava Bay. *Chimois*, of mixed Amerindian and Inuit origin, may be translated as "good cheer". The word is sometimes used as a greeting.

FORT COULONGE   The d'Aillesboust family traded with the Amerindians on the Ottawa River from 1670 to 1760. The fort was probably erected about 1680, being named after Nicolas d'Ailleboust de Coulonge-la-Madeleine. Appears on Arrowsmith map of 1832. *See* Coulonge

FORT GEORGE   Established in 1805 by the Hudson's Bay Company and designated Fort George in honour of King George IV. It is sometimes called Big River Fort or Rivière-la-Grande – a translation of the Amerindian word for a nearby river.

FORTIERVILLE   Once part of the seigniory of Deschaillons and named for a pioneer family in the district.

FORT RUPERT   Built in 1668 by Médard Chouart des Groseilliers (1618?–96?). The earlier names, Fort Charles and Fort St. Jacques, have disappeared. It was marked as abandoned on D'Anville's map of 1775. Sometimes referred to as Rupert's House.

GAGNON   (Saguenay-Nouveau Québec) For J. Onésime Gagnon, Minister of Mines, Game and Fisheries in the Quebec government from 1936 to 1939 and later Lieutenant-Governor of Québec from 1958 to 1961.

GASCONS   Probably for the Gascons of Gascony, France. A local legend suggests that a shipwrecked Gascon sailor was among the first settlers.

GASPÉ Cape, bay, basin, town, and county. Origin is in dispute; however, Ganong lists seven distinct interpretations in *Transactions of the Royal Society of Canada, 1928*. The evidence favours an Amerindian derivation, probably the Micmac for "end" or "extremity", referring to the northern limits of their territory (*see* Aspy, Nova Scotia). In the "Routier" of Jean Fonteneau dit Alphonse (1542), it appears as Bay of Moules or Gaspé. Gaspé (Hakluyt, 1600); Champlain's maps render it as Gachepé in 1603 and as Gaspé in 1613.

GATINEAU Town, county, river, and park. The name commemorates Nicolas Gastineau (?–1683), clerk of the Company of One Hundred Associates, who was active in the fur trade of the region from 1650 to 1683. It appears as Gatteno on a map by Colonel By (1831). In 1974 the city of Gatineau annexed the adjacent municipalities of Pointe-Gatineau, Touraine, Templeton, Templeton-Ouest, and Templeton-Est.

GENTILLY The parish was founded on July 24, 1784, and occupies the territory of the seigniory of Gentilly, granted to Michel Pelletier, Sieur de Gentilly, on June 17, 1669. For Gentilly, a suburb of Paris.

GIFFARD Commemorates Robert Giffard de Moncel (1587–1668), master surgeon and first doctor of the Hôtel-Dieu of Québec. He was granted the seigniory of Beauport in 1634. The settlement was incorporated as a village in 1912 and became a city in 1954.

GIRARDVILLE Named for Joseph Girard (1854–1933), Member of Parliament for Chicoutimi–Saguenay from 1900 to 1917. The settlement dates from 1915.

GODBOUT River and village. The river was named for Nicolas

Godbout, a seventeenth-century naval pilot.

GRACEFIELD   After Samuel Grace, an early merchant in the district. Founded in 1849.

GRANBY   A name taken from a village in Northamptonshire, England. It was established in 1803 and incorporated in 1859.

GRANDE-RIVIÈRE   Descriptive. The Grande and the Petite rivers run through the area, which was part of a seigniory granted in 1697 to Pierre Cochin that later passed to the Robin family. On September 21, 1974, the two municipalities joined to form the town of Grande-Rivière.

GRANDES-BERGERONNES
PETITES-BERGERONNES   Originated with Champlain's voyage of 1603. He named the two small rivers which flow into the St. Lawrence at this point. Exact origin unknown.

GRAND'MÈRE   The name is a French translation of the Amerindian *kokomis*, or "old woman". The form of a rock there resembles an elderly woman in silhouette.

GREAT WHALE RIVER   *See* Poste-de-la-Baleine

GREENFIELD PARK   The name is an English translation of the original French name, Parc-des-Prés-Verts.

GRENVILLE   Honours George Grenville (1712–70), who served as British Prime Minister from 1763 to 1765.

GRINDSTONE ISLAND   *See* Île-du-Cap-aux-Meules

GROSS-ÎLE   Descriptive. The name was applied to distinguish the island from others in the vicinity.

HA HA BAY
HA HA RIVER   Possibly an adaption of an old French term to designate a blind alley or road and so applied to the bay for "it is said that the French on first going up the Saguenay mistook the bay for a continuation of the river and on coming to the end of it said, Ha! Ha!" (CPCGN files). *See* Saint-Louis-du-Ha! Ha!

HAMPSTEAD   After the borough of the same name north of London, England.

HARRICANA RIVER   *See* Rivière Harricana

HAUTERIVE   A new city developed in 1949–50 by Mgr. N. A. Labrie, first bishop of the area. The name was formerly spelled Haut-rive and is a descriptive derived from the local "high bank". The post office was established on September, 29, 1950.

HAVRE-SAINT-PIERRE   Early name: Eskimo Point. The religious parish was founded in 1861 and honours St. Peter, patron saint of fishermen.

HÉBERTVILLE   Hébertville and Hébertville Station commemorate the career of Abbé Nicolas-Hébert, who served the Kamouraska district in the 1850s.

HEMMINGFORD   The name is derived from the twin villages of Hemingford Abbots and Hemingford Grey near Huntingdon, England.

HENRYVILLE   After Edme Henry, who served the district as agent for the local seigniory. Founded in 1810.

HONFLEUR   For the seaport in the Department of Calvados, France.

HOWICK   Named for Charles Grey, Viscount Howick (1764–1845), who served as British Prime Minister from 1831 to 1834. The community was earlier known as La Fourche.

HUDSON

HUDSON HEIGHTS First called Pointe-à-Cavagnal, it was renamed in 1865 by George Matthews (proprietor of an early glass
factory) after his wife, whose maiden name was Hudson.

HULL The name originated with the township. The old county
of York (as the territory along the Ottawa River was once designated) was divided into townships named after districts in Yorkshire, England. The town, founded by Philemon Wright, was first
called Wrightstown, but was renamed Hull after the township in
1875.

HUNTINGDON The settlement dates from 1820 and is named
after Huntingdon, England. *See also reference to* Hemmingford. Incorporated as a town in 1921.

IBERVILLE From 1843 to 1854 the location was known as
Christieville after an early settler, Christie Napier. It was renamed in 1854 for Pierre Le Moyne, Sieur d'Iberville (1661–
1706), soldier, explorer, and colonizer, ". . . the most renowned
son of New France".

ÎLE-AU-MASSACRE *See entry for* Bic

ÎLE-AUX-COUDRES Designated by Cartier in 1535 because of
the abundance of hazelnut bushes found on the island.

ÎLE-AUX-GRUES For the cranes (*grues*) which formerly frequented the area.

ÎLE-AUX-NOIX Discovered by Champlain in 1609 and named
for the profusion of nut trees (*noyers*) found growing there.

ÎLE-DES-SOEURS Once the property of the Grey Nuns of
Montréal, giving rise to the name.

ÎLE-D'ORLÉANS After the Duc d'Orléans, son of Francis I of

France. It was referred to by Cartier as Isle-de-Bacchus because of grapes found growing there. On maps of the mid seventeenth century it was sometimes called Île-Saint-Laurent.

ÎLE-DU-CAP-AUX-MEULES   *See* Cap-aux-Meules

ÎLE-JÉSUS   The island was granted to the Jesuit order in 1699, from which fact the name is derived.

ÎLE-NOTRE-DAME   A man-made island east of Île-Sainte-Hélène created for Expo 67. Name approved on August 28, 1965.

ÎLE-PERROT   Named for François-Marie Perrot (1644?–91), successor of Maisonneuve as Governor of Montréal (1670 to 1684), later Governor of Acadia. Acquired Île-Perrot as a grant in 1672.

ÎLE-SAINTE-HÉLÈNE   Name bestowed by Champlain in 1611 to honour the patron saint of his wife.

ÎLES-DE-LA-MADELEINE   On June 25, 1534, Cartier sighted three islands, "swarming with diverse sea birds", which he named Isles-de-Margaulx (gannets). Champlain, on his map of 1632, designated the major island as La Magdelene, and later this was extended to the whole group. This early use of the name contradicts the assertion that it is traceable to Madeleine Fontaine, whose husband, François Doublet, later owned two of the sixteen islands in the group.

ÎLES-LAVAL   The municipality of Îles-Laval contains Île-Verte and Île-Ronde. *See* Laval

ISLE-MALIGNE   Descriptive. The island is difficult to approach because of turbulent waters; hence "malicious" or "mischievous" was used as a designation. Town incorporated in 1924. Annexed to the city of Alma in 1962.

ISSOUDUN   Named for a town in central France, the capital of an arrondissement in the Department of Indre.

JACQUES CARTIER   Lake, river, and county (*for city, see* Longueuil). Commemorates the career of Jacques Cartier (1491–1557), first explorer of the Gulf of St. Lawrence and discoverer of the St. Lawrence River, ". . . one of the great rivers of the world and starting point of France's occupation of three-quarters of a continent" (Trudel).

JAMES BAY   Although first discovered by Henry Hudson in 1610, it was named by Captain Thomas James (1593–1635?) on a voyage (1631–2) in search of a northwest passage. *See* Severn River, Ontario

JOLIETTE   Named for Barthélemy Joliette (1787–1850), the founder of the town. Incorporated as a city in 1913.

JONQUIÈRE   Marks the career of Jacques-Pierre de Taffanel, Marquis de la Jonquière, who served as Governor of New France from 1749 to 1752. Became a city in 1956.

KAMOURASKA   Of Amerindian origin, the name has had its present form since early times. It may be translated as "beyond or on the other side of the river". Appears on a map by Franquelin (1686) as Camouraska.

KENOGAMI   City and lake. The name is traceable to an Amerindian source meaning "long lake". It was founded in 1911 and incorporated as a city in 1958.

KINGSEY FALLS   Named for a village in Oxfordshire, England.

KINGSMERE   Although associated with the estate of former Prime Minister Mackenzie King, the name is of nineteenth-century origin. The name of the lake, first known as Jeff's Lake for William Jeff, an early settler, was changed to Kingsmere in 1879 upon the suggestion of Lieut.-Col. J. S. Dennis, then

Deputy-Minister of the Interior. The name of nearby Kings Mountain has been attributed to John King, early chief of the Canadian Geodetic Survey; however, it is apparent that it is older and refers to a pioneer King family who once owned land in the area.

KNOB LAKE   The settlement dates from the 1950s and refers to a nearby "knob-like" mountain. *See also* Schefferville

KNOWLTON   For its founder, Colonel Paul Holland Knowlton (?– 1863), who represented Shefford in the Legislative Assembly of Lower Canada.

KOKSOAK RIVER   An Inuit word which may be translated as "big river".

LABELLE   After the Rev. François Xavier Antoine Labelle (1831–91), known as the "apostle of Colonization" for his work in the development of townships north of Montréal. *See* L'Ascension *and* St. Jérôme

LABRIEVILLE   Honours Mgr. N. A. Labrie, Bishop of the Gulf of St. Lawrence. Founded in 1953.

LAC-À-LA-TORTUE   The town takes its name from the lake. This name is probably a descriptive designation by early settlers (*tortue*, "turtle").

LAC-AU-SAUMON   Descriptive. The "lake" is really a widening of the Matapedia River. It was formerly a spawning ground for salmon. The parish dates from 1876.

LAC-BELLEMARE   Honours the Rev. Adélard Bellemare, who founded a mission here in 1872.

LAC-BOUCHETTE   For Joseph Bouchette (1774–1841), Surveyor-General of Lower Canada. Bouchette visited this area in 1828. Parish organized in 1894.

LAC-BRÔME   Lake and town. For the village of Brome in East Suffolk, England.

LAC-CARRÉ   The settlement was known as Saint-Faustin until 1947. The present name of the lake is a descriptive term, *carré* meaning "square".

LAC-CAYAMANT   An Amerindian descriptive meaning "lake with bay at the end".

LAC-DES-COMMISSAIRES   Honours commissioners Andrew and David Stuart, who explored the Saguenay area in the 1820s.

LAC-DES-ÉCORCES   The lake which gave its name to the parish derived its name from the beautiful white birch woods which surround it (*écorce*, "bark"). Parish founded in 1897.

LAC-ETCHEMIN   For a tribe of the Abenaki confederacy. The name is said to mean "where there are hides for snowshoes".

LACHENAIE   For Charles Aubert de la Chesnaye (?–1702), who purchased the local seigniory from Jean-Baptiste Legardeur de Repentigny in 1688.

LACHINE   Part of a land grant to the explorer La Salle. "La Chine" was derisively applied to the seigniory because of the failure of his expedition to discover a passage to China. Dates from 1688. *See* La Salle

LACHUTE   Descriptive. The name is taken from the falls in the nearby North River and was originally written La Chute.

LAC-KEMPT   For Sir James Kempt (1764–1854), Governor from 1828 to 1830.

LAC-MÉGANTIC   County, town, and lake. Possibly from an Abenaki word which means in translation "the place where fish are found" or "where they preserve fish". The original site of a large Abenaki village.

LAC-MOUSSEAU   Formerly Harrington Lake (*see opening chapter*). For Louis Mousseau, who settled on the lakeshore in 1867.

LACOLLE   From the river which was so named because of the difficulties encountered by small boats in navigating its surface – *la colle* means "paste" or "glue".

LAC-SAINT-JEAN   The lake was discovered on July 16, 1647, and named by Abbé Jean De Quen of the Jesuit mission at Tadoussac.

LAC-SAINT-LOUIS   Name bestowed by Champlain in 1611 while inspecting the area for settlement possibilities.

LAC-SAINT-PIERRE   Named for a widening of the St. Lawrence River near Trois-Rivières. Champlain recorded the name on the day of his arrival, June 29, 1603 (St. Peter's Day).

LAFLÈCHE   *See* St. Hubert

LAFONTAINE   Possibly for Louis-Hippolyte Lafontaine (1807–64), who served as Premier of the Canadas from 1848 to 1851.

LA GRANDE-RIVIÈRE   The name is a French translation of the original Amerindian designation meaning Big River. Other names were Fort George River (for George IV) and Big River. Appears on Watkin's map of 1872 as Big River.

LA GUADELOUPE   Originally, from a range of mountains in Spain and later bestowed in honour of Notre Dame de la Guadeloupe, patron saint of the Mexican people. The name was officially adopted in 1949, replacing St. Évariste Station.

LA MALBAIE   Designated Mallebaye (*mal*, "evil" or "bad") by Champlain (1608) because of difficulty experienced in anchoring ships. For many years called Murray Bay.

LAMBTON   For John George Lambton, Lord Durham (1792–1840), Governor General of British North America in 1838 and author of the *Durham Report*.

L'ANNONCIATION   Incorporated in 1908, this town takes its name from that of the religious parish.

LANORAIE   Originally owned by Monsieur de la Noraye, an officer in the Carignan–Salières Regiment, who gave his name to the seigniory. In 1721 it passed into the hands of Jean-Baptiste Neveu, colonel of the militia in Montréal.

LA PÊCHE   The municipality was established in 1974 by the amalgamation of Sainte-Cécile-de-Masham, Wakefield, Aldfield, and Masham-Nord. The name is derived from a river and a lake and means "the fishing".

LA PÉRADE   *See* Sainte-Anne-de-la-Pérade

LA PRAIRIE   Descriptive. A portion of the original seigniory was level prairie land, being granted to Jacques de la Ferte, Abbé de la Magdeleine, one of the Company of One Hundred Associates. First called La-Prairie-de-la-Magdeleine.

LA PROVIDENCE   From the name of the parish. Incorporated in 1899 but now a part of the city of Saint-Hyacinthe.

LAROCHELLE   Named for the seaport of La Rochelle, France.

LA SALLE   For the explorer, René-Robert Cavelier, Sieur de la Salle (1643–87), discoverer of the mouth of the Mississippi River in 1682.

LA SARRE   Taken from the La Sarre Regiment, part of Montcalm's army at Québec in 1759. Founded in 1917. Incorporated on August 17, 1949.

L'ASCENSION   In 1886 Abbé Antoine Labelle visited the area on Ascension Day, planted a cross, and named the parish in honour of the day. *See* Labelle

L'ASSOMPTION   County, town, river, and lake. Named after the seigniory of Saint-Pierre-du-Portage-de-l'Assomption, founded in 1724.

LA STATION-DU-COTEAU   A descriptive name indicating the hills or slopes (*coteaux*) in the region.

LATERRIÈRE   First called Grand-Brûlé, this town changed its name in 1865 to Notre-Dame-de-Laterrière for Dr. Marc-Pascal de Sales Laterrière (1792–1872), a one-time member of the Legislative Assembly of Lower Canada.

LA TUQUE   The name was assigned because a rock on the nearby riverbank was thought to resemble the type of tuque worn by early fur traders. Incorporated in 1911.

LAURENTIAN HIGHLANDS, or LAURENTIANS   From the Latin form of Lawrence, *Laurentius*, the designation is traceable to the writings of François Xavier Garneau (1809–66), noted historian.

LAURENTIDES   After the Laurentian plateau which stretches along the northern shore of the St. Lawrence River. *See above.* It was formerly known as Saint-Lin, but was renamed upon its incorporation in 1883. The birthplace of Sir Wilfrid Laurier.

LAURIER
LAURIERVILLE   Both place names honour Sir Wilfrid Laurier, Prime Minister of Canada from 1896 to 1911.

LAUZON Originally Cap-de-Lévy for Henri de Lévis, Duc de Ventadour, the name was changed upon incorporation in 1867 to honour Jean de Lauzon (1584–1666), the Governor of New France from 1651 to 1656.

LAVAL
LAVAL-DES-RAPIDES Both place names commemorate the career of François de Montmorency Laval (1623–1708), the first Bishop of Québec.

LAVALTRIE After Séraphin Margane, Sieur de la Valtrie (1643–99), to whom the seigniory was granted in 1672.

LEBEL-SUR-QUÉVILLON Named for Louis-Amable Quévillon (1749–1823), a noted architect and sculptor.

LEMOYNE Honours Pierre Le Moyne (1661–1706), explorer and colonizer.

LENNOXVILLE For Charles Gordon Lennox, Duke of Richmond (1764–1819), who served briefly from 1818 to 1819 as Governor General.

L'ÉPIPHANIE The name originated with that of the religious parish. Tradition has it that the first mass here was celebrated on Epiphany.

LÉRY For Gaspard-Joseph Chaussegros de Léry (1682–1756), army officer and engineer, to whom the seigniory was granted in 1735. Earlier forms of the name were De Léry and Ville de Léry.

LES CAPS Descriptive. The place was named for the high cliffs in the area. Post office established in 1914. Officially adopted as a place name in 1955.

LES ÉBOULEMENTS Named for a landslide (*éboulement*) in 1663 which is said to have markedly changed the shoreline.

LES ÉCUREUILS   The nearby point of land which juts into the St. Lawrence was once covered with nut trees and was so overrun with squirrels that the first settlers called it Les Écureuils (The Squirrels). The name spread to the seigniory and then to the parish. Settlement dates from 1742.

LES MÉCHINS   The name possibly refers to the offshore rocks which were a hindrance to early navigation. Once spelled Les Méchants.

LES SAULES   The name is derived from the abundance of willow (*saules*) trees in the vicinity. Annexed by Québec, January 1, 1970.

LÉVIS   Honours François Gaston, Chevalier de Lévis (1719–87), who was in command at Montréal in 1759. On Montcalm's death he assumed charge of the French forces. The name was bestowed in 1861, replacing Aubigny, an earlier attempt to honour the Duke of Richmond and Aubigny.

LINIÈRE   For Linière Taschereau, an early seignior in the region.

L'ISLET
L'ISLETVILLE   The name is derived from a large rock to which early settlers gave the name L'Islet. This term spread afterward to the seigniory and thence to the parish, which was founded in 1679.

L'ISLE VERTE   Descriptive ("green island"). The name is mentioned in the *Jesuit Relations* of 1663 and is possibly traceable to Cartier.

LONGUEUIL   After Charles Le Moyne de Longueil (1626–85), who was born in the Norman village of the same name. By order-in-council in August 1969, Longueuil and Jacques Cartier were amalgamated.

LORETTEVILLE   The name was bestowed in 1673 by Abbé Pierre-Joseph-Marie Chaumonot (1611–93), who lived for a time near Loreto, Italy.

LORRAINVILLE   Founded in 1907 and named for the Rt. Rev. N. Z. Lorrain, Catholic Bishop of Pontiac.

LOTBINIÈRE   The village and county honour René Louis Chartier de Lotbinière (1642–1709), who was a member of the Sovereign Council of New France.

LOUISEVILLE   For Princess Louise, wife of the Governor General, the Marquess of Lorne, who served in this post from 1878 to 1883. *See* Lake Louise, Alberta

LUCERNE   The name was adopted by plebiscite in 1964. It was proposed by Dr. Joseph-Gaston Isabelle, Member of Parliament for Gatineau, and replaced Hull-Sud, which was assigned in 1879.

LUCEVILLE   For Luce Gertrude Drapeau, one-time owner of the seigniory.

LYSTER   Named for Lyster, England, birthplace of William King, pioneer of the lumber industry in the district.

MACAMIC   The name is probably of Amerindian origin and may mean "wonderful". The town takes its name from that of the river. Approved on April 23, 1919.

MACKAYVILLE   *See* Saint-Hubert

MC MASTERVILLE   Named for William McMaster, one-time president of Canadian Industries Limited, operators of a plant in the town. Incorporated in 1917.

MADAWASKA   *See* New Brunswick *entry*

MAGOG   An abbreviated form of the Abenaki word *memphremagog*, translated as either "expanse of water" or "beautiful water".

MALARTIC   Takes its name from that of the first gold mine, opened in 1935. Possibly for Comte de Malartic (1730–1800), who served with Montcalm.

MANICOUAGAN   River and peninsula. The name is possibly of Cree origin and may be translated as "where there is bark" for making canoes; or it may be a French adaptation of *Manicouaganistiku*, "drinking place".

MANIWAK   The name is derived from *Mani* for "Mary" and *aki* for "land" – "Mary's land or land of the Virgin Mary". It was founded in 1849 by the Oblate Fathers and was once called Notre-Dame-du-Désert.

MANSEAU   Honours the first parish priest, Abbé Martial Manseau. Incorporated in 1922.

MAPLE GROVE   Descriptive. The name is for the abundance of maple trees in the vicinity.

MARBLETON   Named for a nearby marble quarry.

MARIA   Bay and township named for Lady Maria Effingham, wife of Lord Dorchester, once Governor General.

MARIEVILLE   Originates with the name of the parish of Sainte-Marie-de-Monnoir, part of the seigniory of Monnoir.

MARSOUI   The name is a variation of *marsouin*, the French for "porpoise" (which are sometimes found in the area).

MASCOUCHE   An Amerindian descriptive, possibly meaning "smooth plain" or "prairie". Parish founded in 1761.

MASKINONGÉ   River, county, and town. The name is from the Algonquin for "pike" or "big pike", once plentiful in the river.

MASSON   Honours Louis François Rodrigue Masson (1833–1903), Lieutenant-Governor of Québec from 1884 to 1887 and later a Senator.

MASSUEVILLE   First called Bonsecours, this town was later re-named for Aimé Massue, a former seignior in the area.

MATAGAMI   River, town, and lake. Spelled as Mattagami on some maps after the 1895 *Geological Survey Report*'s rendering of the name. The name is of Algonquin origin and may mean "where the waters meet".

MATANE   County, town, and river. Of Amerindian origin, this name is perhaps a corruption of the Micmac *mtctan* or Algonquin *matawan*, meaning "beaver pond".

MATAPÉDIA   The name may be traced to Micmac sources. It has been translated by Abbé Pacifique de Valigny as "forked river" or "junction of two rivers" (for the confluence of the Matapédia and Restigouche rivers).

MELOCHEVILLE   Incorporated in 1919 and named for a leading citizen, Joseph Meloche.

MERCIER   Formerly Sainte-Philomène, the name was changed in 1968 as the result of a local petition to the Québec legislature. Possibly for Honoré Mercier (1840–94), Premier of Québec from 1887 to 1891.

MINTO LAKE   Named for Lord Minto (1845–1914), who served as Governor General from 1898 to 1904.

MIRABEL   Of uncertain origin, the name was adopted for the new international airport by order-in-council of the Québec government on December 20, 1972. Legend has it that it is a contraction of the name of Miriam and Isabel, daughters of an early Scottish settler. The name was chosen for the airport because it is easily understood in most languages. *See* Sainte-Scholastique

MISSISQUOI   The name is probably traceable to the Abenaki *mesipskoik*, roughly translated as "place where flint is found".

MISTASSINI   From fur trader James McKenzie's *Journal* of 1808: "We continued for 25 leagues along the lake until we came to the large stone from which it takes its name", the Great Stone Lake, rendered in the Montagnais dialect as Mista-assini. The lake was first discovered in 1672 by Abbé Charles Albanel (1616–96).

MOISIE RIVER   The name is possibly a variation of a Montagnais personal name.

MONTEBELLO   Name bestowed by Louis Joseph Papineau in 1854 for his friend the Duke of Montebello.

MONT-JOLI   Descriptive. The name is a French reference to the "pretty hill" overlooking the St. Lawrence River. Founded in 1881.

MONT-LAURIER   After Sir Wilfrid Laurier, Prime Minister of Canada from 1896 to 1911.

MONT-LOUIS   For King Louis XIV of France. The seigniory was granted in 1725.

MONTMAGNY   Marks the career of Charles Huault de Montmagny (1583–1653), Governor and Lieutenant-General of New France from 1636 to 1648.

MONTMORENCY   Falls, river, town, and county. The name was first applied to the falls by Champlain (1613) in honour of the Duc de Montmorency (1595–1632), who purchased the vice-royalty of New France in 1620.

MONTPELLIER   For the town in southern France, capital of the Department of Hérault.

MONT-RAOUL-BLANCHARD   The name honours geographer François Raoul-Blanchard (1877–1965).

MONTRÉAL   Name bestowed by Jacques Cartier in 1534: "we ascended a great mountain near to [Hochelaga] that is tilled round about, which we named Mont Roiall [*sic*]." The permanent settlement (Ville Marie de Montréal) dates from 1642. Called Montréal from 1724.

MONT ROLLAND   The community was founded in 1918 and named for the Rolland Paper Company, a major source of local employment.

MONT ROYAL   *See* Montréal

MURDOCHVILLE   Named after James Murdoch, the president of a mining company active in the region. Incorporated in 1952.

MURRAY BAY   *See* La Malbaie

NAPIERVILLE   Named for Napier Christie, the son of General Gabriel Christie, who purchased the local seigniory in 1766. *See* Iberville

NAUDVILLE   Incorporated in 1954 and named for Albert Naud, "who figures prominently in its establishment"; annexed to nearby Alma in 1962.

NEUVILLE   An earlier name, Pointe-aux-Trembles, indicating that the area was formerly covered with aspens (*trembles*), was changed in 1919 to Neuville, after Nicolas Dupont de Neuville (1633–1713), a member of the Conseil Souverain and a local land-holder.

NEW CARLISLE   Founded in 1887 and named for Carlisle, England.

NEW QUÉBEC   Formerly the District of Ungava (northern Québec, between Hudson Bay and Ungava Bay), the area became part of the Province of Québec by act of Parliament on December 21, 1912. Officially called territory of Nouveau-Québec.

NEW RICHMOND   The name originates with the Duke of Richmond, who served as Governor General from 1818 to 1819.

NICOLET   Town, county, and river. Dates from early eighteenth century and marks the career of Jean Nicolet (1598–1642), interpreter, explorer, and associate of Champlain.

NITRO   Assigned during the Second World War, the name recognizes the establishment of a defence plant which manufactured high explosives. Post office from 1961.

NOMININGUE   The community takes its name from the lake and is an Amerindian word for "red earth", indicating the presence locally of red ochre.

NORANDA   The name is a contraction of North Canada, for the Noranda Mines Limited, established in 1922. It was incorporated as a town in 1926 and achieved the status of a city in 1948.

NORMANDIN   After Joseph Normandin, who conducted an early survey of the area in 1733.

NORMÉTAL   For the Normetal Mining Corporation, which established a copper and zinc mine in the district in 1938.

NORTH HATLEY   First known as Charleston after the Rev.

Charles Stewart, it was later renamed for Hatley, a parish in Cambridgeshire, England.

NOTRE-DAME-DES-ANGES   Named after a seigniory of the same name granted to the Jesuits.

NOTRE-DAME-D'HÉBERTVILLE   *See* Hébertville

NOTRE-DAME-DU-LAC   Originated with the name of the local parish. The settlement dates from the mid nineteenth century.

NOTTAWAY RIVER   The name is of Amerindian origin and has been translated as meaning "the enemy" or "river of the enemy". It appears as Nottawases on Peter Pond's map of 1785, while Arrowsmith in 1834 renders it as Notaway. Possibly an Algonquin reference to the Iroquois. *See* Nottawasaga, Ontario

NOUVELLE   Commemorates the career of Abbé Henri Nouvel (1621?–1702?), a Jesuit missionary who came to New France in 1662. *See also* Pointe-au-Père

NUNS' ISLAND   *See* Île-des-Soeurs

OKA   Stems from an Algonquin word which may be translated in French as *doré*. It is possibly a reference to the quantities of pickerel once found in the Lake of Two Mountains. Dates from 1717.

OLD CHELSEA   *See* Chelsea

OLD HARRY BAY
OLD HARRY HEAD   For Harry Clarke, an early Scottish settler in the Magdalen Islands. Clarke was for a long time the only resident on this part of Coffin Island.

OMERVILLE   Named for Omer Goudreau, the owner of land on which the village is now located. Incorporated in 1953.

ORFORD, MONT   For Orford, a parish in Suffolk, England.

ORMSTOWN   Named for Orms Ellice, son of Alexander Ellice, who purchased the seigniory of Beauharnois in 1795.

ORSAINVILLE   The name is derived from a property title conferred on Intendant Jean Talon in May 1675.

OTIS   Commemorates the career of Abbé Lucien Otis, who served as parish priest in the area during the mid nineteenth century. The community dates from 1869.

OTTAWA   *See* Ontario *entry*

OTTER LAKE   Probably a descriptive term; however, the exact origin is unknown.

OUTREMONT   The name was determined by the city's geographical position in relation to Montréal, i.e., beyond Mount Royal. From the name of the residence of the Le Bouthillier family.

PABOS   Of uncertain origin. The name may be Basque, but is more probably Micmac. It appears on a map of 1506 as a designation for the nearby bay. The seigniory of Pabos was granted in 1696 to René Hébert.

PAPINEAUVILLE   After Louis Joseph Papineau (1786–1870), whose family owned the seigniory in which the town is located.

PARENT   For Étienne Parent (1801–74), a journalist and member of the legislature of the United Province of the Canadas for Saguenay.

PASPÉBIAC   A descriptive originating in the Micmac language. It probably refers to the basin which forms a natural harbour at this point. Appears on Denys's *Carte de l'Amérique Septentrionale*, 1672.

PERCÉ   Name derived from the offshore rock or island which is "pierced", permitting fishing boats to pass through. It was mentioned by Champlain in 1612 and is one of the oldest parishes on the Gaspé. Percé Rock refers to the bird sanctuary established in 1919.

PÉRIBONCA   From the Great Péribonca River, the name of which is of Amerindian origin and has been translated by Abbé Lemoine as "river cutting through the sand" or "place where sand is displaced". The setting for Louis Hémon's *Maria Chapdelaine*.

PERKINS   Formerly known as the municipality of Templeton North. The name was changed to honour that of the first settler. Amalgamated with adjacent municipalities in 1974 to form the municipality of Val-des-Monts.

PETIT-CAP   A descriptive that refers to the nearby landscape.

PIERREFONDS   For a town in northern France in the Department of Oise. *See also* Sainte-Geneviève-de-Pierrefonds

PIERREVILLE   Originally Saint-Thomas-de-Pierreville, the name was taken from Pierre Philippe, son of the owner of the seigniory, Sieur Laurent Philippe, in 1683. The settlement was incorporated as a village in 1887.

PINCOURT   The area was once a forest of short pine, or *pins courts* – a stopping point for early voyageurs on the Ottawa River. Incorporated in 1950.

PLAINS OF ABRAHAM   Named for Abraham Martin (1589–1664), an early settler who was possibly of Scottish origin.

PLESSISVILLE   Commemorates the career of Mgr. Joseph Octave Plessis (1763–1825), the Bishop of Québec from 1806 to 1825.

POINTE-À-GATINEAU   *See* Gatineau

POINTE-AU-PÈRE   After Abbé Henri Nouvel, a Jesuit priest who landed at this point on December 7, 1663. *See* Nouvelle

POINTE-AU-PIC   Descriptive. The name refers to a peak (*pic*) of rock which juts into the St. Lawrence River at this point.

POINT-AUX-TREMBLES   Designated by early settlers for the "aspen covered point of land which stretched out into the river". Dates from 1674.

POINTE-CALUMET   From an Algonquin word for "pipe of peace".

POINTE-CLAIRE   Descriptive. Named for the clear (*claire*) view of Lac-Saint-Louis which may be obtained at this point. Founded in 1913.

POINTE-DU-LAC   Founded in 1744, this parish derived its name from the fact that it is situated on a point of land running into Lac-Saint-Pierre.

POINTE-FORTUNE   For William Fortune, who settled there in the 1700s.

PONT-ROUGE   For a red bridge (*pont rouge*) that was erected by the first settlers in 1769.

PORT-ALFRED   Dates from the establishment of a paper mill in 1917 by J. E. Alfred Dubuc.

PORT-CARTIER   A new town (includes Shelter Bay area), the name of which was approved on January 23, 1962. For Jacques Cartier.

PORT-DANIEL   Originally Conche-Saint-Martin (discovered July 4, 1534, St. Martin's Day, by Jacques Cartier), it was renamed Port-Daniel in honour of Captain Charles Daniel (?–1661), a member of the Company of One Hundred Associates.

PORT-MENIER   For Henri Menier (?–1914), a French entrepreneur who made a fortune in the chocolate industry. He was once the owner of Anticosti Island.

PORTNEUF   The first settlers established themselves at "the port" at the mouth of the present-day Portneuf River. This element was later combined with the last syllable of Sieur Le Neuf to become Portneuf (Abbé Pierre George Roy).

POSTE-DE-LA-BALEINE   Descriptive. The name originates with the whale (*baleine*) fishery once carried on at the mouth of the Great Whale River. The new designation was adopted in 1965. Note also Grande rivière de la Baleine and Petite rivière de la Baleine.

POVUNGNITUK   River and trading post. The name is of Inuit origin. It has been translated as "place of bad smells".

PRICE   The earlier name, Priceville, was given to the site of a large sawmill operated by Price Brothers.

PRINCEVILLE   Named after Pierre Prince, who was one of the first settlers in the area. It was incorporated in 1857 as a village.

PROULXVILLE   For Abbé Prudent Proulx, an early parish priest.

QUÉBEC   Derived from the Amerindian word *kebek*, indicating a strait or channel that narrows. *See entry regarding province*

QUYON   Of uncertain origin. It is possibly an English misspelling of an earlier French name.

RAWDON　After Lord Francis Rawdon, Marquess of Hastings (1754–1826).

REPENTIGNY　Honours Pierre Le Gardeur de Repentigny (?–1648), a director of the Company of One Hundred Associates and Admiral of the Fleet, who obtained a grant of a seigniory in the area in 1647.

RESTIGOUCHE or **RISTIGOUCHE**　*See* New Brunswick *entry*

RICHELIEU　River, town, and county. All three names commemorate the career of Armand Jean Duplessis, Duke of Richelieu (1585–1642), principal minister of Louis XIII of France.

RICHMOND　Named in 1819 for Charles Lennox, Duke of Richmond (1764–1819), who was Governor General from 1818 to 1819. *See also* Richmond *and* Richmond Hill, Ontario

RIGAUD　Originated with the seigniory of Rigaud, which was granted in 1732 to Pierre and François Rigaud, sons of the Marquis de Vaudreuil (1691–1763), the last Governor of New France.

RIMOUSKI　City and county. The only agreement is that the word is of Micmac or Malecite origin. It has been variously translated as "land of moose" or "haunt of dogs". The seigniory of Rimouski was granted in 1688 to Sieur Augustin Rouer de la Cordonnière.

RIVIÈRE-AU-RENARD　Appears as early as 1744 and is undoubtedly descriptive of an incident in the early history of the region (*renard*, "fox").

RIVIÈRE-AU-TONNERRE　Descriptive. A four-hundred-foot waterfall near the mouth of the river produces a noise like thunder (*tonnerre*). Parish dates from 1871.

RIVIÈRE-AUX-OUTARDES　From the number of wild geese

(*outardes*) that frequent the river.

RIVIÈRE-DES-PRAIRIES   May be descriptive because of nearby "prairie" land, or for a voyageur by this name. *See* Des Prairies

RIVIÈRE-DU-LOUP   Name originated with the river and may be derived from the presence of timber wolves (*loups*) in the seventeenth century. Known briefly as Fraserville for a family which once held seigniorial rights in the district. The present name was officially adopted in 1919.

RIVIÈRE-DU-MOULIN   Descriptive. The location of a mill (*moulin*) on the river in 1750 suggested the name.

RIVIÈRE-EASTMAIN   Also known as La-Grande-Rivière-de-l'Est. The name is traceable to the Hudson's Bay Company post, Fort Eastmain, established in 1672. On White's and Carver's maps of 1778. Sometimes called Slude River (a reference to mica deposits found there); however, the name Eastmain was approved in 1905 and the river was officially designated Rivière-Eastmain on April 30, 1963.

RIVIÈRE-HARRICANA   An Algonquin word, which has been translated as the "place where bark dishes are obtained for cooking". Earlier spelling: Hurricanaw (Robert Bell).

RIVIÈRE-NASTAPOCA   Of uncertain origin, though more probably traceable to Amerindian than to Inuit sources. The exact meaning is unknown.

RIVIÈRE-OUELLE   For a Monsieur Ouel, compatriot of Champlain and member of the Company of One Hundred Associates.

ROBERTSONVILLE   After Joseph Gibb Robertson, who was once president of the Quebec Central Railway. It dates from the opening of the asbestos mines in 1909.

ROBERVAL   For Jean François de la Rocque, Sieur de Roberval (1500–60), explorer and "lieutenant general in the new lands discovered by Cartier".

ROCK ISLAND   The community name was transferred from an island in the Tomifobia River. It was incorporated as a town in 1956.

ROSEMERE   Named for the red and white roses found in the area.

ROUGEMONT   Named after a Captain de Rougemont, the Commandant of Fort Sainte-Thérèse in 1666.

ROUYN   Lake and town. Named for Captain de Rouyn, an officer in the Royal Roussillon Regiment (part of Montcalm's army.)

ROXTON FALLS   Named for a village in Bedfordshire, England.

SACRÉ-COEUR-DE-JÉSUS   First known as Dolbeau for Jean Dolbeau (1586–1652). The community was renamed in 1900 after the religious parish. *See* Dolbeau

SAGUENAY   County and river. The name is probably of Amerindian (Cree) origin, although its meaning is disputed. *Sakinipi*, or "water that goes out", is one possibility.

SAINTE-ADÈLE   After Adèle Raymond, wife of Augustin Norbert Morin, founder of the parish. *See* Val-Morin

SAINT-ADELPHE   A variation of the first name of Abbé Adolphe Dupuis, who erected a cross to mark the location of the parish church.

SAINT-AGAPIT-DE-BEAURIVAGE   May be traced to the seigniory of Beaurivage, granted April 1, 1738, to Gilles Rageot de

Beaurivage. The parish name was added to that of the seigniory.

SAINTE-AGATHE   First settlers were Irish and the parish drew its name from that of the Irish church in Rome.

SAINTE-AGATHE-DES-MONTS   A descriptive to distinguish this settlement from Sainte-Agathe. *See above*

SAINT-ALBAN   After Alban Bond, one of the early settlers in the district.

SAINT-ALEXIS-DES-MONTS   The parish was placed under the patronage of St. Alexis and named in memory of Alexis Boulanger, who donated land for the parish church.

SAINT-ALPHONSE-DE-CAPLAN   The earlier name was Musselyville for the Rev. H. J. Mussely, a Belgian priest who once served this area. Present designation is that of the parish, Saint-Alphonse, joined with the name of Jean Caplan, an early Amerindian resident.

SAINT-ANDRÉ-AVELLIN   For André Trudeau, surveyor and nephew of Joseph Papineau, who surveyed this section of the Petite Nation seigniory.

SAINTE-ANGÈLE-DE-MÉRICI   The parish was established in 1869 under the protection of Ste-Angèle-de-Mérici. The local seignior's wife, Angèle Drapeau, donated candlesticks for the new church and "was later remembered".

SAINTE-ANNE-DE-BEAUPRÉ   For Sainte Anne, the patron saint of sailors. *See also* Beaupré

SAINTE-ANNE-DE-BELLEVUE   A descriptive. The "fine view" was named by Louis and Gabriel de Berthé upon receipt of a land grant in the area about 1672.

SAINTE-ANNE-DE-LA-PÉRADE   Located at the mouth of the Sainte Anne River, the seigniory of La Pérade was granted in 1672 and named after Thomas de Lanouguère (1644–78), acting Governor of Montréal and seignior of Sainte-Anne. According to the *Dictionary of Canadian Biography*, he signed himself Lanaudière, Tarieu de Lanaudière, and Tarieu de la Pérade. From the latter designation the place name has evolved.

SAINTE-ANNE-DE-LA-POCATIÈRE   The parish was established in 1678 and comprised the seigniory of Pocatière granted in 1672 to Marie-Anne Juchereau, widow of François Pollet, Sieur de la Combe-Pocatière. She added her Christian name to that of the freehold to form this name, later bestowed on the parish.

SAINTE-ANNE-DES-MONTS   So named by the first settlers in memory of Sainte-Anne-de-la-Pocatière, their native parish.

SAINT-ANSELME   Reputed to have been inspired by the nearness of the parish to St. Henri (Saint Anselme was persecuted by Henri I of England, hence the linking of the names.)

SAINT-ANTOINE-DES-LAURENTIDES   Marks a separation from the original parish of Saint-Antoine.

SAINT-BASILE   Honours Basile Daignault, one of the builders of the parish church.

SAINT-BONAVENTURE   *See* Bonaventure

SAINT-BONIFACE-DE-SHAWINIGAN   Designated by Mgr. Thomas Cook, the first bishop of Trois-Rivières, on February 3, 1859. Named for Saint Boniface, "the apostle of Germany".

SAINT-BRUNO   After Abbé Bruno Leclerc, curé of Notre-Dame d'Hébertville and founder of the parish in 1910.

SAINT-BRUNO-DE-MONTARVILLE   Possibly traceable to the Boucher de Montarville family.

SAINT-CAMILLE   From the Christian name of Abbé Camille Brochu, priest of the nearby Saint-Magloire parish.

SAINTE-CÉCILE-DE-MASHAM   Masham was named for a town in Yorkshire, England. *See* La Pêche

SAINT-CÉSAIRE   The name is derived from that of the religious parish. There is no known local association.

SAINT-CHARLES   Honours Charles Couillard, local seignior, who donated land for the parish church in 1748. *See* Beaumont

SAINT-CHARLES-DE-MANDEVILLE   The first mission was established by Abbé Charles Turgeon, curé of Saint Didace. Mandeville was derived from Maxime Mandeville, an early settler.

SAINT-CHRYSOSTOME   From the name assigned to the religious parish.

SAINTE-CLAIRE-DE-JOLIETTE   Honours the memory of Claire Françoise Bissot, wife of Louis Jolliet (1645–1700), explorer.

SAINT-COEUR-DE-MARIE   Upon incorporation the village adopted the name of the religious parish. It was originally known as Saint-Mathias.

SAINT-CONSTANT   The name was derived in honour of Constant Cartier.

SAINTE-CROIX   A part of the seigniory of Sainte-Croix that was granted to the Ursuline Order.

SAINT-CUTHBERT   Detached from Berthier in 1770. In 1766 James Cuthbert, seignior, granted a parcel of land to the parish on condition that it be placed under the patronage of St. Cuthbert.

SAINT-CYRILLE　Name may be traced to Cyrille Brassard, an early settler. Founded in 1872. Incorporated in 1905.

SAINT-DAMASE　After Abbé Damase Morisset, curé of the neighbouring parish of Présentation.

SAINT-DAMIEN-DE-BUCKLAND　The name developed from the community's proximity to the villages of Saint-Damien and Buckland. Name adopted in 1934.

SAINT-DAVID-DE-L'AUBERIVIÈRE　Named for the Rev. François-Louis Pourroy de Lauberivière, fifth bishop of Québec, and David Déziel, the first parish priest.

SAINT-DENIS　Derived from Barbe Denis, wife of Louis de Gannes, Sieur de Falaise, to whom the seigniory was granted in 1694.

SAINT-DONAT　The name was bestowed by Abbé Gabriel Nadeau, curé of nearby Sainte-Luce, who established the parish. *See* Saint-Gabriel-de-Rimouski

SAINT-ÉLEUTHÈRE　Suggested by Cardinal Taschereau in 1874 for the martyred Saint Éleuthère.

SAINT-ÉMILE　The community name was derived from that of the religious parish.

SAINT-ÉPHREM-DE-TRING　For Éphrem Proulx, who donated land for the parish church. Incorporated in 1864. Tring is for the township which was named for Tring, Hertfordshire, England.

SAINT-ÉPIPHANE　Parish church was dedicated to Saint-Épiphane in honour of Abbé Épiphane Lapointe, curé of Rimouski.

SAINT-EUSTACHE   Founded in 1768, this town takes its name from Eustache Lambert, once the local seignior. It was the scene of a battle on December 14, 1837, part of the uprising of 1837.

SAINT-FÉLICIEN   The name of the religious parish commemorates Saint Félicien, a martyr for Christianity during the reign of Diocletian.

SAINTE-FÉLICITÉ   The community was formerly known as Pointe-au-Massacre because of a shipwreck which occurred there. It was created as a parish in 1860 and placed under the protection of Sainte Félicité.

SAINT-FÉLIX-DE-VALOIS   *See* Saint-Jean-de-Matha

SAINT-FÉRÉAL   Commemorates the career of Jean Lyon de Saint-Ferréol (1692–1745), the superior of the Seminary of Québec and Vicar General.

SAINT-FLAVIEN   Named after the Rev. Pierre Flavien Turgeon (1787–1867), Archbishop of Québec from 1850 to 1867.

SAINTE-FOY   Parish established in 1698 and named for a village in France.

SAINT-FRANÇOIS, RIVIÈRE   The name of the river is taken from the parish of Saint-François-du-Lac, dating from 1638.

SAINT-FRANÇOIS-D'ASSISE   Named after Abbé François Cinq-Mars, curé of Saint-Alexis-de-Matapédia.

SAINT-FRANÇOIS-DU-LAC   Possibly marks the career of François de Lauzon, whose family were landholders in the area.

SAINT-FULGENCE   The area was first settled in 1839 and called L'Anse-au-Foin, "Hay Cove". The new name evolved from that of the religious parish.

SAINT-GABRIEL   Honours Abbé Gabriel Nadeau, curé of Sainte-Luce, who ministered to the first colonists of the parish.

SAINT-GABRIEL-DE-BRANDON   Named after the religious parish. Brandon may be traced to a town in Suffolk, England.

SAINT-GÉDÉON (Lac-Saint-Jean)   Named for Gédéon Ouimet (1823–1903), who served as Premier of Québec from 1873 to 1874.

SAINTE-GENEVIÈVE-DE-BATISCAN   Selected by early settlers for the patron saint of Paris.

SAINTE-GENEVIÈVE-DE-BERTHIER   Named for Marie-Geneviève Berthier, daughter of the seignior, Alexandre Berthier, who acquired the seigniory in 1674.

SAINTE-GENEVIÈVE-DE-PIERREFONDS   After the religious parish. *See* Pierrefonds. Incorporated as a town in 1959.

SAINT-GEORGES (Beauce)   Name honours an early parish priest, the Rev. Georges Payette. Founded in 1840.

SAINT-GEORGES (Champlain)   After the religious parish.

SAINT-GÉRARD   Incorporated in 1886 as Weedon Lake. The name was changed to that of the parish in 1905.

SAINT-GERMAIN-DE-GRANTHAM   Honours Edward Granville Eliot, third Earl of St. Germain (1798–1877), who accompanied the Prince of Wales to Canada in 1860. Grantham (the township name) is for a town in Lincolnshire, England.

SAINTE-GERMAINE-DU-LAC-ETCHEMIN   Parish is located on the side of Lac-Etchemin. It was founded in 1867, the same year in which Sainte Germaine was canonized, hence the selection of the name.

SAINT-GILLES   Part of the seigniory of Beaurivage and named in 1738 for Gilles Rageot, the first landholder.

SAINT-GRÉGOIRE (Nicolet)   After Grégoire Bourque, who donated land for the parish church.

SAINT-GUILLAUME   The earlier name, Ruisseau des Chênes (Oak Brook), was changed to Saint-Guillaume for Charles William Grant, who gave land for the presbytery and church.

SAINT HELEN'S ISLAND   *See* Île-Sainte-Hélène

SAINTE-HÉNÉDINE   Name honours Hénédine Dionne, wife of the seignior, Elzéar Taschereau.

SAINT-HENRI   For Henri Marie Dubreuil de Pontbriand (1708–60), Bishop of Québec from 1741 to 1760.

SAINT-HILAIRE   After the religious parish named in honour of Élie Saint-Hilaire, M.L.A. for Chicoutimi from 1881 to 1888.

SAINT-HONORÉ (Chicoutimi)   Originated with the name of Honoré Petit (1848–1919), M.L.A. for Chicoutimi and Saguenay from 1892 to 1919.

SAINT-HONORÉ (Témiscouata)   Derived from the name of the first settler, Honoré Morin.

SAINT-HUBERT   The parish was instituted by canon in 1862 and placed under the patronage of Saint-Hubert. By order-in-council on October 20, 1971, the town of Saint-Hubert was amalgamated with the city of Laflèche to become Ville-de-Saint-Hubert.

SAINT-HYACINTHE   For Hyacinthe Simon Delorme, who in 1753 purchased the seigniory from Pierre de Rigaud, Marquis de Vaudreuil-Cavagnal, to whom it had been granted in 1748.

SAINT-ISIDORE (Dorchester)   After the religious parish.

SAINT-JACQUES (Montcalm)   Settled in 1775 by Acadians and placed under the patronage of Saint-Jacques in honour of Abbé Jacques Degeay, the curé.

SAINT-JANVIER   A hill within the parish limits bore the name Saint-Janvier and the name was later ascribed for the parish.

SAINT-JEAN   (The anglicized form, St. John's, was dropped by the passage of a private bill in the Assembly in 1962.) Traces its origin to Fort Saint-Jean, which was established in 1748 and probably named for the French Minister of Marine at the time, Jean Frédéric Phélypeaux, Comte de Pontchartrain.

SAINT-JEAN-DE-BOISCHATEL   After M. de Beauchastel, a major in the La Sarre Regiment during the French regime.

SAINT-JEAN-DE-DIEU   The parish name was selected by Mgr. Jean Pierre François La Force Langevin (1821–92), the Bishop of Rimouski, "because no other parish in the area had chosen that saint as patron" (Roy).

SAINT-JEAN-DE-MATHA   Saint-Félix-de-Valois and Saint-Jean-de-Matha, adjoining parishes, were named because of the close association between their two patron saints.

SAINT-JEAN-EUDES   From the name of the parish priest. The community was annexed on August 15, 1970, to Arvida.

SAINTE-JEANNE-D'ARC   Established in 1920, the year of the canonization of Ste-Jeanne-d'Arc.

SAINT-JEAN-PORT-JOLI   A combination of the parish name with a descriptive of the location on a small harbour formed by the river. Dates from 1721.

SAINT-JÉRÔME (Lac-Saint-Jean)   The name was taken from that of the religious parish, which replaced the earlier Amerindian name, Métabetchouan. Founded in 1834 by the Rev. Antoine Labelle (1833–91). *See* Labelle

SAINT-JÉRÔME (Terrebonne)   First known as Dumontville for a local seignior, the town was then named after the titular saint. Founded in 1852.

SAINT-JOACHIM-DE-MONTMORENCY   Possibly because the titular saint of the adjoining parish (Sainte-Anne-de-Beaupré) was the wife of Saint Joachim. The parish was created in 1685 and the village takes its name from the parish.

SAINT-JOSEPH (Beauce)   Honours Joseph Fleury de la Gorgendière (1676–1755), an early landholder in the area. *See* Sainte-Marie

SAINT-JOSEPH (Saint-Hyacinthe)   For the religious parish.

SAINT-JOSEPH-D'ALMA   *See* Alma

SAINT-JOSEPH-DE-LA-RIVIÈRE-BLEUE   A combination of the parish name with that of the river. Descriptive.

SAINT-JOVITE   The first mass in the parish was celebrated on February 15, 1877, the feast day of St. Jovite.

SAINTE-JUSTINE   For Marie Justine Têtu, wife of Sir Hector Langevin, long-time Minister of Public Works and associate of Sir John A. Macdonald.

SAINT-LAMBERT   Marks the career of Raphael Lambert Closse (1618–62), merchant and sergeant-major of the Ville-Marie garrison.

SAINT LAWRENCE RIVER
LE SAINT-LAURENT   Originally applied to Baie-Saint-Laurent
(formerly known in English as Pillage Bay) on the north shore of
the present-day Gulf of St. Lawrence. The river was discovered by
Cartier on August 10, 1535, St. Lawrence Day. The name was gradually applied to the gulf and the river. In 1553, Gomara designated
the river as "la grande rivière de Saint-Laurent". The Mercator
map of 1569 and Champlain's charts of 1616 and 1632 note the
"Golphe St. Laurens".

SAINT-LÉON-DE-STANDON   Adapted after the first settler,
Léon Rousseau. Standon is a village in Hertfordshire, England.

SAINT-LÉON-LE-GRAND   Originates with Abbé Léon
d'Auteuil, one-time parish priest of Amqui, from which the parish was detached in 1907.

SAINT-LÉONARD-D'ASTON   An association of the parish
name with that of the community. Probably named for one of the
numerous Astons in England, e.g. in Warwickshire.

SAINT LEONARD
SAINT-LÉONARD-DE-PORT-MAURICE   Named for the titular
saint of the religious parish, who was canonized in 1867. The city
name is Saint Leonard, changed from Saint-Léonard-de-Port-
Maurice on November 10, 1962.

SAINT-LIBOIRE   Named for Abbé Liboire Girouard, the first
parish priest.

SAINT-LOUIS-DU-HA! HA!   The community was founded in
1873 and placed under the patronage of St. Louis in honour of
the first settler, Louis Marquis. *See* Ha Ha River

SAINT-LUC   Named by association with the neighbouring parishes of St-Martin and St-Marc.

SAINTE-MADELEINE   From the name assigned to the religious
parish.

SAINT-MAGLOIRE   Honours the first priest in the parish, Abbé Magloire Rioux.

SAINT-MARC-DES-CARRIÈRES   Des Carrières is taken from the limestone quarries (*carrières*) in the vicinity. The parish (Saint-Marc's) dates from 1901 and is named for a church in Rome.

SAINTE-MARIE   For Marie Claire Fleury de la Gorgendière, wife of the seignior, Joseph Fleury de la Gorgendière. *See* Sainte-Joseph-de-Beauce

SAINT-MARTIN   Established in 1882 and placed under the patronage of Saint-Martin-de-Tours by Cardinal Elzéar Alexandre Taschereau.

SAINT-MATHIAS   First known as Pointe-Olivier for Mgr. Jean Olivier Briand (1715–94), Bishop of Québec. The name was changed in 1809 for the titular saint of the parish.

SAINT-MAURICE RIVIÈRE   Discovered in 1535 by Cartier; the name originates with the seigniory granted in 1668 to Maurice Poulin de la Fontaine (1620–70). Early name – Trois-Rivières – was replaced by the Christian name of the head of the Poulin family and gradually extended to the river, the county, and the surrounding region.

SAINT-MICHEL   Part of metropolitan Montréal. The community was named after the patron saint of the parish.

SAINT-MICHEL-DES-SAINTS   Founded in 1860 and placed under the patronage of Saint-Michel-des-Saints because the saint's canonization coincided with the founding of the parish.

SAINT-MICHEL-DE-VAUDREUIL   For Michel Chartier de Lotbinière, seignior of Vaudreuil. The parish was established in 1829 by Mgr. Panet.

SAINT-MOÏSE   Founded in 1870 under the patronage of St. Moïse in honour of Abbé Moïse Duguay.

SAINT-NAZAIRE   For Mgr. Louis Nazaire Bégin (1840–1925), second bishop of Chicoutimi and later a cardinal.

SAINT-NOËL   Commemorates the career of Abbé Noël Chabanel (1613–49), who died a martyr's death at Huronia on December 8, 1649. He was canonized by Pope Pius XI on June 29, 1930.

SAINT-OCTAVE-DE-L'AVENIR   Named for its founder, Abbé Octave Caron. Established in 1933.

SAINT-OMER   Detached from Carleton in 1899 and placed under the patronage of St. Omer in honour of the first missionary in the area, Abbé Omer Normandin.

SAINT-OURS   The name was derived from the owner of the seigniory, Pierre de Saint Ours (1640–1724), a captain of the Carignan-Salières Regiment.

SAINT-PACÔME   The parish was founded in 1851 when it was detached from Rivière-Ouelle. The name is from that of the religious parish which was placed under the patronage of the "hermit saint".

SAINT-PASCAL   The parish was established in 1827 and named for Pascal Taché, seignior of Kamouraska.

SAINT-PAUL-L'ERMITE   After the titular saint of the parish.

SAINT-PAULIN   Detached from the parish of Saint-Léon and instituted canonically on December 27, 1847. The new parish comprises part of the seigniory of Dumontier. The name originates with the religious parish.

SAINT-PHILÉMON   Detached from the parish of Saint-Paul-de-Burton and probably designated Saint-Philémon because the latter was a disciple of St. Paul.

SAINT-PIE   Founded in 1830 and named for St. Pie V, who served as Pope from 1566 to 1572.

SAINT-POLYCARPE   For the titular saint of the parish.

SAINT-PRIME   Honours Abbé Prime Girard, curé of Roberval, who was responsible for establishing a mission in the locality.

SAINT-PROSPER   After Abbé Prosper Meunier, curé of Saint-Zachairie-de-Metgermette, the founder of the mission.

SAINTE-PRUDENTIENNE   The name originates with that of the religious parish.

SAINT-RAPHAEL   Honours the Rev. François-Raphaël Paquet, a benefactor of the parish and curé of nearby Saint-Gervais.

SAINT-RAYMOND   After St. Raymond Nonnat, whose anniversary coincided with the establishment of the parish in 1842.

SAINT-RÉDEMPTEUR   From the name of the religious parish.

SAINT-RÉMI   Commemorates the career of Daniel de Rémy de Courcelle (Courcelles) (1626–98), once Governor of New France. The parish was founded in 1833.

SAINT-ROCH-DE-L'ACHIGAN   Named after Roch-de-Saint-Ours, the owner of the seigniory of La Chevaie, who, reputedly, granted land for the parish church. *Achigan* is the Algonquin word for "small-mouthed bass".

SAINT-ROCH-DES-AULNAIES   The name results from a union of the communities of Saint-Roch and Des Aulnaies (part of the seigniory granted to Nicolas Juchereau de Saint-Denis in 1656). Des Aulnaies is derived from the alder-covered banks of the nearby Ferrée River.

SAINT-ROCH-D'ORFORD   The post office was known as Rock-Forest. "This suggested the idea of putting the parish under the patronage of St. Roch." (Roy)

SAINTE-ROSALIE   The area was once part of the seigniory of Sainte-Hyacinthe, owned by the Dessaules family. Rosalie was a popular Christian name in this family.

SAINTE-ROSE-DU-DÉGELÉ   *See* Dégelis

SAINT-SAUVEUR-DES-MONTS   Descriptive of the location of the parish (surrounded by the Laurentians).

SAINTE-SCHOLASTIQUE   Founded in 1825 and named for the sister of St. Benoît, whose name is applied to a neighbouring parish. Incorporated as a city in 1971. The name was changed to Mirabel in 1973.

SAINT-SIMÉON   The name is taken from that of the religious parish. Established in 1869.

SAINT-STANISLAS   *See* Deux-Rivières

SAINT-SULPICE   The seigniory was once the property of the Seminary of Saint-Sulpice, Montréal. The parish was established in 1706.

SAINTE-THÈCLE   The first mission was conducted by the curé of the nearby Saint-Tite (Saint-Tite and Sainte-Thècle were contemporaries).

SAINTE-THÉRÈSE   The parish was placed under the patronage of Saint-Thérèse in honour of Thérèse de Blainville, granddaughter of the first seignior.

SAINT-TIMOTHÉE   Adopted for the village from the name of the religious parish.

SAINT-TITE   *See* Sainte Thècle *above*

SAINT-TITE-DES-CAPS   Des Caps was added to the parish name because of the location at the foot of the headlands (*caps*) behind Cap-Tourmente. Founded in 1853 when the saint was inscribed on the Roman calendar.

SAINT-UBALD   Named for Ubald Gingras, one of the early settlers.

SAINT-ULRIC   Honours Ulric Joseph Tessier (1817–92), jurist and senator and one of the benefactors of the parish.

SAINT-URBAIN-DE-CHARLEVOIX   After Abbé Urbain Boiret, Superior of the Seminary of Québec.

SAINT-VALLIER   Dates from 1713 and was originally part of the seigniory of La Durantaye, but was later purchased by Jean Baptiste de la Croix de Chevrières de Saint Vallier, second bishop of Québec.

SAINT-VICTOR-DE-TRING   For Victor Hudon, a Montréal wholesale merchant who had many business connections in the Eastern Townships. *See* Saint-Éphrem-de-Tring

SAINT-WENCESLAS   Adopted in 1954 after the name of the religious parish.

SAINT-ZACHARIE   Honours Abbé Zacharie Lacasse (1845–1921), missionary and author.

SAINT-ZÉNON   Founded in 1870 and established as a civil parish on October 7, 1895. The name of the community is derived from the religious parish.

SAINT-ZÉPHIRIN-DE-COURVAL   A combination of the parish name with that of the seigniory of De Courval.

SAINT-ZOTIQUE   Named when Mgr. Bourget brought relics of the saint to Québec.

SALABERRY DE VALLEYFIELD   *See* Valleyfield

SAULT-AU-MOUTON   The name is derived from the river which flows through the village. Its origin is unknown, although the name has been recorded on maps since 1681.

SAWYERVILLE   For Josiah Sawyer, who took up land here in 1742.

SAYABEC   Traceable to the Micmac, this name refers to the fact that the river is often blocked by driftwood and beaver dams.

SCHEFFERVILLE   The area was first known as Knob Lake for a nearby mountain. The present name was adopted in 1955 and honours Mgr. Lionel Scheffer, Bishop of Labrador.

SCOTSTOWN   First settlers were brought to the area in the 1830s from Scotland by the British American Land Company.

SENNETERRE   First known as Nottaway, the name was changed in 1918 in honour of an officer in the Languedoc Regiment of Montcalm's army at the siege of Québec. It was incorporated as a town in 1956.

SENNEVILLE   For Captain Le Ber de Senneville, a local seignior.

SEPT-ÎLES   The islands were identified by Cartier on August 18, 1535, and named Ysles Rondes (round, from their shape). Later referred to as Sept-Isles, familiar to Cartier because of a similar place name near Saint-Malo.

SHAWBRIDGE   Named for William Shaw, the first postmaster in the area and builder of a bridge over the Rivière-du-Nord.

SHAWINIGAN   Lake, river, and falls. The name is of Amerindian origin and probably means "portage on the summit or crest", for the portage over a crest of rocks. Baie-de-Shawinigan is on the river and denotes a slight widening at this point.

SHAWVILLE   Founded in 1840 and named for a pioneer family.

SHELTER BAY   *See* Port Cartier

SHERBROOKE   Named after Sir John Coape Sherbrooke, Governor General from 1816 to 1818.

SHICKSHOCK MOUNTAINS   Referred to as Notre Dame Mountains on Champlain's map of 1632. More recent maps revert to the Amerindian Shickshock (1857). Chic Choc (1858) is a Micmac term, translated as Rocky Mountains. The official spelling is Chic-Chocs.

SHIGAWAKE   Originally a part of the parish of Saint Godefroi, the parish takes its name from the river. Mgr. Eugène Rouillard has translated the Micmac word as "land of the rising sun", since the Indians were in the habit of descending the river to reach Chaleur Bay.

SILLERY   For its founder, Noël Brulart de Sillery (1577–1640), a member of the Company of One Hundred Associates.

SOREL   The site of Fort Richelieu, later named for Pierre de Saurel, a captain in the Carignan-Salières Regiment.

SQUATEC   The name has been variously spelled as Squatteck,

Squateck, and Squatec, from a Micmac word for "a lake form caused by the widening of the river."

STANSTEAD   Probably for Stanstead, Essex, England.

STRATFORD   Possibly named for a section of London, England.

SULLIVAN MINES   The name was derived from the Sullivan Gold Mines.

SUTTON   Named after one of the many English Suttons, possibly for Sutton in Surrey.

SWEETSBURG   The early name, Churchville (for John Church, a local merchant), was changed to honour Gardner Sweet, the first postmaster. Annexed to Cowansville on February 1, 1964.

TADOUSSAC   The name is of Amerindian origin and was probably first mapped by Cartier. One of the earliest spellings is Thadoyzeau, noted by André Thévet, whose source was almost certainly Cartier. The name may be translated as "breasts", a reference to nearby hills.

TALON   Commemorates the career of the "great intendant", Jean-Baptiste Talon (1625–94).

TÉMISCAMING   Lake and river. Sometimes written Témiscamingue-Timiskaming (Delisle, 1733, and D'Anville, 1755), the name is Amerindian in origin and has been translated as "deep water".

TÉMISCOUATA   County and lake. A Cree descriptive, this name may mean "deep lake" or "deep all over". The Témiscouata River drains to the south by the Madawaska to the Saint John River.

TEMPLETON   Named for a village in Devonshire, England.

TERREBONNE Literally "good land", the community was so named by the first seignior, André Daulier Des Landes.

THETFORD MINES Once known as Kingsville for the proprietor of local asbestos mines, the name was changed to that of the township which was given in honour of the town of Thetford, Norfolk, England. Incorporated on September 22, 1892.

THURSO Named for the parish of Thurso, Caithness, Scotland.

TOURAINE Adopted on January 5, 1966, for the old French province of the same name, which corresponded to the modern Department of Indre-et-Loire.

TRACY After the Marquis de Tracy, Lieutenant-General of New France from 1663 to 1667. The community was formerly known as L'Enfant-Jésus-de-Sorel. The name was changed to Tracy in 1954.

TRING JONCTION For a town in Hertfordshire, England. Incorporated in 1918.

TROIS-PISTOLES The name is of uncertain origin. One tradition is that a barque stranded near the mouth of the river sent a sailor to seek fresh water. In his search he lost a silver goblet valued at "trois pistoles" (CPCGN files). The seigniory of Trois-Pistoles was granted in 1687.

TROIS-RIVIÈRES A descriptive which probably dates from the period of Champlain's explorations (the St. Maurice River has three branches at this point). The settlement was founded by Sieur La Violette in 1634.

UNGAVA Of Inuit origin, the name may be translated as "far away".

UPTON Established in 1800 and named for a village in Cheshire, England.

VAL-BARRETTE Named for an early settler in the area. Parish was founded in 1914.

VAL-BÉLAIR Established on December 29, 1973, with the amalgamation of Bélair and Val-Saint-Michel.

VAL-BRILLANT Until 1913 the community was known as Cedar Hall; from 1913 to 1916 it was known as Saint-Pierre-du-Lac. The name was changed to honour Abbé Pierre Brillant, first curé to come to this region in 1889.

VALCARTIER Located in the valley of Rivière-Jacques-Cartier, named for the explorer.

VALCOURT Possibly a descriptive for "short valley".

VAL-DAVID Named in 1931 for Athanase David.

VAL-DES-MONTS A municipality established among the hills east of the Gatineau River and comprising Perkins, Portland-Ouest, and part of Wakefield.

VAL-D'OR Founded in 1934 as a result of gold-mining activity in the region.

VAL-JALBERT The early name of the community was the Amerindian *Ouiatchouan*. It was renamed in 1909 after Damase Jalbert, founder of the local pulp-and-paper industry. Annexed by the parish municipality of Saint-Louis-de-Chambord, January 1, 1971.

VALLÉE-JONCTION Descriptive. The community is named for its location in the Chaudière River valley.

VALLEYFIELD Officially the city is known as Salaberry de Valleyfield. This is a combination of an industrial name (for Valley-field Paper Mills, Edinburgh, Scotland) plus that of Charles Michel d'Irumberry de Salaberry (1778–1829), who commanded the Canadian forces at the Battle of Châteauguay on October 26, 1813.

VAL-MORIN   Established in 1922 and named for Auguste-Norbert Morin (1803 – 65), one of the early residents of the area.

VANIER   The earlier name, Québec-Ouest, was changed to Vanier by order-in-council on May 16, 1966, to honour General Georges Philias Vanier (1888–1967), Governor General of Canada from 1959 to 1967.

VARENNES   Named after Cap-de-Varennes, part of a seigniory granted in 1672 to René Gaultier de Varennes (1635–89), an officer in the Carignan-Salières Regiment, who served as Governor of Trois-Rivières.

VAUDREUIL   Marks the career of Philippe de Rigaud, Marquis de Vaudreuil (1643–1725), Governor of New France from 1705 to 1724.

VERCHÈRES   Named for François Jarret, Sieur de Verchères (1641–1700), who was granted a seigniory in 1672.

VERDUN   A variation of Saverdun, France, the birthplace of Zacharie Dupuis, who was granted land in this vicinity in 1672.

VICTORIAVILLE   The early name, Demersville, was changed in 1861 in honour of Queen Victoria.

VILLE-MARIE   Founded in 1866 by the Oblates of Mary Immaculate, and first known as Sainte-Vierge.

VILLENEUVE   Detached in 1922 from Beauport (Beauport-Est). Named for Abbé Louis Villeneuve, a Sulpician priest.

WAKEFIELD   Named for Wakefield in Yorkshire, England. *See* La Pêche

WARWICK   Established in 1804 and named for Warwickshire, England.

WATERLOO   The name marks the Battle of Waterloo in 1815.

WATERVILLE   Descriptive. Named because of the location of a hydro station on Rivière-Coaticook.

WEEDON CENTRE   Named for the village of Weedon, Buckinghamshire, England.

WESTMOUNT   Incorporated in 1873. A descriptive which is indicative of its location.

WINDSOR   The name originates with the township, which in turn was named for Windsor, Berkshire, England.

WOTTONVILLE   Named for Wotton in Surrey, England. Founded in 1849.

YAMACHICHE   The name is of Algonquin origin and has evolved from that of the river. It may be translated as "muddy" or "clay" river.

YAMASKA   An Algonquin descriptive which was applied to the extensive marshes in the region. It has been variously translated as "where there is grass under the water" or "where the grass and rushes are high".

Saskatchewan

 The name is derived from that which was first applied to the Saskatchewan River. In the Cree language it was known as *Kisiskatchewani Sipi* (Tyrrell), or "swift-flowing river". Henday's spelling was *Keiskatchewan,* with the modern rendering, *Saskatchewan,* being officially adopted in 1882 when a portion of the present-day province was designated a provisional district of the North West Territories. Achieved provincial status in 1905.

ARBORFIELD   It is suggested locally that the original designation, Fairfield, was rejected by postal authorities on Arbor Day, giving rise to the coined name. The post office was established in 1910.

ARCOLA   The name is derived from the Battle of Arcola in northern Italy, November 15–17, 1796, an important confrontation in the Napoleonic Wars. This settlement was incorporated as a town in 1903.

ASSINIBOIA   For the Assiniboine Indians, who once frequented the area. It was called Leeville after Hubbard Lee, the first postmaster, and the name was changed to Assiniboia, November 23, 1913. *See* Manitoba *entry*

ASSINIBOINE RIVER   *See* Manitoba *entry*

ATHABASCA, LAKE   *See* Alberta *entry*

BALCARRES   Probably named for Balcarres in Fifeshire, Scotland.

BATOCHE   Headquarters for Louis Riel during the North West Uprising of 1885, it was named for Xavier Letendre, a Métis trader. His nickname was Batoche, derived from the French *bateau*, meaning "boat".

BATTLEFORD   Named because of its location on a ford of the Battle River, it was the capital of the North West Territories from 1876 to 1883.

BATTLE RIVER   Derived from the number of battles fought on its banks between the Blackfoot and Cree Indians.

BENGOUGH   Honours John Wilson Bengough (1851–1923), one of Canada's best-known cartoonists.

BIENFAIT   A local legend attests that the designation "well done" (*bien fait*) was assigned to the settlement by two French-speaking railway workers. The town was, however, named about 1886 by the C.P.R. for a member of an Amsterdam banking firm (CPCGN file 62 F/3). *See also* Boissevain, Manitoba

BIGGAR   Honours William Hodgins Biggar, one-time general solicitor for the Grand Trunk Pacific Railway Company.

BIG RIVER   The name is an English translation of an earlier Amerindian descriptive term. The village was founded in 1909 and incorporated in 1921.

BIRCH HILLS   Named for the groves of birch trees located on the range of hills near the town.

BLAINE LAKE   A surveyor named Blaine was drowned in the lake prior to the establishment of the settlement in 1911.

BROADVIEW   A descriptive name assigned in 1882 when "nothing could be seen to the west but a great expanse of prairies" (Russell).

BRUNO   Marks the career of the Rev. Bruno Doerfler, the founder of a German–American colony in 1902.

CABRI   Said to be a variation of an Amerindian word for antelope, indicating they were once prevalent in the district (Russell). The word *cabri* is French, meaning the kid of a goat, and was used by French Canadians for the prong-horned antelope (Rayburn).

CANORA   An acronym derived from the first letters of *Ca*nadian *No*rthern *Ra*ilway. Incorporated as a town in 1910.

CARLTON   From Carlton House, a Hudson's Bay Company fort built in 1810 on the North Saskatchewan River. A nearby historic site marks the Carlton Trail, once the major overland route linking Fort Garry and Edmonton House.

CARLYLE   Named in 1882 by J. G. Turriff, probably for the Scottish author Thomas Carlyle (1795–1881).

CARNDUFF   Honours John P. Carnduff, who was a homesteader in the district about 1884. He was named the first postmaster in 1891.

CARROT RIVER   An English translation of a Cree word for the wild carrot, native to this area.

CRAIK   For Robert Craik, a surveyor on the Prince Albert branch of the Canadian Pacific Railway.

CREE LAKE   For the Cree Indians originally known as *Kristeneaux.* The name was suggested by J. C. Sproule, a geologist with the Department of Mines and Resources (Russell). *See* Kinistino

CREIGHTON   A residential suburb of Flin Flon, located west of the Manitoba boundary. Named in 1948 to honour Thomas Creighton (1877–1952), a prominent prospector in the area.

CUDWORTH   Marks the career of Ralph Cudworth (1617–88), English philosopher and Master of Christ's College, Cambridge.

CUMBERLAND HOUSE   The site of the first inland trading post of the Hudson's Bay Company, established in 1774. Probably named after Prince Rupert, Duke of Cumberland (1619–87).

CUSSED CREEK   Scene of an encounter in the North West Uprising of 1885 which gave rise to the "Ballad of the Near Battle of Cussed Creek" (CPCGN file 62 M/SW).

CUT KNIFE   Also scene of a battle in 1885. Derived from Cut Knife Hill, where a Sarcee chief of that name was killed in a fight with a band of Crees.

CYPRESS HILLS   Originally Montagne de Cyprès, the name appears as Cypress Hills on Palliser's map of 1865. The French mistakenly associated the jack pine or lodgepole pine, common in the district, with the gray pine, popularly called *cyprès* by the French in Canada.

DAVIDSON   After Colonel A. D. Davidson, a Minnesota promoter and organizer of the Saskatchewan Valley Land Company. The area was largely settled by American immigrants in the early years of the twentieth century.

DIEFENBAKER, LAKE   A reservoir on the South Saskatchewan River, named for J. G. Diefenbaker, the first resident of Saskatchewan to hold office as Prime Minister. The name was officially adopted on July 14, 1967. *See also* Gardiner Dam

DUCK LAKE   Scene of the first engagement of the North West Uprising, March 26, 1885. The first settlement was at the lake about a mile west of the town. "It was well named the ducks being so plentiful that when generally distributed the vibration of their wings sounds like thunder." (CPCGN files)

EASTEND   Location of a North West Mounted Police detachment, the most easterly group of Division A and located on the east side of the Cypress Hills.

EATONIA   Marks the career of Timothy Eaton (1834–1907) and the contribution of the Eaton mail-order company to the development of the West.

ELDORADO   For the Eldorado Mining and Refining Company which opened uranium mines in the area.

ESTERHAZY   After Count Paul Otto d'Esterhazy (1830–1912), a native of Hungary, who was active in promoting settlement in the area.

Nearby is Kaposvar Settlement, which marks the first major Hungarian settlement in Canada, July 1886. It stems from a village of the same name southeast of Budapest.

ESTEVAN   Commemorates the careers of Sir George Stephen, afterward Baron Mount Stephen (1829–1921), and Sir William Van Horne (1843–1915). The name is said to be formed by a selection of letters from the name of each – George *Ste*phen, W. C. *Van* Horne. Both were prominent in the development of the Canadian Pacific Railway. It is also claimed that the name is a Spanish rendering of Stephen, and an acronym derived from Esther Van Horne, Sir William's daughter (CPCGN files).

ESTON   For a town of the same name in the West Riding of Yorkshire, England.

FOAM LAKE   A descriptive. "The lake is shallow and after a blow there is always foam around the edges" (CPCGN file 62 N/12).

FORT QU'APPELLE   *See* Qu'Appelle

FORT WALSH   A North West Mounted Police post, built in 1875 and named after Inspector James Morrow Walsh (1843–1905), who later became the first Commissioner of the Yukon District, serving from 1897 to 1898.

FRENCHMAN BUTTE   Originated with the death of a Frenchman on the butte around 1800.

GARDINER DAM   On July 21, 1967, the dam across the South Saskatchewan River was officially opened and named in honour of J. G. Gardiner (1883–1962), one-time Premier of Saskatchewan and federal Minister of Agriculture from 1935 to 1948. *See* Diefenbaker, Lake

GRAVELBOURG   After Abbé Louis Pierre Gravel (1868–1926), the founder of the town in 1906.

GREEN LAKE   A descriptive, indicating the colour of the water.

GRENFELL   After Pascoe de P. Grenfell, London merchant, shareholder, and director of the Canadian Pacific Railway.

GULL LAKE   Designated by John Macoun (1832–1920), Dominion botanist, "who was impressed by the number and variety of gulls frequenting the place" (Russell).

GUNNAR   From the Gunnar Mining Company Limited, which opened the local uranium mine in 1955.

HERBERT   After Sir Michael Henry Herbert, who served as British ambassador to the United States from 1902 to 1903.

HUDSON BAY   Town about thirty miles from the Manitoba border. The area was visited as early as 1760 by fur traders. In the 1790s a trading post was established a few miles from the present town at the junction of the Fir, Red Deer, and Etomami rivers. The town was established in 1903 and named for Henry Hudson, the explorer. Originally it was called Hudson Bay Junction; however, the latter part of the name was dropped in 1946 upon incorporation of the town.

HUMBOLDT   For the German scientist and explorer Baron Alexander Von Humboldt (1769–1859). Assigned at the time of the original C.P.R. survey in the 1870s.

ÎLE-À-LA-CROSSE, LAC   May be literally translated as "lake of the crosier" or "lake of the stick", as the lake is supposedly shaped like a bishop's staff (Russell). The name may also be derived from an island in the lake on which the Amerindians played lacrosse.

IMPERIAL   Name chosen by local settlers, who were mainly of British origin. *See* Union Jack

INDIAN HEAD   Originated with a range of hills ten to twelve miles south of the town. One of the hills is reputed to have "the configuration of a man's head" (CPCGN file 62 L/12).

ISLAND FALLS   Located on an island in the Churchill River. A nearby waterfall inspired the name.

ITUNA   Believed named by Grand Trunk Pacific officials who were "familiar with the Celtic name, Ituna, for the Solway Firth which Kipling used in one of his books" (Russell).

KAMSACK   Of Amerindian origin. A local Indian was nick-named *Kamsack,* roughly translated as "big man". This term was applied in derision, since the individual was a dwarf.

KAPOSVAR   *See* Esterhazy

KELVINGTON   For Lord Kelvin (1824–1907), prominent British mathematician. Named in 1905 by Mrs. John McQuarrie, who was raised near Kelvin's estate in Scotland.

KERROBERT   A reversal of the names of Robert Kerr, who served as traffic manager of the Canadian Pacific Railway. The area was first settled in 1906.

KINDERSLEY   Honours Sir Robert Kindersley, a shareholder and supporter of the Canadian Northern Railway.

KINISTINO   For the Cree people who were given the French form of an Amerindian name of unknown meaning.

KIPLING   After Rudyard Kipling (1865–1936). It was originally Kipling Station but was changed January 1, 1954. *See* Ituna

LAFLECHE　Commemorates the career of Louis François Richer Laflèche (1818–98), prominent missionary to the Métis, who later became Bishop of Trois-Rivières.

LANGENBURG　A German settlement named for Prince Victor of Hohenlohe-Langenburg.

LANIGAN　For W. B. Lanigan, a freight manager of the C.P.R.

LA RONGE　Town and lake. The name was probably derived from the French verb *ronger*, "to gnaw", evidence of the work of beaver in the area.

LEADER　First known as Prussia, one of several names changed during the First World War.

LEMBURG　Named in 1905 for the capital of Austrian Galicia. Formerly called Sifton for William Sifton, a Canadian Northern contractor, but Sir Clifford Sifton objected to the use of the name.

LUMSDEN　For Hugh Lumsden, supervising engineer for the Qu'Appelle, Long Lake and Saskatchewan Railway Company.

LUSELAND　From the Luse Land Development Company, St. Paul, Minnesota, which was responsible for the heavy American migration to the district.

MACKLIN　For Harry Macklin, a representative of the *Winnipeg Free Press,* who reported the construction of the Grand Trunk Pacific to the newspaper.

MAIDSTONE　After Maidstone, Kent, England.

MANITOU BEACH　Utilizes the Amerindian name for the foremost god in their mythology. *See* Manitou, Manitoba

MANKOTA   From Mankato, Minnesota, home of the original settlers. The name is of Sioux origin and refers to "a deposit of pigmented earth used by the Indians for paint" (Stewart).

MANOR   Cannington Manor, founded in 1882 (ten miles to the northwest), was an attempt to bring rural life in "the gracious English manner" to Saskatchewan. The attempt failed; however, the nearest rail point retains the name Manor.

MAPLE CREEK   Descriptive of the Manitoba maples which thrive along the banks of the creek. Incorporated as a town in 1903.

MEADOW LAKE   Known to the French as Lac des Prairies. Descriptive of the nearby region.

MELFORT   Early name Stoney Creek; changed to Melfort in 1904 in honour of Melfort, Scotland, birthplace of an early settler, Mary Melfort Campbell, Mrs. Reginald Beatty.

MELVILLE   After Charles Melville Hays (1856–1912), president of the Grand Trunk Railway Company from 1909 to 1912. He was drowned in the *Titanic* disaster, April 15, 1912. Incorporated as a town in 1909, it became a city in 1960.

MIDALE   A combination of the names of two early settlers, Dr. R. M. Mitchell and John Dale.

MOOSE JAW   Traceable to Amerindian sources. The name appears on the Palliser map of 1857 as Moose Jaw Creek, the contours of which reputedly resembled the outline of the jawbone of a moose.

MOOSOMIN   During the North West Uprising, a prominent chief who remained loyal to the government was Moosomin. The name in Cree means "high bush cranberry".

MOSSBANK   Selected by Robert Jolly, this is a variation of Mossgeil, Scotland. He and his brother, Alexander, migrated from there and settled at Mossbank in 1907.

NESSET LAKE   Commemorates the sacrificial career of Miss Inez Nesset, a nursing sister of the Canadian Red Cross Society in northern Saskatchewan. Name officially approved November 21, 1967.

NIPAWIN   Originated with the Cree word indicating "standing place". Refers to a lookout point on the Saskatchewan River.

NOKOMIS   Named by Mrs. Thomas Halstead from Longfellow's *Hiawatha* because "the west represented the romantic domain of the Indians" (Russell).

OLD WIVES LAKE   Formerly Johnstone Lake, the name was changed officially on November 5, 1953, to a translation of the original Amerindian name. Marks the massacre of a group of Cree women by Blackfoot warriors.

ORCADIA   The area was first settled by immigrants from the Orkney Islands. Orcadia is the classical name for these islands. Post office established February 12, 1905.

OUTLOOK   Descriptive of the view or "outlook" of the Saskatchewan River valley.

OXBOW   For a semicircular bend in the Souris River. Russell traces the origin to a nearby school section designated Boscurvis (Latin for Oxbow) by Mrs. T. M. Baird, an early teacher. Later adopted as a townsite on the railway north of Boscurvis.

PERDUE   Settled in 1908 and named for Judge W. E. Perdue of Winnipeg.

PETER POND LAKE   Named for Peter Pond (1740–1807), the explorer who mapped the lake in 1778.

PIAPOT   Commemorates a Cree chieftain, "Pie-a-Pot", who refused to sign a treaty with the whites. In one altercation he managed to temporarily halt construction of the C.P.R. by erecting a tent on the roadbed of the railway.

PONTEIX   The community was first known as Notre Dame d'Auvergne; later the name was changed to Ponteix for a community in France, the home parish of Abbé Albert Royer, a Catholic missionary.

PORCUPINE PLAIN   Named Porcupine in 1929. The word Plain was added to avoid confusion with Porcupine, Ontario.

PREECEVILLE   Originates with the Preece family, early residents of the area.

PRELATE   First settled in 1903. The name was chosen for ecclesiastical reasons, a prelate being of high rank in the Catholic Church.

PRINCE ALBERT   Generally credited to Rev. James Nisbet, who reputedly selected the name in honour of the consort of Queen Victoria. There was a Fort Albert built about 1865 by the Hudson's Bay Company and that may have inspired this name.

QU'APPELLE   Valley, town, and fort are all transfer names from the river which was known to the Cree as *Kah-tep-was,* meaning "the river which calls". The legend of the spirit supposedly haunting the river was perpetuated by the French "Qu'Appelle".

RADVILLE   "An almost unrecognizable corruption of the name of the homesteader on whose land the townsite was located, Conrad Paquin" (Russell).

REDVERS   After General Sir Redvers Buller (1839–1908), Commander of the British Forces in South Africa from 1899 to 1900.

REGINA   Assigned August 23, 1882, by the Governor General, the Marquess of Lorne (1845–1914), in honour of his wife's mother, Queen Victoria. Originally called Pile O'Bones.

REINDEER LAKE   A translation of an earlier Amerindian designation.

ROSETOWN   Named by M. H. MacLeod, General Manager of the Canadian Northern Railway, for James Rose, a pioneer settler in 1904 and 1905, and because of the growth of wild roses in the district.

ROSTHERN   Probably the result of a spelling error. Rosethorn is an earlier version of the same name. CPCGN records mention an incident during railway construction in which a man named Ross drowned south of the town. Russell suggests that Ross-tern (tern being a variant of pool) may have been the original form.

ST. WALBURG   For Mrs. Walburga Musch, a pioneer settler in the area.

SALTCOATS   Named by Sir Hugh Allan for a town in Ayrshire, Scotland, to replace the earlier name, Stirling.

SASKATCHEWAN RIVER   *See provincial entry*

SASKATOON   The site was selected and named in 1882 by John N. Lake of Toronto, acting for the Temperance Colonization Society. *Mis-sask-guah-too-min* is a Cree word for an edible red berry that is native to the area.

SEYMOUR LAKES   For Dr. M. M. Seymour (1857–1929), who served as Director of the Saskatchewan Bureau of Health and later, from 1923 to 1927, as Deputy Minister of Health.

SHAUNAVON Said to have been given by Lord Shaughnessy in 1913 for an area near his ancient family home in Ireland (Russell). It is also thought to be a combination of Shaughnessy and Van Horne. Lord Shaughnessy objected to the use of his name by the Canadian Pacific Railway, and the objection was overcome by this contraction.

SHELLBROOK A descriptive, transferred from the nearby Shell Brook.

STAR CITY After Mr. Walter Starkey, who established a homestead in the district in 1899.

STEELE NARROWS Marks the career of Major Samuel Benfield Steele (1851–1919), Superintendent of the North West Mounted Police.

STOUGHTON After John Stoughton Dennis (1820–85), onetime Surveyor General of Dominion Lands and Deputy Minister of the Interior.

STRASBOURG Settled by German immigrants and named for Strassburg, Germany, now Strasbourg, France. Spelling confirmed by provincial order-in-council June 21, 1919.

STURGIS For Sturgis, South Dakota, the home of early settlers in the district.

SWIFT CURRENT An English translation of *Saskatchewan*, "swift flowing" or "swift current". The place name was approved August 27, 1911. Swift Current River was changed to Swift Current Creek, reflecting local usage, May 13, 1970.

TISDALE For Frederick W. Tisdale, the first local station agent for the Canadian Pacific Railway.

UNION JACK The name was chosen locally for patriotic reasons on May 31, 1928, replacing the earlier name, Vérendrye.

UNITY   After Unity, Wisconsin, the home of the first settlers in the district.

URANIUM CITY   Selected in recognition of the discovery of uranium deposits in the area in 1952.

VANSCOY   From the name of an early homesteader in the district, Vernon VanScoy, a native of Logan, Iowa.

WADENA   For Wadena, Minnesota. Originally an Ojibway word meaning "little round hill" (Stewart).

WAKAW   Cree descriptive from *Wokawkomah* for "crooked lake".

WASKESIU   Traceable to the Cree word for "red deer".

WATROUS   Honours Frank Watrous Morse, vice-president and general manager of the Grand Trunk Pacific Railway.

WATSON   After Senator Robert Watson (1853–1929), who served as provincial M.L.A. for Portage la Prairie, provincial Minister of Public Works, and federal M.P. for Marquette. He was called to the Senate in 1900.

WEYBURN   Possibly for Weybourne, Norfolk, England. It is also suggested that the Souris River, which runs through the town, may have been designated a "wee burn".

WILKIE   Bestowed by the Canadian Pacific Railway in honour of Daniel Robert Wilkie (1846–1914), president of the Imperial Bank of Canada.

WILLOW BUNCH   For the numerous willow bluffs in the vicinity. "Bluff" is commonly used in western Canada for an isolated grove of trees (Rayburn).

WOLLASTON LAKE   After Dr. William Hyde Wollaston (1766
–1828), one-time president of the Royal Society.

WOLSELEY   Honours Sir Garnet Joseph, first Viscount Wolseley (1833–1913), a distinguished British soldier, who commanded the Red River Expedition in 1870.

WOOD MOUNTAIN   Descriptive of the growth of trees and
shrubs along the low range of hills.

WYNYARD   From the English family estate of Mrs. F. W. Peters, whose husband was supervisor of the Land Department of
the Canadian Pacific Railway.

YORKTON   The area was settled in 1882 by the York (Ontario)
Farmers Colonization Company. First known as York City.

Yukon Territory

The territory was established on June 13, 1898, although the name, of Amerindian origin, was first applied to the river and is from *Yu-kun-ah*, meaning "great river". It was first noted in 1846 by John Bell (1799–1868) an employee of the Hudson's Bay Company, "who called it by what he understood to be its Indian appellation" *(Geological Survey Report,* 1887–8).

Northwest Territories

Historically, the term was loosely applied to the vast lands north and west of Lake Superior; later it signified the administrative district which predated Saskatchewan and Alberta; and from January 1, 1920, it has meant "that part of Northern Canada between the Yukon Territory and Hudson Bay, including Baffin Island, the islands in James Bay, Hudson Bay, Hudson Strait, and the Arctic Archipelago." *See also* Franklin, Keewatin, *and* Mackenzie

AKIMISKI ISLAND, NWT Originally Viner's Island, the name was changed in the nineteenth century to a variation of the Cree word for "the land across".

AKLAVIK, NWT The name was suggested in 1910 by Col. G. L. Jennings, an officer in the Royal North West Mounted Police. Of Inuit origin, it may be translated as "place of the barrenland grizzly" or simply "where there are bears".

AKPATOK ISLAND, NWT In Ungava Bay. The name is from the Inuit for "place of birds".

ALASKA HIGHWAY, YT This highway stretches from Dawson Creek, B.C., to Fairbanks, Alaska. The name originates with the Amerindian designation variously spelled as Alaeksu, Alaschka, or Alaxa, meaning "mainland", although Alaska has been in common usage since 1867. The Alaska Highway was officially named on July 19, 1949. (The acronym Alcan is less commonly used.)

ALERT, NWT Named for H.M.S. *Alert,* flagship of a British survey expedition to the Arctic in 1875–6.

ALVERSTONE, MOUNT, YT Honours the Lord Chief Justice of England, Richard Everard Webster, Viscount Alverstone (1842–1915), a member of the Alaska Boundary Commission of 1903. The boundary peaks in the St. Elias Mountains in British Columbia bear the names of all seven men who served on the Commission: Alverstone (1908), Aylesworth (1908), Root (1908), Turner (1908), Lodge (1908), Armour (1923).

AMUNDSEN GULF, NWT Named after Roald Amundsen, who sailed his ship, *Gjöa,* through the Northwest Passage from Atlantic to Pacific in 1903–6. *See* Gjoa Haven

ARCTIC BAY, NWT For the whaling vessel *Arctic,* under the command of Captain William Adams, who visited the area in

1872. The word Arctic is traceable to the Greek *arktos,* "the bear".

ARCTIC RED RIVER, NWT   Descriptive. The name was approved on December 12, 1939, for both the river and the settlement. The location was originally the site of a Hudson's Bay Company post dating from about 1900.

AUGUSTA, MOUNT, YT   Named in 1891 by Professor I. C. Russell for his wife, Augusta Olmsted Russell.

AUYUITTUQ NATIONAL PARK, NWT   (Formerly Baffin Island National Park) The national park, comprising 8,290 square miles and lying along the 66th parallel, was created on February 22, 1972. The Inuit name was chosen locally in Broughton Island and Pangnirtung on February 12, 1975, and may be translated as: "land of the big ice" or "the place where ice does not melt".

AXEL HEIBERG ISLAND, NWT   Named after Axel Heiberg, a patron of the Sverdrup expedition to the Arctic of 1898 to 1902.

BABBAGE RIVER, YT   Named by Sir John Franklin for the mathematician Charles Babbage (1792–1871), one of the founders of the British Astronomical Society.

BACK RIVER, NWT   Named for George Back (later admiral) (1796–1878), who was an Arctic navigator and an officer in the Franklin expedition of 1819 to 1820. The original Amerindian name *Thlew-ee-coh-desseth,* "great fish river", was considered by Back to be "inconveniently long".

BADHAM, MOUNT, YT   Honours Francis Badham, a member of the International Boundary Survey party in 1913 when the peak was located. He was subsequently killed in action during the First World War.

BAFFIN ISLAND, NWT   Named, like the bay between Greenland and Baffin Island, after William Baffin (?–1622), explorer and navigator. The island was discovered by Baffin in 1616 and the name was approved on December 5, 1905. *See* Auyuittuq

BAILLIE-HAMILTON ISLAND, NWT Bestowed in 1851 by William Penny to mark the career of Captain W. A. Baillie-Hamilton, then Secretary of the Admiralty.

BAIRD, MOUNT, YT Named in 1887 for Spencer Fullerton Baird (1823–87), a noted American naturalist.

BAKER LAKE, NWT After Sir William Baker of the Hudson's Bay Company. It was designated by Captains Christopher and Norton of the same company, the discoverers of the lake in 1762.

BANKS ISLAND, NWT The westernmost island of the Arctic Archipelago. The name was assigned by Sir William Parry (1790–1855), Arctic explorer for Sir Joseph Banks (1744–1820), long-time president of the Royal Society.

BATHURST ISLAND, NWT The island was named by W. E. Parry in 1819 for the Earl of Bathurst (1762–1834), then Secretary of the Colonies. The inlet on the south shore of Coronation Gulf was named by John Franklin in 1821 for the same person.

BEAUFORT SEA, YT and NWT Commemorates the career of Sir Francis Beaufort (1774–1857), Rear-Admiral and hydrographer to the Admiralty from 1829 to 1855.

BELCHER ISLAND, NWT The name is sometimes ascribed to Sir Edward Belcher (1799–1877), commander of the 1872 expedition in search of Sir John Franklin; however, it predates Sir Edward. Bellin's *Carte de la Baye de Hudson* (1744) names the feature I. de Roteur (old French form of the verb *roter*, "to belch"). It was probably named for James Belcher, captain of a Hudson's Bay Company vessel (Fraser).

BOMPAS, MOUNT, YT Named for the Rev. William Bompas

(1834–1906), first Anglican Bishop of the Diocese of the Yukon. Bompas spent the years from 1865 to 1905 as a missionary in the north.

BONANZA CREEK, YT   Orignially Rabbit Creek, the name was changed to mark the discovery of gold by George Washington Carmack, August 17, 1896.

BOOTHIA PENINSULA, NWT   The peninsula was discovered by Captain Sir James Ross during his expedition of 1829–33 and named by him for Sir Felix Booth (1775–1850), prominent London distiller and promoter of Arctic expeditions. Ross also named the Gulf of Boothia.

BORDEN ISLAND, NWT   Named after Sir Robert Borden (1854–1937), Prime Minister of Canada from 1911 to 1920.

BROUGHTON ISLAND, NWT   Located off the east coast of Baffin Island, it was named by Ross for Commodore William Robert Broughton (1762–1821). *See* Boothia Peninsula *above*

BROUGHTON ISLAND, NWT   In Hudson Bay. Named for W. K. Broughton, an employee of the Hudson's Bay Company.

BURWASH LANDING, YT   The settlement was established in 1903 and named for Major Lachlan Taylor Burwash (1874–1940), mining engineer and Arctic explorer. A monument to mark his career was erected here on August 31, 1973.

CAMBRIDGE BAY, NWT   Named for the Duke of Cambridge (1774–1850), brother of King William IV.

CARCROSS, YT   Originally known as Caribou Crossing, the new name was coined by Bishop William Bompas and approved in 1905.

CARMACKS, YT   This name marks the career of George Washington Carmack, who struck gold on August 17, 1896, precipitating the Klondike gold rush of 1897–8. *See* Henderson Creek

CENTENNIAL RANGE, YT   A range of the St. Elias Mountains which was climbed as part of Canada's centennial celebrations in 1967. Other nearby peaks were named for each of the provinces and the territories. Name officially approved on February 2, 1967.

CHAMPAGNE, YT   An apocryphal version credits one Jack Dalton with the origin of the name. He is reputed to have celebrated the completion of a cattle drive by opening a case of champagne. Actually the name dates from the establishment of a trading post by Harlow Chambers during the gold rush.

CHESTERFIELD INLET, NWT   The inlet was first visited by Sir Thomas Button in 1612 and 1613. It was later named for the Earl of Chesterfield (1694–1773), the author of *Chesterfield's Letters.*

CLINTON CREEK, YT   The settlement, established in 1969, was named for a nearby stream.

CLYDE, NWT   Name assigned by Captain (later Sir) John Ross in 1818 while on an expedition in search of the Northwest Passage. The settlement was relocated in 1965 on the north shore of Patricia Bay and, although the exact origin of its name is unknown, it may possibly be named for the River Clyde in Scotland.

COLVILLE LAKE, NWT   After Andrew Colville, who was Deputy-Governor of the Hudson's Bay Company from 1839 to 1852 and Governor from 1852 to 1856.

CONSOLATION MOUNTAIN, YT   The name was suggested by the Rev. James Outram "who on climbing the mountain found the main peak inaccessible"(CPCGN files).

COOK, MOUNT, YT   Named in 1874 by W. H. Dall for Captain

James Cook (1728–79), English navigator and explorer.

COPPERMINE, NWT   The name was bestowed in 1771 by Samuel Hearne because the Indians had obtained copper from the region. Early variant of the name: Copper River.

CORAL HARBOUR, NWT   Named by an American whaler, George Comer, "for the peculiar red coral brought to the surface when taking soundings" (Fraser).

CRAIG, MOUNT, YT   Named in 1916 to honour John Davidson Craig (1875–1936) of the International Boundary Survey staff.
    Also Craig Harbour, an abandoned settlement in the Northwest Territories.

DAVIS STRAIT, NWT   After John Davis (1554–1605), navigator and explorer.

DAWSON, YT   Named in honour of George M. Dawson (1849–1901), director of the Geological Survey of Canada from 1895 to 1901. It was originally called Dawson City and served as capital of the territory until 1953.

DEADMEN VALLEY, NWT   The valley is sometimes referred to as Headless Valley. According to R.C.M.P. files at least eight men met death in the area under unexplained circumstances during the period from 1908 to 1960.

DESTRUCTION BAY, YT   During the gold rush a storm wrecked a number of boats in the bay. The settlement name is derived from the bay, which is located on Kluane Lake. Name adopted on April 2, 1953 (Stevenson).

DEVON ISLAND, NWT   Assigned by Sir William Parry (1790–1855), for Devon, England, the native county of a member of his crew, Lieutenant Liddon.

DEZADEASH LAKE, YT   The name of the lake is of Amerindian origin and means "a native fishing method unique to the region. Pieces of white birch bark were placed on the lake bottom to attract trout." (Phillips)

DONJEK RIVER, YT   Named by C. W. Hayes of the United States Geological Survey in 1891. The name was coined from portions of two Amerindian words of uncertain meaning (possibly for wild water and white fox berry). Associated names include: Donjek Mountain, Donjek Glacier, and Donjek Range.

DORSET, CAPE, NWT   First applied by Captain Luke Foxe, September 24, 1631, to the cape and later to Dorset Island. Named after the Earl of Dorset (1590–1652).

ECHO BAY   *See* Port Radium

ELLESMERE ISLAND, NWT   For Francis Leveson-Gower, Earl of Ellesmere (1800–57), and dates from the Inglefield expedition of 1852.

ELSA, YT   From a claim staked in 1900 by Charles Brefalt and "named for a woman in his native Sweden" (Phillips).

ESKIMO POINT, NWT   The site of a permanent Hudson's Bay post in 1921. The earlier name was *Arviak,* Inuit for "the place where the whale is hunted".

FARO, YT   The name is derived from a gambling game in which the cards bore a stylized portrait of an Egyptian pharaoh. The name was officially approved on February 27, 1969, and applied to the townsite which serves the Anvil Mining Corporation.

FIJI ISLAND, NWT   Named for James Asasela, or Jim "Fiji", a Samoan sailor on the *Polar Bear,* part of the Stefansson expedition (Stefansson, *The Friendly Arctic*). *See also* Jim Fiji Harbour

FINLAYSON RIVER, YT   Commemorates the career of Duncan Finlayson (1796?–1862), the chief factor and later a member of the Board of Directors of the Hudson's Bay Company.

FIREWEED CREEK, YT   A descriptive derived from the abundance of fireweed on the south bank. The name was proposed by D. Tempelman-Kluit and officially adopted July 30, 1968. The fireweed (*Epilobium augustfolium*) is the official flower of the Yukon.

FIRTH RIVER, YT   Adopted October 21, 1944, after long local usage. For John Firth, a trader with the Hudson's Bay Company (CPCGN file 0654).

FIVE FINGER RAPIDS, YT   The name is derived from the geographic location, for here the Yukon River divides into five distinct channels.

FORT FRANKLIN, NWT   The original Fort Franklin, on Great Bear Lake, was built in 1825 and named by Sir John Franklin. The present settlement dates from the 1950s.

FORT GOOD HOPE, NWT   Established on the left bank of the Mackenzie by the North West Company in 1804 as a fur-trading post (Arrowsmith, 1857). The fort was named as an expression of optimism on the part of early traders.

FORT LIARD, NWT   It was also built by the North West Company and established some time prior to 1807. *See* Liard River

FORT MCPHERSON, NWT   The earlier name was Fort Peel or Peel River House. It was built by John Bell in 1840 and named for the chief trader of the Hudson's Bay Company, Murdoch McPherson.

FORT NORMAN, NWT   Possibly named after Alexander Norman McLeod or Archibald Norman McLeod, both of whom were prominent traders in the region in the early nineteenth century.

The post dates from 1810. *See* Norman Wells

FORT PROVIDENCE, NWT A fur-trading post built by the Hudson's Bay Company about 1851. Ten years later a Roman Catholic mission, Notre Dame de la Providence, was established. It was named by the company "as an expression of trust".

FORT RELIANCE, YT Founded in 1874 by Leroy Napoleon McQuesten, an early prospector, it was later superseded by Dawson City (Johnstone, 1887).

FORT RELIANCE, NWT A Hudson's Bay Company post which was established in the winter of 1833 at the mouth of Lockhart River for Captain George Back (1796–1878). The fort has long been abandoned; however, the adjacent site is occupied by the settlement of Reliance.

FORT RESOLUTION, NWT The settlement grew up around the original Hudson's Bay Company post and the name is "suggestive of the hardships which had to be overcome". The post was established in 1815.

FORT SIMPSON, NWT Originally known as Fort of the Forks, from 1804 to 1820, it changed its name to Fort Simpson in 1821 in honour of Sir George Simpson (1792–1860), a governor of the Hudson's Bay Company from 1822 to 1860.

FORT SMITH, NWT The early site was known as both Fort York and Rapids of the Drowned. The Hudson's Bay Company post dates from 1874 and honours Donald A. Smith, Baron Strathcona (1820–1914), one-time governor of the Hudson's Bay Company, president of the Canadian Pacific Railway, and a member of the first Council of the Northwest Territories.

FORTY MILE, YT River and settlement. So named because the settlement was forty miles downstream from Fort Reliance. Settlement now a ghost town.

FOXE BASIN, NWT   Named for Luke Foxe (1586–1635), an Arctic explorer.

FRANCES LAKE, YT   After Frances Ramsay (?–1853), who was the wife of Sir George Simpson, Governor of the Hudson's Bay Company.

FRANKLIN, NWT   A district of the Northwest Territories which was set apart by order-in-council on October 2, 1895. It embraces Melville and Boothia peninsulas, and all the islands in Hudson Bay and Hudson Strait and the Arctic Ocean north to the pole. The name commemorates the explorer Sir John Franklin (1786–1847). *See* Keewatin *and* Mackenzie

FROBISHER BAY, NWT   After Sir Martin Frobisher (1535–94), discoverer of the bay in 1576. Frobisher assumed the bay to be a strait and it first appears on maps as Frobishers Strait (Arrowsmith, 1790). Known briefly as Lumley Inlet, a name bestowed by John Davis; however, the latter name did not pass into popular usage. The settlement dates from 1942 and the establishment of a United States Air Force base.

GJOA HAVEN, NWT   For Roald Amundsen's vessel, the *Gjöa,* which wintered there in 1903–4. The Hudson's Bay post was established in 1927.

GODS MERCY, BAY OF, NWT   The name commemorates an escape from shipwreck by G. F. Lyon in 1824.

GOLD BOTTOM CREEK, YT   Named by prospector Robert Henderson, who mistakenly believed that he had struck gold in the area.

GREAT BEAR LAKE, NWT   Also cape and river. Two theories exist as to the origin of the name: (1) from the northern constellation of stars called the Great Bear, which is reflected in the waters of the lake (PAC, Johnson Papers); (2) more probably a translation of the Amerindian *saschohetha*, a reference to the bears in the vicinity. "Great" denotes the size of the lake. The name was officially approved on January 20, 1902.

GREAT SLAVE LAKE, NWT   Lake and river. From the Etchareotine or Dogrib Indians who were taken as "slaves" by the Crees (Peter Pond, 1785).

GRISE FIORD, NWT   Named by Otto Sverdrup (1855–1930), Norwegian explorer, and may be translated as "pig fiord", a possible reference to an incident on board ship. The settlement was established in the 1950s by a group of Inuit relocated from Baffin Island.

HAINES JUNCTION, YT   For Haines, Alaska, which was named in 1910 for Mrs. Francina Electra Haines of the Presbyterian Board of Home Missions. The town was incorporated in 1910.

HALL BEACH, NWT   Proposed and later adopted in 1956 in honour of Captain C. F. Hall, who spent a number of years on Melville Peninsula in the mid nineteenth century.

HAY RIVER, NWT   The Hudson's Bay Company post was established about 1868 and appears on the company lists in 1872. The name is descriptive, indicating an abundance of grass or hay in the area.

HENDERSON CREEK, YT   For Robert Henderson, a native of Merigomish, Nova Scotia, who was an early prospector in the Yukon. Henderson supplied information to George Carmack which resulted in the discovery of gold on August 17, 1896. *See* Carmacks, Gold Bottom Creek, *and* Too Much Gold Creek

HERSCHEL, YT   Island and one-time settlement. The name was bestowed in 1825 by Sir John Franklin to honour the astronomer Sir William Herschel (1738–1822). Herschel Island was formerly an important whaling centre; however, in recent years these activities have died out. Cape Herschel, and Herschel Bay, Northwest Territories, were named for his son, Sir John Herschel (1792-1871), also a noted astronomer.

HESS RIVER, YT   After Michael Hess, an early pioneer.

HOLMAN, NWT   Probably named for John R. Holman, assistant surgeon on the *Diligence,* part of the Inglefield Arctic expedition of 1853–4.

HUBBARD, MOUNT, YT   Named in 1890 by I. C. Russell, United States Geological Survey, for Gardiner Greene Hubbard (1822–97), founder and first president of the National Geographic Society.

HUDSON BAY and **HUDSON STRAIT, NWT**   Named for their discoverer, Henry Hudson (?–1611). His last voyage was made in 1610 when he entered the strait and bay and explored a portion of their coasts.

HUNKER CREEK, YT   After Andrew Hunker, prospector and miner during the Klondike gold rush.

IGLOOLIK, NWT   Settlement and island. Descriptive name derived from the abundance of igloos on the island. This was the site of Parry's winter camp in 1822–3.

INUVIK, NWT   Established in 1955 as an administrative centre for the Mackenzie Delta. The name is from the Inuit for "the place of man".

ITSI, YT   Lake and mountain. Amerindian for "the wind".

JAKES CORNER, YT   For a Teslin Indian, Jake Jackson, who once lived in this area.

JAMES BAY   *See* Quebec *entry*

JEAN MARIE RIVER, NWT   Honours Abbé Jean Marie, an early missionary in the territories.

JENS MUNK ISLAND, NWT   After Jens Munk (1579–1628), a Danish nobleman who explored the Hudson Bay area. *See* Munk River, Manitoba

JIM FIJI HARBOUR, NWT   *See* Fiji Island

KEEWATIN, NWT   From two Cree words which signify the north wind. Since 1912 one of the three districts of the Northwest Territories. The name was officially adopted by Parliament on April 12, 1876. *See* Franklin *and* Mackenzie

KENNEDY, MOUNT, YT   Near Mount Logan, fifteen miles from the Alaska boundary. The mountain was discovered in 1935 by Dr. Bradford Washburn, a famous mountaineer. The name honours United States President J. F. Kennedy and was officially approved on December 22, 1964. A glacier on the northern faces of Mount Alverstone and Mount Kennedy was officially named Kennedy Glacier on February 24, 1969.

KENO HILL, YT   From the name of a popular gambling game, it is an adaptation of the French *quine* – the five winning numbers in a lottery.

KING PEAK, YT   For Dr. W. F. King, a member of the International Boundary Commission.

KLONDIKE, YT   Village and river. The name is of uncertain Amerindian origin and the popular meaning "hammer creek" is disputed. G. M. Dawson wrote to G. Johnson: "I am by no means satisfied that we actually know either its correct Indian pronunciation or meaning" (Johnson Papers, PAC MG30).

KLUANE, YT   Lake and national park. Of Amerindian origin, this name has been variously translated as "large fish lake" and "white fish place". The park reaches from the Alaska boundary on the west to part of the Haines Highway on the east, and from Kluane Lake on the north to the British Columbia border on the south.

LABERGE, LAKE, YT   Named for Michel Laberge, an employee of the Western Union Telegraph Company, who explored the area in 1867 for a proposed telegraph line. The setting for Robert Service's poem *The Cremation of Sam McGee.*

LAC LA MARTRE, NWT   Descriptive name, referring to the pine marten, *Martes americana.* Appears as Martin Lake (Arrowsmith, 1795).

LEACOCK, MOUNT, YT   Name approved on April 24, 1970, in honour of humorist Stephen Leacock (1876–1944). The mountain was first ascended by M. E. Alford and party, Easter, 1971.

LIARD RIVER, YT   Named for the liards, or cottonwood trees (a species of poplar), found on its banks. Appears as Rivière aux Liards on early maps.

LOGAN, MOUNT, YT   The second-highest mountain in North America, and the highest in Canada, with an elevation of 19,850 feet. It was named for Sir William Edmond Logan (1798–1875), founder and director of the Geological Survey of Canada from 1842 to 1869. The first successful ascent was on June 23, 1925.

LUCANIA, MOUNT, YT   Named in 1897 by the Duke of Abruzzi, an Italian naval officer and explorer, after the Cunard liner on which he had crossed the Atlantic. It was ascended in 1937.

MC ARTHUR PEAK, YT   Marks the career of James Joseph McArthur (1856–1925), a member of the International Boundary Commission involved in establishing the border between Alaska and the Yukon.

MACKENZIE, YT　The most westerly of the three districts of the Northwest Territories. Named for the explorer Alexander Mackenzie (1764–1820), it was created by an order-in-council in 1895. *See* Keewatin *and* Franklin

MACKENZIE KING ISLAND, NWT　Commemorates the career of William Lyon Mackenzie King (1874–1950), long-time Prime Minister of Canada.

MACKENZIE MOUNTAINS, YT　Honours Canada's second Prime Minister, Alexander Mackenzie (1822–92).

MACKENZIE RIVER, NWT　Named after Alexander Mackenzie, who explored the river from Great Slave Lake to the Arctic in 1789. It was once known as Disappointment River.

MACMILLAN PASS, YT　After a chief factor of the Hudson's Bay Company. The river heads in Macmillan Pass.

MC QUESTEN, YT　For Leroy Napoleon McQuesten, an American who was known locally as "the father of the Yukon". *See* Mayo

MALASPINA, MOUNT, YT　Named in 1874, by W. H. Dall of the United States Geological Survey, for Alessandro Malaspina, Italian navigator and explorer, who in 1791, while in the service of Spain, explored the northwest coast.

MAYO, YT　The earlier name was Mayo Landing, for Al Mayo, a legendary pre-gold-rush trader. He was a partner of Leroy McQuesten (referred to above). Name changed to Mayo on August 2, 1958.

MELVILLE ISLAND, NWT　Named by Parry for Robert Saunders Dundas, Viscount Melville (1771–1851), one-time First Lord of the Admiralty. Viscount Melville Sound was also named after him.

MILES CANYON, YT   Named for Nelson A. Miles (1839–1925), a United States major-general, who was once Commandant of Alaska.

MINTO, YT   An abandoned riverboat landing named for the Earl of Minto (1845–1914), Governor General from 1898 to 1904.

NAHANNI, NWT   Butte, mountain, range, and national park. After the Nahanni people, an Athapascan Amerindian division. The name is translated either as "people of the west" or "people of the buttes". The national park was established on February 22, 1972, in the area of South Nahanni River.

NEWTON, MOUNT, YT   Named by I. C. Russell for Henry Newton, American geologist.

NORMAN WELLS, NWT   Alexander Mackenzie noted in 1789 "pieces of petroleum which bear a resemblance to yellow wax" in this location; however, it was not until 1919 that the first oil well was drilled. *See* Fort Norman (latter on Arrowsmith map, 1857)

OLD CROW, YT   From a translation of the Amerindian name *Te-Tahim-Gevtik,* "Walking Crow", for one of the chiefs of the district who died in the 1870s (CPCGN files).

PANGNIRTUNG, NWT   Settlement and fiord. An adaptation of an Inuit word said to mean "place of the bull caribou".

PAULATUK, NWT   The settlement dates from 1935 and the name may be translated from the Inuit as "soot of coal".

PELLY BAY, NWT   Island, lake, mountain, and point (NWT); river (YT). Named for Sir John Henry Pelly (1772–1852), Governor of the Hudson's Bay Company from 1822 to 1852.

PINE POINT, NWT   A descriptive which was officially adopted on May 1, 1958. Incorporated as a town in 1974.

POND INLET, NWT   Named Ponds Bay in 1828 by John Ross for John Ponds (1767–1836), the Astronomer Royal. Name officially adopted as Pond Inlet on March 1, 1951.

PORT BURWELL, NWT   Honours Herbert Mahlon Burwell, a land surveyor, who was in charge of an observation post at this location in 1884.

PORT RADIUM, NWT   Originally Cameron Bay, the name was changed in 1937 after the discovery of radium in the pitchblende ore mined in the area. Now Echo Bay.

PRINCE PATRICK ISLAND, NWT   For Prince Arthur William Patrick Albert, Duke of Connaught (1850–1942), who served as Governor General from 1911 to 1916.

PRINCE OF WALES ISLAND, NWT   After Prince Albert Edward, Prince of Wales (1841–1910), later King Edward VII.

RAE, NWT   Originally a Hudson's Bay Company fort dating from about 1790. It was moved from present-day Rae Point to the new location in the 1850s. Named in honour of Dr. John Rae (1813–1893). Appears on Arrowsmith map 1857 (original location) and on Mackenzie River topographical survey map 1923 (new location). The strait and river were also named for Dr. Rae.

RANCHERIA, YT   River and settlement. The name was first applied to an Amerindian settlement by American settlers and is derived from the Spanish word for farm compound.

RANKIN INLET, NWT   The settlement dates from the establishment of a nickel mine in the mid 1950s. For John Rankin (fl. 1741–8), discoverer of the inlet in 1741 and a lieutenant on the *Furnace*, commanded by Christopher Middleton, Arctic explorer.

REPULSE BAY, NWT   Explored by Captain Christopher Middleton (?–1770) in 1741–2. The name indicates his disappointment in a fruitless search for the Northwest Passage.

RESOLUTE, NWT   For the ship *Resolute,* which wintered at this location in 1850 under the command of H. T. Austin.

RESOLUTION ISLAND, NWT   Probably named by Sir Thomas Button for his ship, *Resolution,* on a voyage during 1612 and 1613.

RICHARDSON MOUNTAINS, YT   After Sir John Richardson (1787–1866), surgeon and naturalist on Franklin's expedition to the western Arctic.

ROBERT SERVICE, MOUNT, YT   Named in 1968 in honour of Robert Service (1874–1958), poet and novelist of the Yukon. Also Robert Service Creek.

ROSS RIVER, YT   Named in 1843 in honour of the chief factor of the Hudson's Bay Company, Donald Ross.

RUPERT'S LAND   The territory granted to the Hudson's Bay Company in 1670 and transferred to Canada in 1870. For Prince Rupert (1619–82), first governor of the company.

SACHS HARBOUR, NWT   For the schooner *Mary Sachs,* a part of the Stefansson expedition of 1913.

ST. ELIAS, MOUNT, YT   The most westerly peak in the Yukon, it was sighted by the explorer Vitus Bering on St. Elias Day, July 16, 1741.

SANIKILUAQ, NWT   Settlement name officially approved on November 27, 1970, and taken from an Inuit family residing on the Belcher Islands.

SAPPER RANGE, NWT   Name adopted August 18, 1966, as a memorial to the Royal Canadian Engineers. The name is derived from the French *saper*, "to sap or undermine", and is a rank within the Royal Canadian Engineers.

SEATTLE, MOUNT, YT   Named by the United States Geological Survey in 1890 after the city of Seattle.

SELWYN MOUNTAINS, YT   Honours Dr. A. R. C. Selwyn (1824–1902), who served as Director of the Geological Survey of Canada from 1869 to 1895.

SNAG, YT   First designated as Snag Creek in 1898 by the United States Geological Survey, possibly because the creek was choked with dead trees.

SNOWDRIFT, NWT   River and settlement. The settlement dates from about 1929. The name is probably descriptive and was first applied to the river by Samuel Hearne.

SOMERSET ISLAND, NWT   Chosen by Sir W. E. Parry (1790–1855), Arctic explorer, for his native county in England.

SOUTHAMPTON ISLAND, NWT   Named in 1631 by Luke Foxe (1586–1635), Arctic explorer, in honour of the third Earl of Southampton (1573–1624).

SPENCE BAY, NWT   This area was explored by Captain John Ross (1777–1856) in the period from 1829 to 1833, and was named "in compliment to a relative of that name".

STEELE, MOUNT, YT   After Sir Samuel Benfield Steele (1849–1919), who joined the Royal North West Mounted Police in 1873 and was placed in charge of the Mounted Police posts during the gold rush of 1898–9.

STEFANSSON ISLAND, NWT   Honours Vilhjalmur Stefansson (1879–1962), noted explorer.

STEWART RIVER, YT   Name assigned by Robert Campbell

(1808–94) of the Hudson's Bay Company for James G. Stewart (?–1881), who assisted Campbell in the exploration of the Yukon in 1850.

STRICKLAND MOUNTAIN, YT   After Inspector D'Arcy Edward Strickland (1868–1908), early member of the Royal North West Mounted Police and Yukon pioneer.

SVERDRUP ISLANDS, YT   For Otto Sverdrup (1885–1930), Arctic explorer.

TATAMAGOUCHE CREEK, YT   Named during the Klondike gold rush; probably for Tatamagouche, Nova Scotia.

TESLIN, YT   Lake, river, and town. The name is from an Amerindian designation translated as "long waters".

THREE GUARDSMEN, YT   Referred to by gold-rush miners as "the three guardsmen" because of their prominent location. The name was officially adopted on August 1, 1898. Individual peaks: Mounts Porthos, Aramis, and Athos.

TOO MUCH GOLD CREEK, YT   Name attributed to Robert Henderson's sense of humour, since he found the creek "goldless". *See* Henderson Creek *and* Gold Bottom Creek

TUKTOYAKTUK, NWT   Formerly known as Port Brabant. The Inuit name was officially adopted on December 7, 1950, and may be translated *tuktu,* "caribou", *yaktuk,* "looks like", or "reindeer that look like caribou".

ULU MOUNTAIN, YT   Named for the ulu, an Inuit knife having a crescent-shaped blade and a handle of bone or wood. The mountain was climbed on March 6, 1972, as part of the second Canada Winter Games. The name was approved on April 17, 1972.

VICTORIA ISLAND, NWT   Named in 1839 by Thomas Simpson to honour Queen Victoria (1819–1901).

VISCOUNT MELVILLE SOUND, NWT   Name assigned by Sir William Parry (1790–1855) after Robert Saunders Dundas, Viscount Melville, who served as Lord Privy Seal and First Lord of the Admiralty in the British Cabinet. *See* Melville Island

WALSH, MOUNT, YT   For James Morrow Walsh (1843–1905), who was the first commissioner of the Yukon District. He served in the North West Mounted Police from 1873 to 1883.

WATSON LAKE, YT   Town and lake. Named after Frank Watson, a pioneer Yukon trapper and miner.

WERNECKE, YT   Settlement and mountains. Named for Livingston Wernecke (?–1941), a Klondike prospector. The settlement name was approved on December 12, 1939, and the name of the mountains on April 2, 1948.

WHALE COVE, NWT   Although the area was explored in the seventeenth century by Thomas Button the settlement dates from 1959. Descriptive name.

WHITEHORSE, YT   The capital of the Yukon since 1953. Named for the Whitehorse Rapids which are said to resemble the mane of a white horse.

WOOD, MOUNT, YT   For Zachary Taylor Wood (1860–1915), Assistant Commissioner of the Royal North West Mounted Police and Yukon pioneer. Wood was a great-grandson of the twelfth president of the United States, Zachary Taylor.

WOOD BUFFALO NATIONAL PARK, NWT   Located on the Alberta–Northwest Territories boundary, the park was established in 1922 to protect the wood bison or buffalo.

WRIGLEY, NWT   After Joseph Wrigley, an employee of the Hudson's Bay Company.

YELLOWKNIFE, NWT   The community was established following the discovery of gold in 1934. The name is derived from the Athapaskan band of Amerindians, who possessed tools made from yellow copper. It is now capital of the Northwest Territories, and was incorporated as a city on January 1, 1970.

YUKON   River, mountain, and crossing. *See entry at the beginning of the chapter.*

Bibliography

Primary Sources
The major primary source consulted was the files of the CPCGN, Department of Energy, Mines and Resources. Certain provincial records such as those of the Ontario Geographic Names Board also revealed much useful material. A significant amount of information was gleaned from the Public Archives of Canada, notably in MG30, the Johnson Papers. The most useful historical maps are mentioned in the individual entries.

Secondary Sources
No attempt has been made to provide a detailed bibliography; only the works most frequently consulted are listed below. Readers who may be interested in a more complete bibliography are directed to:

SEALOCK, R. B., and SEELEY, P. A. *Bibliography of Place Name Literature.* Chicago: American Literary Association, 1948.

Selected Bibliography on Canadian Toponymy. Ottawa: Department of Mines and Technical Surveys, 1964.

AKRIGG, G. P. V., and AKRIGG, HELEN B. *1001 British Columbia Place Names.* Vancouver: Discovery Press, 1973.

ARMSTRONG, G. H. *The Origin and Meaning of Place Names in Canada.* Toronto: Macmillan of Canada, 1970.

BACK, GEORGE. *Narrative of the Arctic Land Expedition.* London: John Murray, 1836.

BAGARA, R. R. *A Dictionary of the Otchipwe Language.* Minneapolis: Ross and Haines, 1973.

BEAUREGARD, LUDGER. *Toponymie de la Région Métropolitaine de Montréal.* Québec: Commission de Géographie, 1968.

BIGGAR, H. P. *The Works of Samuel de Champlain.* 6 vols. Toronto: The Champlain Society, 1936.

BROWN, THOMAS J. *Nova Scotia Place Names.* Halifax: Royal Print, 1922.

Canadian Permanent Committee on Geographical Names. *Principles and Procedures.* Ottawa: Department of Energy, Mines and Resources, 1975.

CARTWRIGHT, GEORGE. *A Journal of Transactions and Events.* Newark, Allin and Ridge, 1792.

CLARK, ANDREW H. *Three Centuries and the Island.* Toronto: University of Toronto Press, 1959.

————. *Acadia: The Geography of Early Nova Scotia to 1760.* Madison: University of Wisconsin Press, 1968.

Commission de Géographie de Québec. *Nomenclature des noms Géographiques de la province de Québec.* Québec: Ministère des Terres et Forêts, 1926.

CORMACK, W. E. *Narrative of a Journey Across the Island of Newfoundland.* St. John's, Nfld.: Morning Chronicle, 1873.

DE GRÂCE, ÉLOI. *Noms Géographiques de l'Acadie.* Moncton, N.B.: La Société Historique Acadienne, 1974.

DEMPSEY, H. A. *Indian Names for Alberta Communities.* Calgary: Glenbow Institute, 1969.

DORION, HENRI, and POIRIER, JEAN. *Lexique des Termes Utiles à l'Étude des Noms de Lieux.* Québec: Les Presses de l'Université Laval, 1972.

DOUGLAS, ROBERT. *Place Names of Prince Edward Island.* Ottawa: King's Printer, 1925.

————. *Place Names of Alberta.* Ottawa: King's Printer, 1928.

————. *Place Names of Manitoba.* Ottawa: King's Printer, 1933.

DROLET, JEAN-PAUL. *Map Lore.* Ottawa: Department of Energy, Mines and Resources, 1975.

ECKSTORM, F. H. *Indian Place Names of the Penobscot Valley and the Maine Coast.* Orono: University of Maine, 1974.

EKWALL, E. *The Concise Oxford Dictionary of English Place Names.* Oxford: Clarendon Press, 1960.

FERGUSSON, BRUCE. *Place Names of Nova Scotia.* Halifax: Public Archives of Nova Scotia, 1967.

FRASER, J. K. *Place Names of the Hudson Bay Region.* Ottawa: Department of Energy, Mines and Resources, 1970.

GANONG, WILLIAM F. *Crucial Maps in the Early Cartography . . . of the Atlantic Coast.* Toronto: University of Toronto Press, 1964.

————. *A Monograph on the Place Nomenclature of New Brunswick.* Toronto: Canadiana House, 1973.

GARDINER, HERBERT F. *Nothing But Names.* Toronto: G. N. Morang, 1889.

GATES, CHARLES M., ed. *Five Furtraders of the Northwest.* Minneapolis, Minn. 1933.

Geographic Board of Canada:

First Annual Report of the Geographic Board of Canada – 1898. Published as a supplement to the *31st Annual Report* of the Department of Marine and Fisheries.

Second Annual Report of the Geographic Board of Canada – 1900. Published as a supplement to the *33rd Annual Report* of the Department of Marine and Fisheries.

Third Annual Report of the Geographic Board of Canada – 1901. Published as a supplement to the *34th Annual Report* of the Department of Marine and Fisheries.

Ninth Report of the Geographic Board of Canada, for year ending June 30, 1910. Supplement to the *Annual Report* of the Department of Marine and Fisheries.

Part II: *Place Names in Quebec*, by James White

Part III: *Place Names – Thousand Islands*, by James White

Part IV: *Place Names – Northern Canada*, by James White

(a) Introduction

(b) Expeditions – Northern Canada

(c) Explorers – Northern Canada

(d) Ships – Northern Canada Expeditions

(e) Bibliography for Place Names – Northern Canada

(f) Place Names.

Tenth Report of the Geographic Board of Canada, for year ending June 30, 1911. Supplement to the *Annual Report* of the Department of Marine and Fisheries. Appendix – "Handbook of Indians of Canada", a reprint from the *Handbook of American Indians North of Mexico*.

Eleventh Report of the Geographic Board of Canada, for year ending June 30, 1912. Supplement to the *Annual Report* of the Department of Marine and Fisheries.

Twelfth Report of the Geographic Board of Canada, containing all decisions to June 30, 1913. Supplement to the *Annual Report* of the Department of the Interior.

Sixteenth Report of the Geographic Board of Canada, containing all decisions from April 1, 1917, to March 31, 1919. Supplement to the *Annual Report* of the Department of the Interior. Appendix A – Nomenclature of the Mountains of Western Canada. Appendix B – Division of the Northwest Territories into the Provisional Districts of Mackenzie, Keewatin, and Franklin.

Seventeenth Report of the Geographic Board of Canada, containing all decisions from April 1, 1919, to March 31, 1921. Supplement to the *Annual Report* of the Department of the Interior. Part II: *Meaning of Canadian City Names*, compiled by R. Douglas. Part III: *Place Names on Anticosti Island, Quebec*, by Lt.-Col. W. P. Anderson. Part IV: *Place Names in Magdalen Islands, Quebec,* compiled by R. Douglas.

Eighteenth Report of the Geographic Board of Canada, containing all decisions to March 31, 1924. Supplement to the *Annual Report* of the Department of the Interior.

Nineteenth Report of the Geographic Board of Canada, containing all decisions from April 1, 1924, to July 31, 1927. Published for the Geographic Board by the Department of the Interior.

A Guide to the Pronunciation of Canadian Place Names. Toronto: Canadian Broadcasting Corporation, 1959.

GUINARD, J. E. *Les Noms Indiens de mon pays.* Montréal: Rayonnement, n.d.

HAMILTON, WILLIAM B. *Local History in Atlantic Canada.* Toronto: Macmillan of Canada, 1974.

HEARNE, SAMUEL. *A Journey . . . to the Northern Ocean.* Toronto: The Champlain Society, 1911.

HOFFMAN, BERNARD G. *Cabot to Cartier: Sources for a Historical Ethnography of Northeastern North America.* Toronto: University of Toronto Press, 1961.

HOLMGREN, E. J., and HOLMGREN, P. M. *2000 Place Names of Alberta.* Saskatoon: Modern Press, 1972.

HOWLEY, M. F. "Newfoundland Name Lore". *Newfoundland Quarterly,* 1932-1940.

JENNESS, DIAMOND. *Indians of Canada.* Ottawa: National Museum of Canada, 1967.

JOHNSON, J. B. *Place Names of Scotland.* London: n.p., 1934.

KIRKCONNELL, WATSON. *Place Names in Kings County Nova Scotia.* n.p., 1971.

LEMOINE, J. M. *The Chronicles of the St. Lawrence.* Montreal: Dawson, 1878.

MACKENZIE, ALEXANDER. *Voyages . . . Through the Continent of North America.* London: Cadell, 1801.

MARDON, ERNEST G. *The History of Place Names in Southern Alberta.* Winnipeg: The Canadian Institute of Onomastic Sciences, 1972.

MATTHEWS, C. M. *Place Names of the English Speaking World.* New York: Charles Scribner, 1972.

MILTON, W. F., and CHEADLE, W. B. *The Northwest Passage by Land.* London: Cassell, 1865.

MORSE, WILLIAM INGLIS. *Acadiensia Nova.* 2 vols. London: Bernard Quaritch, 1935.

Le Nord de l'Outaouais: Manuel-Répertoire d'Histoire et de Géographie Régionales. Ottawa: Le Droit, 1938.

ORKIN, MARK M. *Speaking Canadian English.* Toronto: General Publishing Company, 1970.

PACIFIQUE, PIERRE. *Noms Géographiques des Provinces Maritimes.* Sainte Anne de Ristigouche, 1935.

PALLISER, JOHN, et al. *The Journals . . . Relative to the Exploration of a Portion of British North America.* London: H. M. Stationery Office, 1863.

PEDLEY, CHARLES. *The History of Newfoundland.* London: Longmans, 1863.

PHILLIPS, JAMES W. *Alaska–Yukon Place Names.* Seattle: University of Washington Press, 1973.

Principles of Geographical Naming. Toronto: Ontario Geographic Names Board, 1975.

PROWSE, D. W. *A History of Newfoundland.* London: Macmillan, 1895.

RAND, S. T. *Dictionary of the Language of the Micmac Indians.* Halifax: n.p., 1888.

RAYBURN, ALAN. *Geographical Names of Renfrew County.* Ottawa: Department of Energy, Mines and Resources, 1967.

————. *English Geographical Names in Canada with Generic Terms of French Origin.* Ottawa: Department of Energy, Mines and Resources, 1971.

————. *Characteristics of Toponymic Generics in New Brunswick.* Ottawa: Department of Energy, Mines and Resources, 1972.

———— . *Acadia: The Origin of the Name and its Geographical and Historical Utilization.* Ottawa: Department of Energy, Mines and Resources, 1973.

———— . *Geographical Names of Prince Edward Island.* Ottawa: CPCGN, 1973.

———— . *Geographical Names of New Brunswick.* Ottawa: CPCGN, 1975.

ROSS, SIR JOHN. *Narrative of a Second Voyage in Search of a Northwest Passage.* London: A. W. Webster, 1835.

ROUILLARD, E. *Noms Géographiques de la Province de Québec.* Québec: Marcotte, 1906.

ROY, P. G. *Les Noms Géographiques de la Province de Québec.* Lévis, 1906.

RUDNYCKYJ, J. B. *Manitoba, Mosaic of Place Names.* Winnipeg: Canadian Institute of Onomastic Sciences, 1970.

RUSSELL, R. T. *What's in a Name?* Saskatoon: Western Producer Book Service, 1973.

SEARY, E. R. *Toponymy of the Island of Newfoundland.* St. John's: Memorial University, 1959.

———— . *Place Names of the Avalon Peninsula of the Island of Newfoundland.* Toronto: University of Toronto Press, 1971.

SEARY, E. R.; STORY, G. M.; KIRWIN, W. J. *The Avalon Peninsula of Newfoundland: An Ethno-linguistic Study.* Ottawa: Department of the Secretary of State, 1968.

SEBERT, L. M. *Every Square Inch.* Ottawa: Department of Energy, Mines and Resources, 1970.

SHEPPE, WALTER, ed. *First Man West: Alexander Mackenzie's Journal.* Berkeley: University of California Press, 1962.

Société de Géographie de Québec, *Annual Bulletins.*

STEFANSSON, V. *The Friendly Arctic.* New York: Ginn & Co., 1921.

STEWART, GEORGE R. *American Place Names.* New York: Oxford University Press, 1970.

THOMPSON, D. W. *Men and Meridians.* 3 vols. Ottawa, Queen's Printer, 1966–9.

TYRRELL, J. B., *Algonquin Names of Places in Northern Canada.* Toronto: University of Toronto Press, 1915.

————— . *David Thompson's Narrative of His Explorations.* Toronto: The Champlain Society, 1916. (New edition edited by R. Glover, 1963.)

VOORHIS, ERNEST. *Historic Forts and Trading Posts.* Ottawa: Department of the Interior, 1930.

WALBRAN, JOHN T. *British Columbia Coast Names.* West Vancouver: J. J. Douglas, 1971.

WIX, EDWARD. *Six Months of a Newfoundland Missionary's Journal.* London: Smith and Elder, 1836.

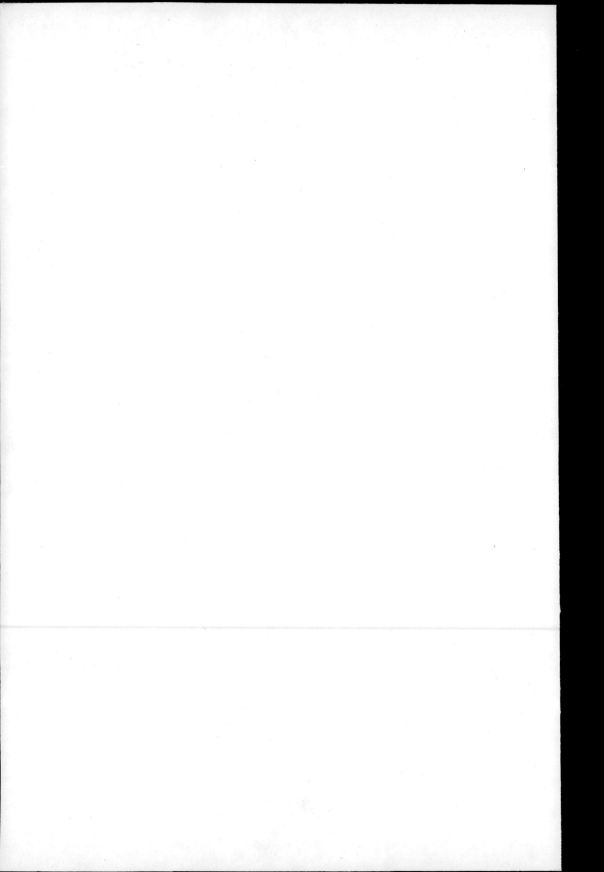